KT-134-040

Achieving QTS

Primary
Mathematics

Teaching Theory and Practice

Seventh edition

Achieving QTS

Primary Mathematics

Teaching Theory and Practice

Seventh edition

Clare Mooney • Mary Briggs • Mike Fletcher •
Alice Hansen • Judith McCullouch

SAGE | LearningMatters

Los Angeles | London | New Delhi
Singapore | Washington DC

Learning Matters
An imprint of SAGE Publications Ltd
1 Oliver's Yard
55 City Road
London EC1Y 1SP

SAGE Publications Inc.
2455 Teller Road
Thousand Oaks, California 91320

SAGE Publications India Pvt Ltd
B 1/I 1 Mohan Cooperative Industrial Area
Mathura Road
New Delhi 110 044

SAGE Publications Asia-Pacific Pte Ltd
3 Church Street
#10–04 Samsung Hub
Singapore 049483

Editor: Amy Thornton
Production controller: Chris Marke
Project management: Deer Park Productions
Marketing manager: Catherine Slinn
Cover design: Toucan Design
Typeset by: C&M Digitals (P) Ltd, Chennai, India
Printed by Henry Ling Limited at The Dorset Press,
Dorchester DT1 1HD

Library of Congress Control Number: 2014935443

British Library Cataloguing in Publication data

A catalogue record for this book is available from the British Library

ISBN 978-1-4462-9559-5 (pbk)
ISBN 978-1-4462-9550-2

MIX
Paper from
responsible sources
FSC
www.fsc.org   FSC™ C013985

Contents

1
Introduction

About this book

This book has been written to satisfy the needs of all primary trainees on all courses of initial teacher training in England and other parts of the UK where a secure knowledge and understanding of how to teach mathematics is required for the award of Qualified Teacher Status (QTS) or its equivalent. This book will also be found useful by Newly Qualified Teachers (NQTs), mentors, curriculum co-ordinators and other professionals working in education who have identified aspects of their mathematics practice which require attention or who need a single resource to recommend to colleagues.

Features of the chapters of this book include:

- clear links with the Teachers' Standards in England;
- references to required mathematics knowledge and understanding;
- research summaries that give insights into how the theory of mathematics teaching has developed, including seminal studies on children's ideas about mathematics and how their understanding develops;
- examples of practice in the classroom to illustrate important points;
- suggestions for embedding ICT in your practice;
- reminders of how planning for teaching mathematics fits in with the bigger picture, across the curriculum and with other aspects of school life;
- reflective tasks and practical activities for you to undertake;
- a summary of key learning points;
- references to key texts and suggestions for further reading.

For those undertaking credits for a Master's Degree, we have included suggestions for further work and extended study at the end of each chapter in a section called 'M-Level Extension'. The book also contains a glossary of terms.

What is primary mathematics and why is it taught?

Children need to develop a good mathematical understanding in order to function effectively as members of our society. The expression 'functional literacy' is frequently used when discussing children learning aspects of English language and literacy. However, we also need to consider 'functional numeracy', that which is required by children in order to operate and interact effectively in today's society. The number of occasions throughout the day when we all encounter mathematical concepts is manifold. An understanding of different aspects of number is required to find the correct house in the street, to call someone on the phone or to lay the table. Measures are used every day, either accurate or estimated, when shopping (mass, length, capacity, money), when driving a car, riding a bike or crossing the road (speed, distance, time), and when telling the time or acknowledging the passing of time. We live in a three-dimensional world, hence an understanding of spatial concepts is vital if we are to interact with and make sense of our physical environment. Each day we encounter data, we evaluate data and we interpret data. All of this demonstrates just how important for children a clear knowledge and understanding of mathematics really are.

In order to achieve the aim of 'functional numeracy' children need to be able to think flexibly and to apply their knowledge to new situations, to solve practical problems, to experiment within mathematics itself, to develop the ability to reason mathematically and to communicate their reasoning to others. We cannot assume a child is 'functionally numerate' if they can only answer pages of questions. They need to be able to abstract and generalise from specific situations in order to demonstrate their mathematical thinking. These elements of generalising and communicating mathematical thinking need to be foremost in our teaching. However, we must also not lose sight of the awe and wonder of mathematics, the creativity and elegance that ensure the stimulation, challenge and enjoyment.

RESEARCH SUMMARY RESEARCH SUMMARY RESEARCH SUMMARY

In order to achieve the aim of 'functional numeracy' successfully we need to consider how we are building a community of learners within our mathematics classrooms. Bruce (2007) identified student interaction as one of the essential characteristics of effective mathematics teaching. However, she also found that, left to their own devices, the children did not necessarily engage in high-quality maths talk. She identifies five features that encourage high-quality student interactions, that establish a learning community within the mathematics classroom and that increase levels of achievement in mathematics.

1. The use of rich maths tasks

When a task allows for multiple strategies and/or has multiple solutions, children have greater opportunity to explain and justify their reasoning.

2. Justification of solutions

Encouraging the children to engage in productive arguments and justification in class discussion, rather than simply recounting procedures, leads to greater understanding.

3. Students questioning one another

Another powerful strategy is getting the children to ask higher-order questions of one another. Using prompt cards with question stems such as *'how are... and... similar?* can usefully support children in this. A child might use the prompt here to ask *'How are squares and parallelograms similar?'* within the context of geometry. The children retained more when using prompt cards than when they spent the same amount of time in small group discussion without prompts.

4. Use of wait time

Asking questions that require higher-level thinking is only useful if children are given sufficient time to do the related thinking. Children's attitude towards learning improves if this wait time is combined with higher-level questioning.

5. Use of guidelines for maths-talk

Explain: 'This is what we ...'

Agree with reason: 'I agree because ...'

Disagree with reason: 'I disagree because ...'

Build on: 'I want to build on ...'

Go beyond: 'That makes me think about ...'

Wait time

The use of appropriate guidelines can help teachers and children engage in high-quality interactions leading to richer mathematical thinking and deeper understanding.

Throughout this book we aim to support you in developing successful approaches to teaching mathematics, in building communities of learners within your classrooms and ensuring appropriate levels of attainment in mathematics for the children you teach.

The Teachers' Standards

This book is written to support the development of the knowledge and skills required by teachers in order to demonstrate attainment in *The Teachers' Standards* (DfE, 2011b).

In order to demonstrate this attainment, it is important to know and understand certain things by the time a course of initial teacher training is completed. Within mathematics these include:

- the key aspects of mathematics underpinning children's progress;
- methods of developing children's mathematical knowledge, understanding and skills;
- how to plan and pace mathematics lessons;
- the selection and use of mathematical resources;
- how to lead oral work and use interactive methods;
- recognising common mathematical errors and misconceptions and how to prevent and remedy them;
- assessing and evaluating mathematics teaching and learning;
- recognising standards of attainment in mathematics that should be expected of pupils;
- the importance of engaging pupils' interest in and enthusiasm for mathematics.

Curriculum context

This book will support you to teach the mathematics early learning goals in the Early Years Foundation Stage and the Key Stages 1 and 2 content of the mathematics National Curriculum for England (Dfe, 2013). Because schools have the freedom to design their own school curriculum, which might include aspects of mathematics beyond the National Curriculum, we have focused in this book on giving you the insights into the development of the theory behind the core areas of mathematics teaching that you will need to inform your practice, as you plan to promote the mathematical understanding of

If you feel that you need more help with your own knowledge and understanding, see the companion title in this series **Primary Mathematics: Knowledge and Understanding** *(Learning Matters, 2014)*

the children you work with and to ensure that they develop effective skills of using and applying mathematics.

Early Years Foundation Stage

The *Statutory Framework for the Early Years Foundation Stage* (EYFS) (DfE, 2014) sets the standards that all early years providers must meet to ensure that children learn and develop well and are kept healthy and safe. It promotes teaching and learning to ensure children's 'school readiness' and gives children the broad range of knowledge and skills that provide the right foundation for good future progress through school and life. Children will remain in the EYFS until the end of the academic year in which they turn five years of age. In practice this will mean that children will follow EYFS until they finish their Reception year.

There are seven areas of learning and development that shape the educational programmes in early years settings. The three *prime* areas are:

- communication and language;
- physical development; and
- personal, social and emotional development.

The four *specific* areas are:

- literacy;
- mathematics;
- understanding the world; and
- expressive arts and design.

For the purposes of this book we shall focus on the area of learning and development 'mathematics', which *involves providing children with opportunities to develop and improve their skills in counting, understanding and using numbers, calculating simple addition and subtraction problems; and to describe shapes, spaces, and measures* (DfE, 2014, p. 8). Crucially, the focus in mathematics is that children talk about and apply mathematics in a way that makes common sense to them (Tickell, 2011, p. 103).

Mathematics in the National Curriculum

The mathematics primary National Curriculum in England is split into three key stages: Key Stage 1 (5–7 years), lower Key Stage 2 (7–9 years) and upper Key Stage 2 (9–11 years). Each key stage includes attainment targets and by the end of each key stage, *pupils are expected to know, apply and understand the matters, skills and processes specified in the mathematics programme of study* (DfE, 2013a, p. 89). The mathematics National Curriculum in England has three aims to ensure that all pupils:

- become **fluent** in the fundamentals of mathematics, including through varied and frequent practice with increasingly complex problems over time, so that pupils develop conceptual understanding and the ability to recall and apply knowledge rapidly and accurately;
- **reason mathematically** by following a line of enquiry, conjecturing relationships and generalisations, and developing an argument, justification or proof using mathematical language;

- can **solve problems** by applying their mathematics to a variety of routine and non-routine problems with increasing sophistication, including breaking down problems into a series of simpler steps and persevering in seeking solutions.

Furthermore, the National Curriculum explains how mathematics is an interconnected subject in which pupils need to be able to move fluently between representations of mathematical ideas. In order to support pupils with this, you need a good subject knowledge to see the connections, be fluent, reason mathematically and solve problems yourself.

At the time of publication, the Department for Education was analysing feedback to their consultation on primary assessment and accountability. As part of this, they planned to consult on core principles for a school's curriculum and assessment system. It was outlined that schools would be able to introduce their own approaches to formative assessment, to support pupil attainment and progression. Each school's assessment framework should be built into their school curriculum, so that schools can check what children have learned and whether or not they are on track to meet expectations at the end of the key stage, and so that they can report regularly to parents.

External testing for mathematics continues at the end of Key Stage 2. In the Government's response (DfE, 2011a) to the Bew Review (2011) into Key Stage 2 testing, assessment and accountability they stated:

> *It is important that mathematics tests are accessible to all pupils and do not unfairly disadvantage weaker readers. At the time of publication, The Standards and Testing Agency was reviewing all future National Curriculum Tests in mathematics to ensure that they remain accessible to all pupils, and that they are primarily tests of mathematics rather than reading.*

(DfE, 2011a, p. 10)

It was envisaged that new end of Key Stage assessments would be introduced in summer 2016 and that these would be of a *higher and more ambitious expected standard* (DfE, 2013b, p. 7) than existing tests.

The Primary Framework for Literacy and Mathematics

The National Numeracy Strategy (NNS) was made available to primary schools throughout England from 1999. The NNS Framework for Teaching Mathematics was intended to supplement the NC Order and offer a sort of national 'scheme of work' for mathematics. The Secretary of State's publication of *Excellence and Enjoyment – A strategy for primary schools* in 2003 resulted in the establishment of the Primary National Strategy. This national strategy brought the National Numeracy Strategy and the National Literacy Strategy together as the Primary Framework for Literacy and Mathematics. This Framework was designed to offer a flexible structure to meet the learning needs of all children. Although the requirement to have regard for the primary national strategies has been discontinued, you may find that schools and individual teachers you work with are still using whole blocks or adapted units of this framework in their medium-term and long-term planning for mathematics, or other elements, such as the three-part numeracy lesson.

REFERENCES REFERENCES **REFERENCES** REFERENCES REFERENCES

Bew, P. (2011) *Independent Review of Key Stage 2 Testing, Assessment and Accountability: Final Report.* London: DfE.

Bruce C. (2007) 'Student Interaction in the Math Classroom: Stealing Ideas or Building Understanding'. *What Works? Research into Practice.* Toronto: Literacy and Numeracy Secretariat.

DfE (2011a) *Independent Review of Key Stage 2 Testing, Assessment and Accountability: Government Response.* London: DfE.

DfE (2011b) Teachers' Standards. Available at www.gov.uk/government/publications/teachers-standards (accessed 13/4/14).

DfE (2013a) *The National Curriculum in England: Framework document.* London: DfE. Available at: www.gov.uk/government/uploads/system/uploads/attachment_data/file/210969/NC_framework_document_-_FINAL.pdf (accessed 13/4/14).

DfE (2013b) *Primary Assessment and Accountability under the New National Curriculum.* London: DfE. Available at:www.gov.uk/government/uploads/system/uploads/attachment_data/file/298568/Primary_assessment_and_accountability_under_the_new_curriculum_consultation_document.pdf (accessed 13/4/14).

DfE (2014) *Statutory Framework for the Early Years Foundation Stage: Setting the standards for learning, development and care for children from birth to five.* London: DfE. Available at: http://www.gov.uk/government/uploads/system/uploads/attachment_data/file/299391/DFE-00337–2014.pdf (accessed 23/4/14).

DfES (2003) *Excellence and Enjoyment – A Strategy for Primary Schools.* London: DfES.

Tickell, C. (2011) *The Early Years: Foundations for Life, Health and Learning. An Independent Report on the Early Years Foundation Stage to Her Majesty's Government.* London: DfE.

FURTHER READING FURTHER READING **FURTHER READING**

To support you in understanding the curriculum context, you may find it helpful to refer to some of the following documentation:

DfE (2013) *Mathematics Programmes of Study: Key Stages 1 and 2. National Curriculum for England*. London: DfE. Available at: www.gov.uk/government/uploads/system/uploads/attachment_data/file/239129/PRIMARY_National_Curriculum_-_Mathematics.pdf

DfE (2014) *Statutory Framework for the Early Years Foundation Stage: Setting the standards for learning, development and care for children from birth to five*. London: DfE. Available at: http://www.gov.uk/government/uploads/system/uploads/attachment_data/file/299391/DFE-00337–2014.pdf (accessed 23/4/14).

Ofsted (2009) *Mathematics: Understanding the Score. Improving practice in mathematics teaching at primary level*. London: Ofsted.

Williams, P. (2008) *Independent Review of Mathematics Teaching in Early Years Settings and Primary Schools*. Nottingham: DCSF.

In addition, you may want to use the websites of the following mathematics education organisations, which have resource materials, online discussions and information on upcoming courses and conferences:

The Association of Teachers of Mathematics: www.atm.org.uk

The Mathematical Association: www.m-a.org.uk

The National Centre for Excellence in the Teaching of Mathematics: www.ncetm.org.uk

2
Teaching strategies

Introduction

The introduction of the mathematics National Curriculum for England (DfE, 2013) prompted teachers to rethink their school curriculum and their teaching and learning strategies for mathematics.

Teaching strategies need to be carefully chosen and planned for each lesson in order to make the most effective use of time and resources, especially the use of teachers and other adults working in the classroom. Mathematics can be enjoyable to teach and to learn, and fun for both the adults and the children. The most successful teachers are those who make the links between aspects of mathematics. The following Research Summary shows the different teaching strategies identified in the research and how this relates to looking at learning theories as part of your training course.

RESEARCH SUMMARY RESEARCH SUMMARY RESEARCH SUMMARY

Askew *et al.* (1997), in their study of effective teachers of numeracy at King's College, London, identified different teacher orientations and their effectiveness in teaching numeracy.

- **Transmission.** The teachers with this orientation emphasise the role of the teacher as the source of mathematical knowledge and they impart the knowledge to pupils focusing on mathematics as a discrete set of rules and procedures. The pupils' role is receivers of knowledge and subordinate to that of the teacher.

If you have looked at learning theories you will recognise links with a behaviourist approach to teaching and learning.

- **Discovery.** Teachers with this orientation emphasise the pupil at the centre of the learning process where the pupils construct or discover mathematical ideas for themselves. The teacher is the provider of activities, resources and support for the learners' discoveries. Mathematics is not seen as purely rules and procedures.

Again the links here are with the constructivist approaches to learning, discovery rather than telling and potentially scaffolding the learning for pupils.

- **Connectionist.** Teachers with this orientation emphasise sharing the work on the complexity of mathematics – pupils and teachers together. In their lessons they share their own strategies for doing mathematics. Teachers are not seen as the only source of mathematical knowledge. They value pupils' methods and explanations. They establish connections within the mathematics curriculum – for example, linking addition and multiplication. These teachers are considered to be the most effective in terms of learning in relation to a test of mathematics.

This is considered the closest to the apprenticeship model of learning which you may have been introduced to, usually associated with Rogoff and Lave (1999) who focused on learning in quite different environments than the classroom and often with older learners.

REFLECTIVE TASK

Think about the teaching strategies you have experienced as a learner. How would you categorise the teachers in relation to Askew *et al.*'s (1997) orientations?

Consider the teachers you have observed teaching mathematics. How would you categorise them? Which teaching strategies were effective for which learners?

The physical organisation of the classroom for mathematics teaching

How you organise your classroom for mathematics teaching will reflect the type of teacher you are and you should consider the arrangement of the furniture in your classroom. For example, making use of whole-class teaching means that children need a focus in the classroom at which they could all look for teacher demonstrations.

This is also necessary if y⬛⬛⬛ use of data projectors and interactive whiteboards (IWBs).

If a carpet area is used for whole-class teaching, there needs to be enough space around for the movement of children between the phases of the lesson while retaining sufficient space for all of them to sit and work comfortably on the carpet and at tables. Some classes have spaces marked out on the carpet to ensure that children have their own area, and these can be allocated to individuals to avoid the potential for disruptive behaviour during the lesson. Children requiring the support of an additional adult during whole-class teaching can be positioned at the edge to enable the adult to sit next to them while not obscuring the rest of the class's view of the whiteboard or disturbing the attention of the rest of the class. Wherever the children are sitting they need to be able to see the IWB without the sun streaming onto the screen and making it difficult for them to see the images used in teaching. This may sound like a common sense issue but many older classrooms have limited options for the installation of IWBs and so they are not always positioned in the most logical place in the room. Problems with wiring, cables and wall space have influenced the location of these resources. Check the organisation in relation to the windows and the lighting in the room when you are moving tables around (Levy, 2002; Smith, 2001). This is also important for children in the EYFS. They need to be able to see clearly when things are demonstrated by adults and other children and not to be squinting into bright sunlight, and the IWB needs to be positioned at a height where they can comfortably reach it.

Many classrooms do not have enough space to sit the whole class on the carpet and at tables without moving furniture during the lesson. The arrangement of tables and chairs must enable maximum flexibility while retaining a focal point. Horseshoes can provide the solution for this, particularly in upper Key Stage 2 where pupils may feel unhappy about sitting on the carpet, seeing this as 'babyish', or where there is insufficient room for these larger pupils.

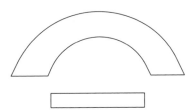

Within this arrangement or others used in whole-class teaching you will also need to consider where to place children who receive support from other adults or require additional resources to support their access to the content of the lesson. You will also need to organise the space so that you have easy access to all children to enable you to monitor and/or work with individuals, groups and the class. This should also include the children who are being supported by others during the lesson as you need to check that all children have the opportunity to achieve their potential.

One technique that has found favour recently is the use of 'brain gym' activities during the lesson. While there have been criticisms of the science behind this approach (see 'A Brain Gym Amnesty for Schools?' (the *Guardian*, March 2006) for the critique), children need focusing during the lesson to maintain their attention. Any physical organisation of the furniture in the classroom needs to take account of the space required for activities such as the 'brain gym'. A direct criticism of children sitting at their tables for up to an hour without any movement is that this can result in a lack of motivation and concentration during the lesson. In Chapters 3 and 4 we will be considering the need to plan linked activities in focusing the learners' attention.

In this situation it is easy to monitor behaviour and attention to tasks, particularly during whole-class teaching. It does, however, have the disadvantage of potentially making it difficult to work with groups or for groups to work together in the main activity. Children who are being supported can be isolated at the edge of the class. This can be a bigger issue in EYFS as children may be distracted by other activities in the room when working with an adult in a small group.

Tables facing in together can focus children on the task within a group and facilitate discussion, while tables in lines or similar formations focus the child either on the whole-class task or on their own work.

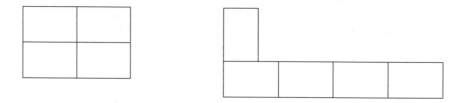

In choosing the layout of tables you also need to consider how easy each arrangement is for additional adults to work with individuals and/or groups.

Organising children on the carpet is equally important, to ensure everyone can see what is going on and to make it easy for you to monitor behaviour and focus on learning. You can also pick up on changes in posture and facial expression that can give you clues about children's understanding, which you can check through questioning. Small boards on the carpet can be better than working on an IWB.

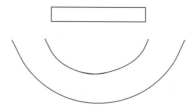

Objectives and how to share them

It is common practice for teachers to be explicit about what they are teaching and what children are expected to learn. You may have been into a classroom and seen the objectives/targets on the board or wall for mathematics lessons. Merely having them on display, however, is not sufficient.

June, a Mathematics Specialist Teacher (MaST) in an infant school, described what she does:

> *I have a clear child-friendly written objective for the lesson. Right at the begin-*
> *ning I get the class, or sometimes an individual, to read the objective with me*
> *and say what we are going to do, e.g. to improve our counting in tens and fives*
> *from any number and back again.*

She then counts with her class using a counting stick as a prompt. When the counting has finished and all the questions have been asked, June then reviews the objective with her class, asking them if they think they have improved and specifically praising particular children who have worked hard. She then moves on to the main activity part of the lesson, again asking the class or an individual to remind the class of the objective. During the plenary she returns to the objective and it is reviewed. In this way the teaching and learning of the lesson are made explicit to all learners.

Once objectives have been shared with the children, they should be displayed on the board or somewhere prominent in the classroom so that the teacher or the children can refer to them at any point in the lesson. This emphasises exactly what you are all working towards.

EMBEDDING ICT EMBEDDING ICT EMBEDDING ICT EMBEDDING ICT

Many teachers use projected PowerPoint presentations as part of their teaching. In relation to the objectives this has a significant advantage as the objectives can be shared on a slide with the class and can be left on display during their work. Some teachers find it useful to copy the slide with the objectives on and add this to the end of their presentation, ensuring that they return to the objectives in the plenary when reviewing the learning that has taken place. These could even be annotated using the IWB facilities to assist with evaluation and assessment.

Sharing the objectives with children remains an issue in observed lessons as it is clear from the following comment in the 2005 evaluation of the Primary National Strategy: *Objectives are not always clear or discussed fully so that pupils are left wondering where the lesson is heading* (Ofsted, 2005). For trainees it is often the first thing to be forgotten when they are being observed so this is an important teaching strategy that needs to be embedded into your practice. Please note that many schools now refer to learning objectives as learning intentions.

The role of talk in the classroom

Some tend not to think of mathematics as a subject that promotes discussion and the development of language skills yet there is a wealth of opportunities for talk in the mathematics lesson. The first area that will be explored here is questioning.

Questioning pupils is a key teaching strategy. It can be used to:

- assess children's understanding;
- assess errors and misconceptions;
- unpack children's methods;
- focus discussion by using children's ideas;
- elicit concrete examples of principles or concepts;
- explore language and vocabulary;
- encourage reflection.

There are two main types of questions that you will use in teaching, closed and open. Closed questions usually require one-word or brief responses whereas open questions require more extensive responses.

There are different times in the mathematics lesson when you will want to use these types of questions. Sometimes you will be keeping the pace brisk and therefore you won't want extended explanations from children. The questions are likely to include:

- How many ...?
- How much ...?
- What would ...?
- What are ...?

At other times you will want to find out more about children's understanding and to use their ideas to focus discussion about concepts. The questions are likely to include:

- How did you work that out?
- How did you decide to work it out that way?
- What does this mean and can you give me an example?
- Can you explain how you did that?

When the children are reflecting on their work, perhaps towards the end of the lesson, you will want to know what they have learnt. The questions are likely to include:

- What have you learnt today?
- If you were doing this again, what would you do differently?
- Having done this, when could you use this method/information/idea again?
- Did you use any new words today? What do they mean?
- What are the key ideas that you need to remember for the next lesson?

Brown and Wragg (1993, p. 18) describe the common errors in questioning:

- asking too many questions;
- asking a question and answering it yourself;
- asking questions only of the brightest or most likeable;
- asking a really difficult question too early;
- asking irrelevant questions;
- asking the same types of questions;
- asking questions in a threatening way;
- not indicating a change in the type of question;
- not using probing questions;
- not giving pupils the time to think;
- not correcting wrong answers;

- failing to see the implications of answers;
- failing to build on answers.

Some of the issues raised by Brown and Wragg have implications for different parts of the lesson. Not giving children time to answer can be difficult in the mental/oral phase as, if they are given too long, the pace drops and children lose the brisk start to their lesson. The match of question to child is also crucial to allow children to be able to answer while providing the right level of challenge.

A strategy that can be employed to avoid this occurring is to ask a child a question and give them time to think about an answer and, while they are doing that, perhaps supported by an additional adult, you can ask several further questions of others in the class. You then return to the child who has been given time for a response which enables you to keep the pace high and helps everyone reach their potential. It also assists with classroom management as the majority of the class are not losing their attention on the tasks given. An alternative strategy can be to use talk partners where children talk to a partner, rehearsing their responses to questions. Everyone is involved and everyone has time to consider their response. Talk partners can be used to solve questions where they share a small whiteboard to jot down their ideas and any notes required to assist them. These ideas for extending the strategies used link to the following Research Summary from the area of assessment.

RESEARCH SUMMARY RESEARCH SUMMARY RESEARCH SUMMARY

From work on formative assessment or assessment for learning, Black and Wiliam (2006) discussed the issue of asking questions in the right way. Questioning can be an effective means of finding out what children have understood. All too often, as research has shown, teachers unconsciously inhibited learning by:

- trying to direct the child towards giving the expected answer;
- not providing enough quiet time for children to think out the answer;
- asking mainly questions of fact.

Black and Wiliam suggest that teachers can break this cycle when they give children:

- time to respond;
- opportunities to discuss their thinking in small groups;
- a choice between several possible answers and the chance to vote on the options;
- opportunities to write down their answers from which teachers then read out a few.

All these strategies can be used in all phases of the daily mathematics lesson.

REFLECTIVE TASK

Review the last mathematics lesson you observed or taught. Using the suggestions from Black and Wiliam, did the lesson allow children any of these opportunities? How could you alter your next lesson in order to allow these suggestions to be incorporated?

'Follow-me' cards can be helpful here as giving the answer – for example, the doubles of numbers – can give children an opportunity to work out which question they should be listening for. What can also help children with the pace of the mental/oral phase is to tell them what kinds of question you are going to ask and when you are going to change the format of the questions. This will particularly support the less able children in any class.

For more detail on probing questions see Chapter 5.

In the main activity and plenary phases, the type of questions will probe children's understanding. In these phases you will be able to allow children longer to answer questions and to explore their ideas and those of others.

Not seeing the implications of the answers to questions is more difficult to address and relies on your own understanding of the connections between areas of mathematics. An example of this might be the able child who is able to see connections and also flouts the rules by moving the decimal point when dividing and multiplying by ten. While this is all right for the child who has a clear understanding of the underlying principles involved, there are problems with this type of explanation being articulated in the classroom for all to hear. The decimal point doesn't actually move – it is the digits that move places and change their value, and children who do not have a clear understanding of place value could potentially increase their misconceptions if you do not intervene after a response such as this. The child who offered this explanation should be thanked and a clear model should be provided for the whole class. The same applies to short cuts that are not generalisable, such as adding a zero when you multiply by ten, which does not make any difference with decimals.

It is very easy to fall into the trap of asking questions of children that merely elicit information about what they already know and do not assist in the progression of their learning. Across the daily lesson there must be a balance of asking and telling through demonstration and modelling. This needs to start in the EYFS, with space given to children to explain their mathematical ideas using the appropriate vocabulary.

Gender

One issue in relation to talk in mathematics is gender. If you are asking questions, who are you asking? Do you ask as many girls as boys? This is a difficult question if the class you are working with has a disproportionate number of one or the other gender but it is an important question to ask. Groups can dominate questioning sessions as they want to get noticed, or you may be using a question to refocus a child's attention on the lesson, putting them on the spot to check if they have been paying attention.

PRACTICAL TASK PRACTICAL TASK **PRACTICAL TASK** PRACTICAL TASK

Record yourself during a mathematics lesson and then listen for the type of questions you use. Do you use some types of questions more than others? Are these types of questions used at particular times during the lesson? How could you increase the range of questions you use? Try writing down the starts of questions to use in your lessons. You might also find that particular groups of children are asked more questions than others. What kind of questions assist you in helping children to make connections between areas of mathematics? After you have worked on this aspect of your teaching you might suggest that it is an agreed focus for observation by your tutor or class teacher.

Introducing and using vocabulary

Once you have the vocabulary that you need for a specific topic then you need to think about how you will introduce this to the class. Try to look for words that go together rather than just going through the vocabulary associated with a topic in the first lesson and assuming that the children will be able to use the appropriate language when required. Children need to be introduced to the words to know what they mean, have their use modelled for them in lessons and have opportunities for practising their use in the appropriate contexts. As each new word is introduced try to give an example of what it means, such as 'factor, one of two numbers which when multiplied together give another number – for example, two factors of 12 are 2 and 6'. Over a number of lessons using the same vocabulary, different examples could be added each day. Single examples can lead children to think that the vocabulary applies only for specific cases rather than generalisable items. This links to the discussion earlier in the chapter about questioning and how this can help children make connections.

You could also select a number of words and ask the class if they are associated with the topic or not. If they are, you can ask children to give you an example of the connection between the vocabulary and the topic. An example of this would be 'how many?' This is an interesting example as it can apply to a number of topics: 'How many would I have if I multiplied 3 by 4?', 'How many would I have if I added 4 to 2?', 'How many is 16 divided by 4?' Other vocabulary is more specific such as the terms 'product' or 'parallel'.

EMBEDDING ICT EMBEDDING ICT EMBEDDING ICT EMBEDDING ICT

You can build up your own word bank as you plan so that you have a set of small labels that can be printed out on A4 paper for display or for use with a group and larger size labels for a whole class.

Demonstrating and modelling

In relation to teaching strategies, demonstrating and modelling are of key importance to delivering an effective lesson. A key aspect of successful and effective lessons is the way that the teacher demonstrates and models for the children during all phases of the lesson.

Mental mathematics

The National Curriculum for England encourages Key Stage 1 children to be confident in their mental mathematics.

> *The principal focus of mathematics teaching in key stage 1 is to ensure that pupils develop confidence and mental fluency with whole numbers, counting and place value. This should involve working with numerals, words and the four operations, including with practical resources [for example, concrete objects and measuring tools].*

(DfE, 2013, p. 5)

As children move through the primary school, mental methods are advised as a precursor to formal algorithms. There is considerable debate about whether it is actually possible to teach mental methods. It is possible to teach a range of strategies from which children can choose the most appropriate for the particular question.

RESEARCH SUMMARY RESEARCH SUMMARY RESEARCH SUMMARY

Tall *et al.* (2001) discussed many of the key issues relating to procedural and conceptual thinking. They focused on the pupils' attention during actions on objects when calculating. Often 5 + 3 can be seen as arrays of objects which pupils imagine in order to combine the quantities. For some pupils seeing arithmetic in terms of mental images of objects persists and this prevents them from moving into the higher realms of mathematics. These pupils rely heavily on counting strategies, which increase the possibilities for errors with increasing number size. The higher achievers seem to focus more on the symbolism itself. They utilise known facts and move away from counting strategies more quickly, seeing the relationships between numbers.

The reason for highlighting the ongoing research above is that it has an important message for teachers. Counting methods are fine as a starting point but children cannot continue to rely on them if they are to be successful with mathematics. When you teach mental methods you will need to emphasise the relationship between counting activities and move towards known facts. If counting in 3s, for example, the links should be made to the 3 times table if counting starts at 0. Showing children that it is easier to count on from the larger of two numbers than to continue to 'count all' is important before children begin to work with larger numbers. An example reported by a student involved a child counting out 62 Multilink cubes in order to add on another two-digit number. The potential for errors using this method is great. The counting strategy here is not appropriate.

Encouraging children to hold numbers in their head during calculation can be assisted by using arrow or number cards to act as a store and provide a visual reminder of the number to be held.

Holding numbers in your head requires practice and will not come easily to all children. Different children will need differing kinds of support. Some will find the visual support helpful; others will find listening to the sound of the numbers easier to work with.

Mental strategies will be taught in the introduction to the main activity to the whole class. The pace of the teaching will be slower than the mental/oral phase where the emphasis is on rapid recall and rehearsal of skills. The main activity is where the clear demonstration and modelling occur.

One concern over the emphasis on mental methods in the previous National Curriculum was that these would become the 'new algorithms' and the only ways of working. However, this was addressed in the 2014 National Curriculum by the introduction of clear objectives related to the teaching of formal algorithms for addition, subtraction, multiplication and division. The important issue with mental methods is that to work effectively they need to be generalisable, that is work for a range of situations, not just one specific case. A good strategy is to show children the different ways that you might have worked out a calculation mentally. The reason for this is that if you are teaching strategies to children then they tend to apply the strategies you have taught or use those that they have confidence with. The latter are likely to be earlier strategies that children revert to if not clear about new ways of working. Your demonstrations offer children the opportunity to see different ways of thinking.

You can also model your own use of known facts to show children how you can explain what you did without just saying 'I knew it'. For example, to double 60 you might say you know that 'double' is the same as ×2, that 2×6 is 12 and that 60 is ten times bigger than 6. So the answer will also be ten times bigger, or 120. Developing number facts can be emphasised by looking at 'turn arounds' or commutativity, i.e. for addition and multiplication the order of the calculation doesn't matter: $2 \times 3 = 6$ and $3 \times 2 = 6$ or $6 + 3 = 9$ and $3 + 6 = 9$. If we know one of each pair of known facts we automatically know the other in the case of addition and multiplication.

Other ways of encouraging mental mathematics are as follows.

- Place a number on the back of a child or on a headband and either they can ask questions of the rest of the class or the class can make statements to assist them in guessing what the number is.
- The same activity can be used with a shape displayed on the child.
- The same kind of activity can be undertaken except that the child out at the front has the number or shape and the rest of the class have to ask questions of the individual in order to find out what it is. This strategy can be problematic with younger or less able children and so the number, a picture of a shape or the shape itself can assist children to remember the item chosen.
- Children can do this activity in pairs where they write a number to attach to each other's headband and then have to ask each other questions to find out what they have.
- Quick draw tables – the class is in two teams; each selects a player and when a question is asked the child who answers first gains a point for their team. You need to make sure that the teams are reasonably evenly matched.

The empty number line

RESEARCH SUMMARY RESEARCH SUMMARY **RESEARCH SUMMARY**

Meindert Beishuizen (1999) described the use of an empty number line for teaching calculating strategies in Holland, which developed out of experiences with the new 'realistic' textbooks during the 1980s. Research at Leiden University led to a new project with the empty number line between 1992 and 1996, from an idea by Treffers and De Moor (1990).

The empty number line combines the partitioning of numbers with mental methods of calculating. Beishuizen gives four arguments for the empty number line:

1. a higher level of mental activation in providing learning support;
2. a more natural and transparent model for number operations;
3. a model open to informal strategies which also provides support for pupils to develop more formal and efficient strategies;
4. a model enhancing the flexibility of mental strategies, in particular variations of N10.

(Adapted from Beishuizen, 1999)

Below are two examples that show how a child can use this strategy to add and subtract:

For more on using an empty number line see Chapter 8.

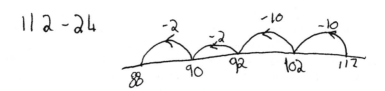

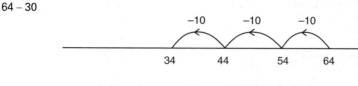

Demonstrating the empty number line

This is one informal calculating method on route towards the use of formal written algorithms based on understanding. It must be stressed that this is not the only strategy that you will teach children but it is a natural progression from mental methods and informal written strategies.

The strategy described here is for subtraction but it can be used for different kinds of calculation. To begin with, you would demonstrate subtracting multiples of 10, first singly then as multiples:

64 – 30

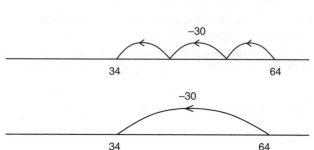

Then partition the number, which could be achieved by counting back to find the answer:

64 – 33

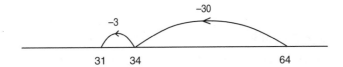

Or focus on the difference and count up from the number to be subtracted:

64 – 33

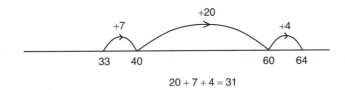

20 + 7 + 4 = 31

The choice between these two ways of using the number line depends on the mental methods that you are emphasising. Children are also likely to adapt these methods to link them with their own mental strategies. This method can be seen as a bridge between mental strategies and written algorithms. Once you have decided how you will demonstrate the use of the empty number line you will also need to ask children to demonstrate this strategy. It can be a particularly useful method to reinforce the proximity of numbers:

For more on the progression of written strategies, see Chapter 8.

101 – 97

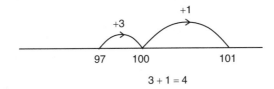

3 + 1 = 4

When larger numbers are introduced children can often think that it means the answers are going to be large. They are not looking at the relative size of both numbers.

Creative and alternative starting points for teaching

In this chapter we will look briefly at creative teaching strategies and we will return to planning these in the following chapter. Using children to physically model mathematics gives an alternative approach and makes the learning memorable for the learners.

Starting with sales advertisements from magazines and newspapers to begin a lesson on percentages gives you a teaching strategy that can link with setting an appropriate homework task. Since children do not all learn in the same way it is important to offer different approaches to teaching and learning.

THE BIGGER PICTURE THE BIGGER PICTURE THE BIGGER PICTURE

When you are planning creative and alternative starting points for mathematics teaching, consider the needs of children with different learning styles. Check if the school as a whole or the class teacher you are working with routinely uses a model of learning styles. There are several different theories; the most straightforward one that is often used in schools divides children into three different types of preferred learning style:

- visual;
- auditory;
- kinaesthetic (or tactile).

Consider innovative stimuli for lessons, such as:

- different things to look at (visual), including pictures, patterns, objects, posters;
- a range of opportunities to listen (auditory), including songs, rhymes, pieces of music, stories;
- unusual activities (kinaesthetic/tactile), including artefacts to handle, tasks set up out of doors or along the corridor, a themed treasure trail around the school site.

For more on the different teaching strategies that best suit each style, read Neil Fleming's (2001) book *Teaching and Learning Styles*.

Using a book as a starting point

English is not the only subject for which books can be used as part of the teaching strategy. Many commercial mathematics schemes include large textbooks to introduce topics either through text, which includes worked examples of calculation strategies for example, or stories which are used to introduce concepts like subtraction. Ordinary storybooks can also provide a different way to start the main activity.

IN THE CLASSROOM

In order to introduce multiplication x2 to a class of Year 1 children, Sue started by telling a short version of the story of Noah's Ark where the animals were entering two by two. Sue had prepared a display of the Ark with a ramp to the door, which she then used to allow pairs of animals to enter, counting in twos with the class. The differentiated worksheets she gave the class were all about the animals entering the Ark.

Although this could be seen as creating an artificial context for the mathematics, Sue wanted to make the lesson interesting and offer images that might assist the children in remembering multiples of two. It also provided interest and a different approach for the class, so adding the notion of novelty.

It can be helpful in focusing children's attention if you sometimes present things in different and novel ways. The important issue for teaching like this is that the mathematics must be explicit regardless of the context.

Below is part of the lesson plan to show how Sue planned to use the story as a starting point.

Multiplication x2	Learning objectives *By the end of the lesson most pupils will be able to recognise even numbers. By the end of the lesson most pupils will be able to count in twos.*
Vocabulary *Even, lots of, how many?, altogether, more, counted.*	
Resources *Where next, Mr Noah?* *Differentiated worksheets*	Assessment criteria *Pupils can give examples of even numbers. Pupils can count in twos – note how far.*
Use of story *This story is familiar to the class but I have not used this for mathematics. I want to offer a different image for pupils to assist them in recalling multiples of two. Provides a varied main activity and should motivate pupils to take part.*	Use of display *Before lesson prepared a display board with an ark and cut-outs of pairs of animals. Later I plan for the pupils to add pairs of animals to the display.*

PRACTICAL TASK PRACTICAL TASK **PRACTICAL TASK** PRACTICAL TASK

Find a book that you could use as the starting point for introducing vocabulary, a specific concept or investigation for a class. Think about how the book would assist the children's visualisation, concept definition or concept image.

The use of the review in mathematics

In plenary sessions at the end of lessons, teachers typically revisited the learning objectives, and asked pupils to assess their own understanding, often through 'thumbs', 'smiley faces' or traffic lights. However, such assessment was often superficial and may be unreliable.

(Ofsted, 2012)

The review/plenary is the most challenging part of the mathematics lesson and can be swallowed up by tidying up or becomes a reporting-back session for the groups/individuals that the teacher has not worked with. Think about setting up challenges during the main activity teaching time to return to in the review/plenary. Some examples of this would be to use one of the wipe-off sheets that are now more widely available which have scales, rulers or other measures on. On one of these sheets add the appropriate objects to be weighed and the scale. Ask specific groups or the whole class to think about how they might solve the challenge for the review and ask them to think about it as they are working during the main activity. A question could be raised, again to be solved during the review/plenary, and put on a board for reference during the main activity working time. Alternatively, set a challenging problem with the intention that pupils should think about it ready for the start of new learning in the next lesson. Or set a practical task, say a bag of different length snakes that you want the children to sort by length from longest to shortest. This task would give you another opportunity to use the appropriate vocabulary of shorter, longer, longest, shortest or shorter than, etc. This kind of activity would also be suitable for a review in EYFS.

Mini-plenaries can also be used throughout the lesson. You can use a mini-plenary when you realise that a number of children have yet to understand the task or when a child has something interesting to share with the class.

> **PRACTICAL TASK** PRACTICAL TASK **PRACTICAL TASK** PRACTICAL TASK
>
> Design three challenges that you might use in a review/plenary for a lesson on measures.

Classroom management in mathematics lessons

Classroom management can support an effective mathematics lesson. One area that you can develop is setting the time and expectations for the children, especially when they are given more independent work.

When you move from whole-class work during the introduction of the main activity to group/paired/individual work, the pace of work will inevitably fall. Even though the pace will be different it is your job as teacher to keep the children focused on their task. Before they move to their tables or begin to work more independently, they need you to tell them what you expect in terms of the amount of work to be completed during this part of the lesson.

One strategy used by a Year 3 teacher involves setting the clock hands. One of the children then draws what the clock will look like when the time is up and the class knows at that point they need to stop work and return to the carpet for the plenary. This reinforces work on the concept of time, which is one of the hardest in mathematics, as well as the expectations of the children, particularly those not working with the teacher. When seen in action, the children in this class are obviously used to this way of working. It is a strategy you would have to introduce gradually before the class members are able to look at the work, look at the clock and stop on time.

Working with a group

When working with a group the first thing is to ensure that the rest of the class are settled, so you might give your chosen group time to write the date and the objective while you check on everyone else. You could give them a reinforcing activity with a time limit, e.g. how many number sentences they can answer in five minutes. Once you know everyone is settled, you can sit with the group. Make sure that you position yourself where you can see the whole class by looking up and scanning the room even though you are predominantly focusing on one group, and ensure that the children know you can see them all too, by praising some children who have settled to their work quickly and are displaying behaviours you wish to see during the lesson.

This is an important teaching and management strategy since, as the teacher, you are responsible for the whole class, regardless of who else is working in the class. You can't assume that a group will be all right if they have adult support. The adult, as well as the children, might want your support during the lesson.

Another good teaching strategy is, where possible, to have the group near to a board on which everyone can record words, ways of working, questions and answers. This can be quite difficult for every group in the class and can mean that some groups spend a lot of the lesson on the carpet when during the main activity you might want them to record or work with equipment. An alternative is to take a small board to the group to use with them; if one is not available then a small easel with flipchart paper attached is a good substitute.

Transitions and how to manage them

Transitions between the phases of the lesson can be one of the most difficult areas for the trainee teacher. It is the time when children have more opportunity to talk and interact with one another and consequently the noise level often rises. Time is often lost from the mathematics lesson as a result of children not settling to the next part of the lesson. Below are a few ways which you might consider to manage these transitions.

- Keep children at their tables during the whole lesson – this has the disadvantage of not providing a slight break so they can refocus their attention but it does cut down the movement around the class.
- Move groups one at a time, so from the mental/oral and introduction of the main activity send one group at a time to settle to the main activity in groups/pairs or individually. This way you can see the group settle before sending the others. It might be useful to keep the group you are going to work with until last when the rest of the class are settled and you can move with this

last group and be able to start work with them. The disadvantage is the amount of time this might take at least to begin with until the class is used to settling quickly. You could either have equipment out on the tables ready or have specific children responsible for collecting materials for class.

- Don't clear up at the end of the main activity before the review. The review can often be swallowed up by the tidying up time. Do the review first, then send the class or one per table back to tidy quickly before moving on to the next lesson or a break. Before a break children are definitely quicker to tidy.
- Use the time and expectations to trigger children moving to the review.
- You may also use the transitions to introduce a 'brain gym' activity, which will allow children some movement before refocusing on their work.

Practical mathematics activities and how to organise them

The practical aspects of mathematics concern many teachers because of the organisational issues. The idea of having 30 children all working with water at the same time is clearly the stuff of nightmares! Doing some aspects of practical mathematics as a whole class is a non-starter unless you have a lot of assistance in the class. There are also the obvious considerations of the amount of equipment needed for a whole class to undertake practical work at the same time. If you haven't got assistance in the classroom then many children may make significant errors or continue to hold misconceptions if you or another adult are not there to check and to interact with them. Nor will you be in a position to assess children's understanding accurately without observation.

So how can you organise things in order that you can see what children are doing? You need to consider what some children can do by themselves while you work with another group or two. It may be possible to consider a more limited differentiation for these lessons, at least to begin with. You might decide to work with half the class while the other half are working on reinforcing their number skills in a measures context, e.g. adding and subtracting weights. Working with half the class means that you have the opportunity directly to teach children how to use a bucket balance or scales before they have an opportunity to practise these skills. In the next lesson the halves of the class would swap over. If you work with just one group you would possibly be looking at three lessons to fit in each of the levels of differentiation.

The first thing that you need to make sure is that the level of the work given to children who will work on their own is right. The match between children and task is crucial in enabling them to get on by themselves when practising a skill or using a strategy you have demonstrated in the introduction to the main activity.

In all situations where you are working with a group, children need to be 'trained' to know when it is appropriate to interrupt you. You could give them a set of ideas to follow before coming to you. A suggested list might be as follows.

- Read through any instructions carefully.
- Ask a friend.
- Read through your work to check answers.

- Make sure that you have not got any other work that you can do first before going to your teacher.
- Use a calculator to check your answers.

You also need to plan times to monitor the rest of the class during the main activity and pick up on children who might be off task.

Many texts for teaching measures ask children to estimate and then measure. One of the difficulties that children have is they can find the estimating difficult. A misconception many children hold is that the estimate has to be accurate. In order to move children away from this view of measures and, particularly, estimating, first give them plenty of opportunity to measure items. Once children have had experience of measuring they can then make sensible estimates for items. Thinking about estimating to the nearest 100 g or nearest 10 cm, depending on the item to be measured, can give children a clearer idea of how they might begin to estimate. Activities like 'show me 1 cm or 10 cm' and 'how far can you hold your fingers apart?' in a mental/oral phase of a lesson can also assist children in visualising measures.

Using displays

Displays of mathematics in many classrooms have been limited to tessellation and data handling. Mathematics displayed around the classroom gives a different view children might otherwise only associate with the images in their books. It also offers an opportunity to celebrate mathematics. For example, you may also set up a PowerPoint presentation to leave running for parents' evenings that displays and celebrates children's mathematics work.

Displays can form part of your teaching strategies for mathematics as they can offer children different images of mathematics to assist them in making the connections between the various aspects of the subject. For example, displays of calculation strategies used in previous lessons can be referred to during future lessons to remind children about the strategies you have already introduced and/or how these link to new strategies.

Number lines and number squares might be part of a semi-permanent display but can also be used to emphasise specific issues such as 'difference'.

Some other suggestions of displays that would support your teaching strategies are as follows:

- details of the controls for a computer program/interactive whiteboard program that you are going to use with your class;
- vocabulary and the children's explanations of the terms;
- problems to be solved, which can act as extension/homework tasks associated with the series of lessons being taught (this will need to be changed as the topic changes);
- examples of strategies being taught;
- a record of an activity – for example, children in a Reception class had to walk along a tree on the floor which had two branches, to decide if they liked apples or not, and place their name on an apple on the appropriate branch of the tree. This work was later displayed on the wall and referred back to by the teacher;

- examples of practical applications of topics, particularly measure;
- examples of practical applications of number e.g. percentage reductions and the language that is used to describe this in shops;
- how to use a calculator and its function keys;
- number or shape of the day/week as a focus of a collection of items for younger children to add to;
- display of storybooks associated with a topic, e.g. size – *'You'll soon grow into them, Titch'*;
- display of non-fiction books about numbers, shapes or measures, encouraging children to read mathematics information books.

PRACTICAL TASK PRACTICAL TASK **PRACTICAL TASK** PRACTICAL TASK

Make a note of the displays in classrooms you visit and any ways in which the teachers use the displays in their teaching.

Teaching strategies in the Early Years Foundation Stage (EYFS)

All of the teaching strategies discussed in this chapter can apply across the full age range but there are some differences when working with the youngest learners.

Types of activity

There are often two distinct types of activities where mathematical ideas are explored: first the adult-planned and -led activity and second the child-initiated and -led activity. You may feel much happier about adult-led activities with potentially clearer outcomes than child-initiated activities as you may feel more in control. This can depend on your experiences prior to your teacher-training course. If you have had experience of working with the youngest children then a more structured approach can feel like more of a straitjacket.

REFLECTIVE TASK

1. Consider the strategies that you could use in an adult-planned and -led activity. Remember those already introduced in this chapter and, although they will not all be in use at once, you will need to think about how you will take account of them as you teach.

- Classroom organisation.
- Learning objectives and how you share them.
- The role of talk and vocabulary.
- Demonstrating and modelling.

- Review.
- The use of display.
- The use of ICT.

2. Consider the strategies for a child-initiated activity. Sometimes this can appear initially more difficult as you are reacting to the path of the individual child's learning and you will need to watch and listen very carefully in order to intervene appropriately. Think about:

- the role of talk and vocabulary;
- demonstrating and modelling as part of appropriate intervention and extension of the learning;
- how you will use review;
- how you could use display;
- whether or not this will involve ICT.

Using the outdoor classroom

Another area of difference for the EYFS is that mathematical learning takes place indoors and outdoors, with children having opportunities for a free flow of activities between the two. However, learning mathematics outdoors should not be exclusively for children in the EYFS – look for opportunities for all children to experience mathematics and mathematical concepts in other locations around the school besides the classroom.

PRACTICAL TASK PRACTICAL TASK **PRACTICAL TASK** PRACTICAL TASK

How will working outdoors alter the teaching strategies that you use? Try a similar activity indoors and out and note the differences in the teaching strategies possible.

The number of adults involved

One key difference is that there are more adults working with children in this stage and so the teacher is only one of the people who will be doing the teaching. Therefore one of the teaching strategies has to be about supporting the other adults who will also be doing the teaching. First they need to be part of the initial planning process if possible. They need to know what their role is in any given activity and, as the teacher, you will need to ensure that they use the appropriate mathematical vocabulary and understand the mathematics within the activity. You may find a sheet such as the one in Chapter 3 helpful to give to other adults for specifically planned activities. For table-top activities it can be helpful to display a note for any adult working on that activity with children about the purpose of the activity, reference to EYFS, key useful questions, key vocabulary and any assessment points as a guide to interactions and a support for less experienced colleagues. This can be made to sit on the table top by using a triangular prism shape, as below.

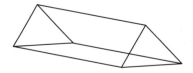

Observe a class teacher in the EYFS working with other members of the team. How do they ensure that everyone knows what is expected from activities?

The use of ICT in teaching mathematics

Information communication and technology (ICT) covers a wide range of resources to support the teaching and learning of mathematics in the primary classroom.

Using an overhead projector

If you still have an overhead projector (OHP) in your school, it can be used in a variety of ways to enhance teaching strategies. If not, these ideas can be adapted for use on an IWB (see following section). The following is a starting point for thinking about how you might use this piece of equipment in teaching mathematics.

Focusing on visual scanning

By putting number sequences or patterns on the OHP with items missing or pieces added, you can use questions such as' What is missing?', 'What has changed?' and 'What is the pattern?' The following list provides some examples.

- For Reception children, a number sequence could read '1, 2, 3, □, 5'. The question would be 'What number is missing?' You could either ask the pupils as a group to show you what is missing or ask an individual to come out and write the missing number in the gap.
- For Year 2 children, the sequence could be '85, □, 91, □, 97'. As before, you could either ask the group as a whole to fill in the gaps or get an individual child to write in what is missing.
- For Year 5 children, you could use a similar technique with the sequence'-9, □,–5, □,–1'.

Focusing on predicting

By gradually uncovering a whole image, or by showing an incomplete picture or diagram, you could try the following.

- Using a shape under a piece of paper – What is the shape? Does your prediction change as you gain more information?
- Using an unfinished shape drawn just with lines or maybe using co-ordinates – At what point can you decide what the shape is?
- Using children as a function machine where they record the number they are given by another child and the result after they have performed an operation on the number – After more recording does the prediction change? Which numbers are useful to try in order to work out what has happened to the number? Does the same apply if there are two operations used?
- For Year 2 children, as an example on a number line placing in the halves from 0-5: □, $1\frac{1}{2}$, etc.

Focusing on checking procedures

Here the OHP is clearly a useful means of checking the accuracy of children working with other technology such as a calculator or with specific mathematical methods.

- Using an overhead calculator to check correct strategies for using a calculator.
- Children explaining written methods e.g. informal, empty number line or towards formal algorithms, or a grid method for multiplication.

You could also allow the children themselves to ask the questions. With any of the above suggestions they could be in control of setting the questions to other members of the class.

Using the interactive whiteboard

Many of the features in the activities using an overhead projector can be exploited using an interactive whiteboard (IWB). These are usually connected to a tablet or individual laptop or PC, enabling access to a wide range of resources on the web or to the local authority's virtual learning environment (VLE). Here are two examples:

Big talking calculator

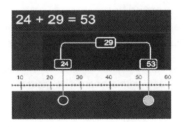

Number lines

This type of equipment means that you don't have to reinvent resources; you can use programs already available. Many exploit the interactive functions of the IWBs so that children can touch the screen and move items around or write with the special pens. IWBs can enhance mathematical modelling and improve the quality of interactions during whole-class teaching. Using an IWB enables the teacher to increase the pace of the lesson when appropriate and can help redress the balance in sourcing resources and planning for teaching.

It is important to note that although an IWB can be used effectively to support interactive whole-class teaching it should only be used when it contributes to the specific development of mathematics objectives. An IWB should be used to complement alternative teaching and learning strategies such as the use of practical apparatus, digit cards, number fans, counters and dice. Showing images on the IWB will support visual learners in particular but those who are kinaesthetic learners will be supported by the use of practical equipment so it is important to balance the use of different kinds of resources.

Using a computer

In Chapter 4 we suggest a way of organising a mathematics lesson in a computer suite. In terms of teaching strategies we will look here at a situation where there is only one computer for the class during a mathematics lesson.

Look carefully at the objectives for the lesson. How might they be enhanced by the use of ICT?

The following examples are brief descriptions of lessons that incorporate ICT. The plans are not given in detail but are designed to give you an outline of how you might think about the situation in different ways.

Key Stage 2, Year 6

Key objective
Make turns; estimate, draw and measure angles.

Introduction
Activities focusing on the degrees needed to add to a given angle to make a right angle (90°) or straight line (180°), or how many more degrees a given angle is than a right angle or a straight line. Rapid recall of facts. Then each child has a set of cards with the following words on: acute, right angle, obtuse, reflex, and they are asked to choose an appropriate card when the teacher says a number of degrees.

Main activity
Recap on the definitions and vocabulary and ways of remembering acute and obtuse: *a* before *o* in the alphabet, A looks like an acute angle. Draw on ideas from the class.

Using a protractor demonstrate on the board how to measure. Get children to come out and try with a board-size protractor or one on an overhead projector.

Group activities
1. *Higher attainers*. Challenge to draw triangles with acute, obtuse, right angles and combinations. Which can you draw, which can't you draw and why? Draw several different triangles and rearrange the angles to show the sum of internal angles in a triangle.
2. *Average attainers*. Worksheet with angles to estimate and then measure. This group will then draw angles for each other.
3. *Lower attainers*. Worksheet and pairs on the computer. The program offers opportunities to estimate angles of different sizes and gain instant feedback of the accuracy of the estimates. They can start with estimates to the nearest 10°.

Teacher to work with groups 2 and 3, paying particular attention to the measuring of angles and the use of the protractor which need to be checked individually.

Review – plenary
Brief feedback on the computer program from those working on this during the lesson. Over a series of lessons more children will work on the computer. Split class in

half: one half to ask questions of the other about the types of angles and/or questions such as 'give an example of an acute angle'.

Key Stage 1, Year 1

Key objective
Know by heart addition and subtraction facts – for all numbers up to and including 5 and pairs of numbers that total 10.

Introduction
Using paddles, rapid recall of $+/-$ facts up to 20 to cover range of ability.

Main activity
Focus on increasing known facts and modelling number sentences from the same three numbers, for example:

$$4 + 5 = 9 \qquad 5 + 4 = 9 \qquad 9 - 5 = 4 \qquad \text{and} \qquad 9 - 4 = 5$$

Group activities
1. *Higher attainers.* Box of numbers from which group chooses two different numbers to form as many sentences as they can, as in the introduction of the main activity. Record favourite set of different numbers for display. Teacher to work with this group.
2. *Average attainers.* Developing number software: complement of numbers to 10. Children to work in pairs with a teaching assistant to practise number bonds. Others to practise number bonds to 10, addition and subtraction. The teaching assistant will need to know what kinds of questions to ask children and the kinds of interventions that would be appropriate.
3. *Lower attainers.* Number facts to 5. This group to use stamps of objects to record their sentences and/or stamps of numbers to record sentences. Large strip of card on which to record their favourite sentences for display.

Review – plenary
Using the activity that the higher attainers have been working on, focus on introducing the idea of the missing number in a sentence and how children can use known facts to solve these problems. More work on this in the next lesson.

Alternative strategies using ICT

1. Alternative strategies for using a computer would be to teach the use of a specific program to an individual, pair or small group and then get the children to teach others in the class how to use the same program. This is the cascade model.
2. Not all children need to use the same program as programs meet children's needs in different ways. It is not always necessary to use ICT with all children. Sometimes you may find yourself under pressure to ensure that everyone in the class has had a turn, particularly with regard to computer use. Doing so may mean not so much focusing on the objectives for teaching mathematics but rather focusing on the need to increase ICT skills. These are not the same things and in mathematics teaching it is the mathematics objectives that are important.

3. You could demonstrate with ICT to the whole class with the IWB.
4. You might use a program for checking specific cases if children are working on an investigative task. An example of this for Reception/Year 1 is the river crossing problem where you have two girls and two women to get across a river. The boat will only take one woman or two girls and all have to travel across the river. Children can work on the problem away from the computer but then check their solutions on the computer at different points in their investigation. For Year 5/6, you might have the class working on the handshakes problem where people are introduced and must shake hands once with one another. The number of people increases and hence the number of handshakes. How many handshakes for 10 people? For 20 more? You could use a program like Mystic Rose to enable children to check answers to specific cases as they work towards generalisation.

A SUMMARY OF **KEY POINTS**

➢ **Teaching strategies should encourage children to make connections between aspects of mathematics that will assist progression in learning.**

➢ **Effective teaching strategies include sharing the learning objectives with the children.**

➢ **Effective teaching strategies include using a variety of stimuli to aid children's mathematical thinking.**

➢ **Effective teaching strategies make full use of the time available for teaching and learning.**

➢ **Effective teaching strategies make use of a range of questions with an awareness of the implications of your choice of questions on teaching and learning.**

➢ **Children need to be set clear targets for the amount of work to be completed, particularly in the main activity.**

➢ **There is a variety of strategies for effective classroom organisation.**

➢ **There is a range of strategies for effective teacher demonstration and modelling.**

➢ **There are many strategies for the use of resources in the teaching and learning of mathematics.**

➢ **Effective teaching strategies make appropriate use of ICT when it supports the progress of learning against the objectives for the lesson or series of lessons.**

M-LEVEL EXTENSION > > > > M-LEVEL EXTENSION > > > >

Find out more about the different models of learning styles. How will meeting the needs of children with different learning styles affect your choice of teaching strategies for introducing key concepts, the planning for series of lessons and your choices of activities for different parts of your daily mathematics lessons? Are there any implications for differentiation as you achieve inclusion of all children? Does your own learning style preference have any bearing on your natural teaching strategies?

REFERENCES REFERENCES **REFERENCES** REFERENCES REFERENCES

Askew, M., Brown, M., Rhodes, V., Wiliam, D. and Johnson, D. (1997) *Effective Teachers of Numeracy: Report of a study carried out for the Teacher Training Agency.* London: King's College, University of London.

Beishuizen, M. (1999 'The empty number line as a new model', in Thompson, I. (ed.), *Issues in Teaching Numeracy in Primary Schools.* Buckingham: Open University Press.

Black, P. and Wiliam, D. (2006) *Inside the Black Box: Raising Standards Through Classroom Assessment.* London: King's College.

Brown, G. and Wragg, E. C. (1993) *Questioning.* London: Routledge.

DfE (2011) *Teachers' Standards.* Available at www.education.gov.uk/publications

DfE (2013) *Mathematics Programmes of Study: Key Stages 1 and 2. National Curriculum for England.* London: DfE. Available at: www.gov.uk/government/uploads/system/uploads/attachment_data/file/239129/PRIMARY_National_Curriculum_-_Mathematics.pdf (accessed 13/4/14).

DfE (2014) *Statutory Framework for the Early Years Foundation Stage: Setting the standards for learning, development and care for children from birth to five.* London: DfE. Available at: http://www.gov.uk/government/uploads/system/uploads/attachment_data/file/299391/DfE-00337-2014.pdf (accessed 23/4/14).

Guardian (2006) 'A Brain Gym Amnesty for Schools?' available at: www.theguardian.com/commentisfree/2006/mar/18/comment.badscience (accessed 13/4/14).

Levy, P. (2002) *Interactive Whiteboards in Learning and Teaching in Two Sheffield Schools: A Developmental Study.* Sheffield: Department of Information Studies, University of Sheffield.

Ofsted (2005) *Primary National Strategy: An evaluation of its impact in primary schools 2004/05.* London: Ofsted.

Ofsted (2012) *Mathematics: Made to measure.* London: Ofsted.

Rogoff, B. and Lave, J. (eds) (1999) *Everyday Cognition: Its Development in a Social Context. Cambridge*, MA: Harvard University Press.

Smith, H. (2001) SmartBoard Evaluation: Final Report. Kent NGfL. See: www.kenttrust-web.org.uk (accessed 6/5/11).

Tall, D., Gray, E., Bin Ali, M., Crowley, L., DeMarois, P., McGowen, M., Pitta, D., Pinto, M., Thomas, M. and Yusof, Y. (2001) 'Symbols and the bifurcation between procedural and conceptual thinking'. *Canadian Journal of Mathematics and Technology Education*, 1 (1): 81–104.

Treffers, A. and De Moor, E. (1990) *Specimen of a National Program for Primary Mathematics Teaching. Part 2: Basic Mental Skills and Written Algorithms.* Tilsburg: Zwijsen.

FURTHER READING FURTHER READING FURTHER READING

Anghileri, J. (ed.) (2001) *Principles and Practices in Arithmetic Teaching: Innovative Approaches for the Primary Classroom.* Buckingham: Open University Press.

Briggs, M. with Davis, S. (2007) *Creative Teaching: Mathematics in the Early Years and Primary Classroom.* London: David Fulton.

Briggs, M. and Pritchard, A. (2002) *Using ICT in Primary Mathematics Teaching.* London: Sage/Learning Matters.

Fox, B., Montague-Smith, A. and Wilkes, S. (2000) *Using ICT in Primary Mathematics: Practice and Possibilities.* London: David Fulton.

Harries, T. and Spooner, M. (2000) *Mental Mathematics for the Numeracy Hour.* London: David Fulton.

Houssart, J. and Mason, J. (eds) (2009) *Listening Counts! Listening to Young Learners of Mathematics.* Staffordshire: Trentham Books.

Jacques, K. and Hyland, R. (eds) (2007) *Professional Studies: Primary and Early Years.* Exeter: Learning Matters.

Thompson, I. (ed.) (2008) *Teaching and Learning Early Number.* Buckingham: Open University Press.

Turvey, K., Allen, J., Potter, J. and Sharp, J. (2014) *Primary ICT and Computing Knowledge, Understanding and Practice.* London: Sage/Learning Matters.

Wragg, E. C. and Brown, G. (2001) *Questioning in the Primary School.* London: Routledge.

3
Planning

Introduction

In order to plan effective lessons and sequences of lessons for mathematics there are a number of areas that need to be explored. As a trainee teacher observing experienced teachers, you will notice that they can perform without any apparent planning and very little written down. This can be misleading as it can make you think that this is how you need to operate. The experienced teacher is only able to operate effectively in this way through building up their expertise by initially planning lessons in more detail as this helps with the thought processes needed to plan good lessons. It is tempting to short-cut this process as it is very time-consuming and feels like an unnecessary work-load. This can be a source of conflict between trainees and their teacher training institutions. The model of written planning you may see in school can be less detailed than is required of trainees but teachers in school are not being assessed against the initial training part of the Standards. It is worth seeing this as part of the training process like any other. You would not want a surgeon operating on you if he or she had not planned each part of the operation in detail several times before working unsupervised. Although as a teacher you are not in a life-and-death situation, your teaching of a specific topic could be the only time children are introduced to that area during the year so it should be well planned, organised and taught. In time you will be able to plan good lessons without the weight of apparent paperwork but you will have still undertaken the cognitive activity of thinking through the lesson in detail and it will be no less rigorous as a result. This will include the necessary consideration of elements of contingency planning, which may well initially look intuitive to the observer, but are skills developed over time. The other side of the planning process is that not all your time will be spent on producing written plans but will be on considering the teaching and learning strategies and resources which are an integral part of the process as a whole.

Another key reason for planning is that you do then have a plan to follow. It is easy when you first start teaching to become concerned about control and classroom management. If your planning is clear and detailed you will be able to pick up the threads of a lesson even after dealing with the children in the classroom. With your mentor and/or class teacher it can be the focus of discussion for setting targets for you and the children. Effective planning should be seen as a support to enhance the teaching and learning, not purely as a chore. It will also enable you to stay closer to your objectives rather than to be drawn into discussions not relevant to the lesson.

The following areas are the general starting points for any planning regardless of the amount of detail that is actually recorded. Your ITT course will have guidance about the requirements and expectations for planning at each stage of your course, which will also guide your thinking and your actions.

Children's previous experiences

You need to consider the previous experience of the topic by the age group you will be teaching. This has two elements: the detail of the activities and tasks given to the children, i.e. the teaching that has been undertaken and, more importantly, the assessments of the children's learning and indications of any misconceptions that occurred during the lessons. It is also useful to know how long ago the group or class last undertook this area of mathematics. It is also helpful to know what the lesson was immediately prior to the lesson that you will be planning as you can then think about making connections for the children as you introduce the area to be taught.

The teacher's subject knowledge

In order to plan and teach effectively you will need to look at the progression within a specific topic and the links between the topic to be planned and other areas of mathematics. Once you know what you will be teaching and you have asked your class teacher and/or mentor about the children's previous experiences, attainments and misconceptions, you are ready to explore your own subject knowledge. Your ITT course will focus on mathematics subject knowledge and pedagogic knowledge. You will want to look at your notes for the specific topic you are planning, to explore the details of the progression. You will want to know where the sessions/lessons you will be planning and teaching fit into this progression. Try to identify any aspects that you may want to revisit in relation to your own understanding. Explain the key aspects to a colleague on the course or the class teacher/mentor to try out your approaches and check your understanding. Be honest with yourself at this point as it is possible to make assumptions about your knowledge. If you need to improve your mathematics subject knowledge, the companion book *Primary Mathematics: Knowledge and Understanding* (Learning Matters, 2014) is a good place to start.

If you are concerned about your subject knowledge and understanding, refer to the companion title in this series Primary Mathematics: Knowledge and Understanding *(Learning Matters, 2014).*

Vocabulary

Check your understanding of the vocabulary that is needed during the session/lesson. Think about how you will explain what each of the words means in a mathematical context, particularly if they are everyday words that are used for a specific meaning in mathematics, e.g. 'difference'. Part of your planning will be to have the words available to introduce to the children on the IWB, a poster, display and/or cards.

Resources

What kind of resources will be needed to help you teach this topic? What resources are available in the school or setting you will be working in? Do they use an IWB on which images can be displayed? How can you vary the resources that you plan to use to support different learning styles? The kinds of things to consider here are posters, images for the IWB, physical resources from different length caterpillars for Reception age children to examples of percentage from papers and magazines for Year 6. Part of your planning process will be to become a collector of resources that you can dip in and out of when needed.

Levels of planning in settings and schools

There are three levels of planning: long term, medium term and short term, although, including the weekly and daily sheets which many settings and schools now use, there can be up to four levels.

Long-term planning

This planning is usually the focus for the whole setting or school and is designed to ensure continuity and progression throughout the age group of the school for children in an area of learning or subject. A school is expected to design its own curriculum, which covers the EYFS and National Curriculum requirements but also takes into consideration the particular needs of the children in the school and the specific context of the school. A school must publish its curriculum for parents on the school website. As a trainee, the long- and medium-term planning are probably the levels you are likely to be given by your placement setting/school, though you are not as likely to have access to the staff discussion about this level while you are on placement, particularly if it is of short duration. If you do have the opportunity it is good experience to join in the discussions even if you will mainly be listening to the other teachers. It would also be worthwhile talking to teachers about how this plan was developed so that you can gain a sense of the process.

A further aspect of long-term planning is to look for opportunities in other curriculum subjects to support children's mathematics. Indeed, the National Curriculum dedicates a whole section to this important consideration:

> *5.1 Teachers should use every relevant subject to develop pupils' mathematical fluency. Confidence in numeracy and other mathematical skills is a precondition of success across the National Curriculum.*
>
> *5.2 Teachers should develop pupils' numeracy and mathematical reasoning in all subjects so that they understand and appreciate the importance of mathematics. Pupils should be taught to apply arithmetic fluently to problems, understand and use measures, make estimates and sense check their work. Pupils should apply their geometric and algebraic understanding, and relate their understanding of probability to the notions of risk and uncertainty. They should also understand the cycle of collecting, presenting and analysing data. They should be taught to apply their mathematics to both routine and non-routine problems, including breaking down more complex problems into a series of simpler steps.*
>
> (DfE, 2013a)

Identifying these links and helping children to make connections between the various experiences they have in school enhances their mathematical development.

Medium-term planning

Medium-term planning is in greater detail than long-term planning and usually comprises half-term to termly plans. As a trainee you may find yourself being given a setting/school's existing medium-term plan or scheme of work. It can be difficult to work from someone else's plans as you may not have been part of the discussion about the order of topics or the time to be given for teaching those topics. For the trainee it is worth making these plans your own by looking at the medium-term plan to cover the time of your placement and adding appropriate detail to support your work and to address the specific standards related to planning in mathematics.

It can be particularly important to gain an overview of what is to be taught when dealing with a mixed year group class. You will need to ensure the areas of mathematics to be covered by both years (if say a Year 1/2 class) coincide so that the same areas are being taught to the two year groups at the same time. This will make it easier to plan in the short term and for you to offer a coherent approach to all children regardless of the year group.

Here is a suggested list of headings for a scheme of work or medium-term plan that you could use to add to a plan from a school or use for planning from scratch for the length of your placement.

Curriculum objective	Time scale	Previous knowledge	Teaching and learning objectives	Vocabulary, terms, definitions	Resources for mental/ oral and review	Resources for main activity

Organisation	Activities/ tasks	Assessment opportunities	Assessment criteria	Differentiation and challenge ref. to IEPs	H/work or home activities	Adult support for specific activities

In this level of planning the important issue to consider is the progression in learning expected of the children over the period of time the plan covers. It should take account of the children's prior knowledge and understanding and enable them to progress through the activities planned. This level of planning then acts as the guide to the short-term planning.

Learning objectives should appear in both medium-and short-term planning. In the medium-term plans these will be broad; for example, children will be taught to derive near doubles. In the short-term plans they will be more specific, showing what you will be looking for in terms of a learning outcome; for example, children will give examples of known facts of doubles and explain how they will use these to derive near doubles. These need to be clearly defined and written in such a way that you will be able to collect evidence of whether or not children have achieved the objectives set. As an example of this, an objective could be stated as 'pupils will be able to describe the features of a triangle', or 'pupils will be able to explain orally their methods of calculating using short division'. If you state the objectives in terms of what children will know or understand, how will you be able to collect evidence of knowledge and/or understanding? When writing objectives the following words could be used to phrase an objective in order to make it easier for you to collect evidence of achievement:

state	**describe**	**give examples**
suggest reasons	**explain**	**evaluate**
pick out	**distinguish between**	**analyse**
carry out	**summarise**	**show diagrammatically**
compare	**demonstrate**	

This is not an extensive list but does give you some examples. If you use one of these starting points it is possible to include knowledge and understanding, for example 'pupils will be able to demonstrate their knowledge and understanding of multiplication by explaining orally their methods of calculating a two-digit by one-digit multiplication'. How do you know if you have worded the objectives for the lesson in an appropriate way? If you can see or hear a response to the statement then you have worded your objective to make initial assessment easier. Making judgements about whether or not children have achieved the objectives set for a lesson is part of the assessment process.

Assessment should be an integral part of the medium- and short-term planning; it should not be seen as a bolt-on extra. It is worth finding out what schools are using – whether they are using specific assessment tools, perhaps from a commercial scheme, or developing their own assessment and review materials.

Block plans

When schools are mapping out blocks and units over the term or year the inter-relatedness of the content and pitch of the units needs to be taken into account. There are various ways that the units can be pieced together to provide children with a coherent learning experience and the example provided can be adapted to suit the specific school context and the children's needs. This will be based on previous teaching and assessment of children's learning.

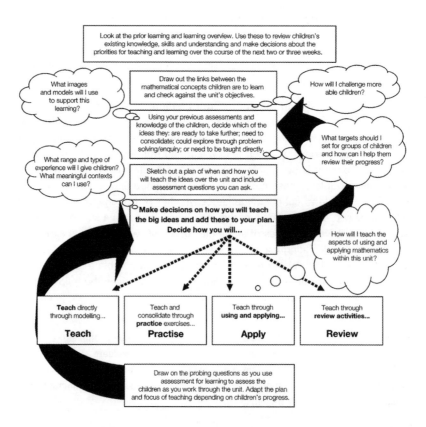

PRACTICAL TASK PRACTICAL TASK **PRACTICAL TASK** PRACTICAL TASK

For the year group you will be teaching next, ask for a copy of the plans for the block or unit(s) that you will be teaching.

- Consider the objectives for the unit in relation to the most able and the least able and ensure that you are matching the content of the plans to all groups of children and their needs.

- Think about the different parts of the lesson and which will offer children opportunities to achieve the objectives. Opportunities could be provided within mental/oral work either for the whole class or a small group.

- Consider the questions you will use to prompt, probe and promote children's learning of the objectives.

- Consider how ICT can be incorporated in the lessons for the unit to support your teaching and to promote children's learning.

- When you consider all these factors plan the initial part of the unit for discussion and review with your class teacher/mentor (you may find the headings suggested at the start of the section on medium-term planning useful to help you with this task).

Short-term planning – weekly plans

Weekly planning is likely to include an overview of the week's lessons and an evaluation of the week's work in order to inform the following week's plans for teaching and learning. This is the beginning of translating the long- and medium-term plans into actual teaching and learning for the children in your class. This plan will enable you to ensure a variety of teaching strategies is employed throughout the week to enhance pupil participation and motivation for learning (see Figure 3.1).

| | Objectives | Key vocabulary | Resources/adults | Key questions | Intro | Main | | | Plenary | Assessment |
						Low attainers	Middle attainers	High attainers		
Mon										
Tues										
Wed										
Thurs										
Fri										

Figure 3.1 Suggested outline headings for weekly planning

The key vocabulary might need to be different in the mental/oral phase from the main activity. In the mental/oral phase one of the reasons for listing the vocabulary is to remind you, as the teacher, of the emphasis on the language you will use for phrasing the questions. In the main activity the emphasis will be on reinforcing known vocabulary and introducing the new.

Commercial schemes

You will find commercial scheme material in most settings/schools. As planning is time-consuming this can be very helpful for ideas for activities and how to put lessons together. Some of these will include prepared lessons. What you need to think about is the match between the lesson and its pitch and expectation in relation to the children you will be teaching. It is tempting to use this type of material straight out of the book but you need to remember that these plans are written for a general class of children of that age group. This kind of lesson plan can only be a guide as each class is different. What is very useful for you starting out as a teacher is that it gives you a very clear guide about the structure of lessons. It is important to recognise here that it is the teacher's responsibility to break down any barriers to learning and so teachers must be aware of how their planning of lessons will allow access for all children to the mathematics curriculum and enable them to make progress in their learning.

PRACTICAL TASK PRACTICAL TASK **PRACTICAL TASK** PRACTICAL TASK

Look at the commercial scheme material available to you on placement.

- Read through the lesson plans and any guidance.
- Adapt the plans to take account of the least and most able children.
- Annotate a copy of the plans to meet your children's needs.
- What ideas could you take for activities from the material?
- How could you change the worksheet offered into a practically based activity?
- If you intend to use a prepared plan as part of your planning, consider how you will intervene to monitor progress during the lesson and inform and redirect learning when necessary.
- Discuss any use of scheme materials with your class teacher/mentor.

Daily or lesson planning and lesson formats

Some teachers use their weekly or block plans as the main short-term planning rather than working on individual lessons, though you will find settings and schools where teachers plan lessons for each day. However, as a trainee you are likely to be required to plan individual lessons, especially when you are being observed. This will also allow you to gain evidence against a number of standards for QTS.

Templates that can be photocopied can restrict you if there are set sizes for boxes for specific aspects of the plans. What is important is that your plans include all the key elements required to ensure a clear effective plan that will support your teaching and progress in learning in the classroom. You may find it helpful to create your own template as a Word document that you can use for all your planning, or your ITT institution may offer you a format with which to work.

You may find that some teachers use a three-part lesson format to structure their lessons, but others vary the format according to what is being taught. You will still need to consider an introduction at the beginning of the lesson where you make the links to previous learning and connections between aspects in mathematics. A review/plenary at the end of the lesson will assist with assessment and give children time to reflect on their learning as well as discuss how today's learning will be used or developed in later lessons. The lesson can be stopped at any point for a mini-review which would allow you to monitor progress, pick up on any misconceptions and extend or redirect learning where needed.

Planning for the Early Years Foundation Stage

When teaching the youngest children, a lesson plan may not be the most appropriate approach as there may not be a clear mathematics time identified. The critical aspects of planning are that the objectives are identified clearly and any mental/oral activities are planned for the whole class/groups, as are activities that ensure that children have opportunities to practise skills learnt. These do not need to be all adult-led activities but children can be encouraged to explore aspects of their mathematical development with the environment and resources that are offered. An area for development after the Williams Review of mathematics (Williams, 2008) is mathematical mark-making in EYFS. Children will need to have opportunities to make marks that represent numbers and shapes through their play. Any planning will need to include opportunities for both indoor and outdoor activities to explore, enjoy, learn, practise and talk about their developing mathematical understanding. Children's mathematical experiences in the Early Years must be fun, meaningful and build their confidence. This will promote positive attitudes towards mathematics and deeply rooted learning.

Vocabulary and the use of mathematical language are crucial with young children as this forms the basis of work in Key Stages 1 and 2. Reviews or plenaries may not have as clear a place as at the end of a specific lesson but a review time is needed so that children have an opportunity to talk about their learning and reflect on the connections they are making. It can also be another space to allow children to express their mathematical ideas orally and continue the development of mathematical language. Preparation of resources and the activities will be even more crucial for the youngest learners along with guidance for the other adults working with the children.

There is a template later in this chapter to give you an example of how you might start to think about planning mathematics development activities for the EYFS (see Figure 3.2). Some settings/schools have mathematics days, in which case you would need to consider more activities. Other settings/schools organise more of an integrated day where the areas of learning and development do not have clearly separate times. Many schools, however, move towards a dedicated lesson during the latter part of the summer term in Reception to give children a planned transition for moving into Year 1. In this case the planning format for Key Stages 1 and 2 may be more appropriate (see Figure 3.3).

The activities are going to be different ones focusing on the same objectives to provide a range of experiences for reinforcement of basic concepts such as counting. The activities are likely to be shorter if adult-led than in the numeracy lesson, though you may find children can sustain a long period of concentration on a task when child-centred. These activities will include puzzles, sand and water, construction toys, play dough, cutting, sticking, sorting, threading, and games linked to the objectives and mathematics that occur in play situations.

General issues about lesson planning

Lesson plans provide the structure of the lesson in detail so that as a trainee you know what you need to prepare in order to teach the lesson and, anyone observing will know what is intended to happen during the lesson. The plan can also act as a prompt as you are teaching so that you remember key vocabulary, for example, what you will be introducing and how you will be explaining definitions and use of terms.

If you have adults working in the classroom they will also need copies of the overall lesson structure including timings and then specific details of what is expected of them and the pupils with whom they will be working. It is also useful to indicate the kinds of questions you would use to elicit responses from pupils as an aid for these people. Clearly the amount of guidance you provide depends on the adults' experience with the pupils and whether or not you have time to sit down with them and go through the lesson plan; this is not always possible with adults who come in for short periods during a week. It is, though, your responsibility as the teacher to plan, guide the adults and monitor the teaching and learning for any groups working with other adults. Alternatively you may use a focus and assessment sheet (see p. 44) prepared for the adult.

You cannot make assumptions about the quality of the experience that a group of learners will have without monitoring during and after the lesson. With experienced and qualified teaching assistants the partnership will be different and as a trainee you can often learn a lot from them about the pupils and how to organise and interact with them.

PRACTICAL TASK PRACTICAL TASK **PRACTICAL TASK** PRACTICAL TASK

Read the Statutory Framework for the Early Years Foundation Stage and the mathematics National Curriculum in England. Choose a year group and a topic related to number and think about what kinds of evidence you would want in order to be able to judge if a child had achieved the objective. Try to word the objective in such a way that this task is as easy as possible.

Planning for mathematics

With all the levels of planning described above, the initial starting point has to be the previous experiences and knowledge of the children you will be working with. The school you will be working in may use a commercial scheme that you can consult for ideas and for the structuring of the lesson and the specific activities. You will also need to look closely at the mathematics the children will be learning. For example, if you are going to be teaching subtraction, look at the progression in skills, knowledge and understanding required. What do you know about common errors and misconceptions that will inform the planning of specific activities and focus your teaching? Then match this to the age group and experience of the children you are

Introductory activities:	Mathematics Learning and Development refs:	Vocabulary: Rhymes and stories:	Resources:		
Whole-class larger group teaching time:	Mathematics Learning and Development refs:	Vocabulary:	Resources:		
Group/pairs/individuals activities:	1.	2.	3.	4.	5.	6.
Objectives and EYFS mathematics refs:						
Vocabulary:						
Time for activity and/or when during the day:						
Resources:						
Adult involvement:						
Questions to ask:						
Assessment:						
Possible extension:						
Review opportunities:						
Assessment issues to note for future planning in terms of learning and in terms of evaluation of activities:						

**Figure 3.2 Suggested template for a lesson plan at the Early
Years Foundation Stage**

Date	Class/year group or set
Notes from assessment of the previous lesson, including errors and misconceptions that need to be addressed in this lesson	
Learning objectives: curriculum references (you might also wish to include standards that you are addressing particularly if you are being observed during this lesson)	
Cross-curricular focus: *e.g. Literacy links, other subjects/areas of learning* **Learning Style:** e.g. VAK	

Resources, including ICT: *Mental/oral:* *Main activity:* *Plenary:*	**Mathematical language:**

Mental/oral starter: *Activity and questions to ask:* Can the children…?	**Assessment:**

Introduction to the main activity *Teacher*	*Children*

Main activity: **Phase:** **Assessment:** Can the children…?	*Less confident:* *Extension/challenge:*	*Average:* *Extension/challenge:*	*More confident:* *Extension/challenge:*

Teacher's role during the main activity:

Differentiation/target setting for specific needs:	**Use of in-class support, including guidance for supporting adult** (this may require additional written guidance for the individual adults):

Review: Key questions to ask/areas to discuss: Introduce homework where appropriate: Note any errors/misconceptions to focus on in the next lesson on this area:

Figure 3.3 Suggested template for a lesson plan at Key Stages 1 and 2

For adult support in the classroom during the numeracy lesson.
Teaching focus and assessment sheet

Teacher:... **Class:** ....

Date:... **Focus for the lesson:** ....

Name of classroom assistant/additional adult:...

Activity: *Brief account of the activity and focus for additional support.*

Equipment needed for group:

Vocabulary: *Key vocabulary to be used by adult and introduced to the children.*

Questions: *Key questions to be used.*

Learning objectives: *These are from the main objectives but likely to be broken down into smaller and more manageable steps.*

1.

2.

3.

For the adult to complete:

Children's names		Can do	Needs help	Note: difficulties/issues for teacher to plan next lesson/support
	1			
	2			
	3			
	1			
	2			
	3			
	1			
	2			
	3			
	1			
	2			
	3			
	1			
	2			
	3			

Figure 3.4 Teaching focus and assessment sheet to share with other adults

planning for and decide what you want them to learn during the lessons allocated to this topic. At this point you can begin to look for activities that will assist you in teaching your key focus, rather than deciding on the activities and then fitting the lesson around them as this may or may not assist in teaching, or enable practice of, the key ideas.

See Figures 3.5 to 3.7 for more examples of developing plans: for progression in multiplication (long-term planning), addition using counting on and counting all (lesson plan for Reception) and recalling multiplication facts and arrays (lesson plan for Year 4).

Since there are increasing numbers of 'off-the-shelf' plans available, which, as a trainee, you might think will cut down your workload, try the following task.

REFLECTIVE TASK

Pick a unit plan or lesson from a commercial scheme and see if this matches what you will be teaching. Think about the children's previous knowledge and their experiences. How much can you use this material without adaptation to meet the children's learning needs? To make it fully effective, what would you need to change?

Though a source of good ideas, particularly for the style of activities for each of the phases of the lesson, 'off-the-shelf' plans do not always match with classes/individuals and need to be used carefully by trainees. However, as you develop experience with planning, teaching and assessing you will be able to make more effective use of all resources available to you.

Now you are ready to try a task unpicking an experienced teacher's planning.

PRACTICAL TASK   PRACTICAL TASK   PRACTICAL TASK   PRACTICAL TASK

Observe a mathematics lesson. If possible, arrange for this to be one taught by an experienced class teacher, mathematics subject leader or Mathematics Specialist Teacher (MaST). Write down what you would need to have planned in order to have taught the lesson. This will give you an idea of how important the planning of each lesson is. If you can, discuss the lesson with the teacher afterwards and ask him/her to talk you through the thinking process while planning.

Differentiation

This is the matching of the teaching and learning activities to the needs of all learners in order to ensure that all children make progress. The ways in which this has been achieved in the classroom have varied. In the past mathematics teaching has resulted in high levels of differentiation with extremes of different work for each member of the class but often there are no more than three or four levels of differentiation within a class. There can be some difficulties in small schools with mixed-age classes and wide ability ranges. For example, a child with specific learning difficulties may have problems reading but be quite able in mathematics. The form of differentiation required

Multiplication and division facts	EYFS/NC	Key concepts	Example activities
Reception	They solve problems, including doubling, halving and sharing.	Halving and doubling	Sharing items between children in the role play area.
Year 1	Pupils should be taught to solve one-step problems involving multiplication and division, by calculating the answer using concrete objects, pictorial representations and arrays with the support of the teacher.	Begin to understand: multiplication and division; doubling numbers and quantities; and finding simple fractions of objects, numbers and quantities. The children make connections between arrays, number patterns, and counting in twos, fives and tens.	Grouping and sharing small quantities. Arrays, number patterns, counting in twos, fives and tens.
Year 2	Pupils should be taught to • recall and use multiplication and division facts for the 2, 5 and 10 multiplication tables, including recognising odd and even numbers • show that multiplication of two numbers can be done in any order (commutative) and division of one number by another cannot • solve problems involving multiplication and division, using materials, arrays, repeated addition, mental methods, and multiplication and division facts, including problems in contexts.	Use a variety of language to describe multiplication and division. Practise to become fluent in the 2, 5 and 10 multiplication tables and connect them to each other. Children connect the 10 multiplication table to place value, and the 5 multiplication table to the divisions on the clock face. Begin to use other multiplication tables and recall multiplication facts, including using related division facts to perform written and mental calculations. Begin to relate materials and contexts to fractions and measures (for example, $40 \div 2 = 20$, 20 is a half of 40). Use commutativity and inverse relations to develop multiplicative reasoning (for example, $4 \times 5 = 20$ and $20 \div 5 = 4$).	Mentally doubling numbers. Arrays $2 \times 5 = 10$ Children work with a range of materials and contexts in which multiplication and division relate to grouping and sharing discrete and continuous quantities, to arrays and to repeated addition.
Year 3	Pupils should be taught to: • recall and use multiplication and division facts for the 3, 4 and 8 multiplication tables.	Continue to practise their mental recall of multiplication tables when calculating mathematical statements in order to improve fluency. Through doubling, connect the 2, 4 and 8 multiplication tables. Develop efficient mental methods, for example, using commutativity and associativity (for example, $4 \times 12 \times 5 = 4 \times 5 \times 12 = 20 \times 12 = 240$) and multiplication and division facts (for example, using $3 \times 2 = 6$, $6 \div 3 = 2$ and $2 = 6 \div 3$) to derive related facts (for example, $30 \times 2 = 60$, $60 \div 3 = 20$ and $20 = 60 \div 3$).	$\square \times 6 = 30$ $\square \times \square = 30$ $13 \times 5 = \square$

(Continued)

Year 4	Pupils should be taught to: • recall multiplication and division facts for multiplication tables up to 12 × 12 • use place value, known and derived facts to multiply and divide mentally, including: multiplying by 0 and 1; dividing by 1; multiplying together three numbers • recognise and use factor pairs and commutativity in mental calculations.	Pupils continue to practise recalling and using multiplication tables and related division facts to aid fluency. Pupils practise mental methods and extend this to three-digit numbers to derive facts, (for example 600 ÷ 3 = 200 can be derived from 2 x 3 = 6).	Writing sentences using vocabulary. Completing multiplication squares.
Year 5	Pupils should be taught to: • identify multiples and factors, including finding all factor pairs of a number, and common factors of two numbers • know and use the vocabulary of prime numbers, prime factors and composite (non-prime) numbers • establish whether a number up to 100 is prime and recall prime numbers up to 19.	Use and understand the terms factor, multiple and prime, square and cube numbers. Use multiplication and division as inverses to support the introduction of ratio in Year 6. Understand the terms factor, multiple and prime, square and cube numbers and use them to construct equivalence statements (for example, 4 x 35 = 2 x 2 x 35; 3 x 270 = 3 x 3 x 9 x 10 = 9² x 10).	Apply all the multiplication tables and related division facts frequently, commit them to memory and use them confidently to make larger calculations. Multiplying and dividing by powers of 10 in scale drawings or by multiplying and dividing by powers of a 1000 in converting between units such as kilometres and metres.
Year 6	Pupils should be taught to: • perform mental calculations, including with mixed operations and large numbers • identify common factors, common multiples and prime numbers • solve problems involving addition, subtraction, multiplication and division • use estimation to check answers to calculations and determine, in the context of a problem, an appropriate degree of accuracy.	Common factors can be related to finding equivalent fractions.	Practise addition, subtraction, multiplication and division for larger numbers. Use all the multiplication tables to calculate mathematical statements in order to maintain their fluency.

Figure 3.5 Outline progression plan for multiplication

Lesson: Addition using counting on and counting all strategies	Date: N/A
Year group/class: Reception (mixed ability)	Size of class: 30

Children's previous experience:
Children have spent several lessons on addition of numerals 1–10 using methods of counting on and counting all – including both written and practical work. Also have experience of counting up to 10 objects and chanting numbers 1–20.

Notes from previous lesson's assessment including errors and misconceptions that need to be addressed:
Some children find it difficult to 'add one' to numbers 1–10 because they are uncertain of the number sequence 1–10 (lower ability group) – need to improve their counting accuracy. Other children have difficulty counting / drawing more than five objects in a group – because they lose count if trying to count and draw at the same time (middle group). Need more practice with this.

Learning objectives:
Pupils should be able to:
- Add 'one more' to numbers 1–10 (or 1–5 for lower ability group).
- Begin to count up to 10 objects to solve addition problems (1–5 for lower ability group).
- Identify numerals 1–10 (or 1–5 for lower ability group).

EYFS-PSRN and NC references:
EYFS-PSRN: p. 76
NC KS1: Ma 2, 3a

Resources:	Health and safety:
• Selection of toys for counting out objects. • Worksheet (×10). • Small dice (×20). Paper (×10). • Puppet for demo. • Washing line – numbers 1–10	• Children to sit in a circle during introduction but individuals doing action to stand in the middle. • Adult support for each group of up to 10 children.

Mental/oral starter (10-15 mins):
Activity A: Children to sit in a circle and in turn say the numbers 1, 2, 3, … 10. Stop the children on a number – the child involved is then invited to select the number from the washing line and to count this many objects.
Aim to stop the lower ability children on numbers 1–5 and the more able children on numbers 5–10 for differentiation. Carry out activity for 5 minutes.

Activity B: Children to sit in circle as before. Invite children not involved in the last activity to come up and quietly tell the teacher what the number is that she shows them. The child then has to do an action this many times
(e.g. clapping, hopping) and the rest of the class have to guess what the number is by counting the number of actions.
Aim to have the lower ability children do actions/count numbers 1–5 and the more able children do numbers 5–10 for differentiation. Carry out activity for 5 minutes.

Introduction to main activity (5 mins):
Explain and demonstrate how we can use our counting skills to solve addition. Show them that if it is an 'add one more' question we can look at the next number in the sequence and if we don't know the next number we can 'count all' the objects to get the answer. Give several examples of inaccurate counting using a puppet to count objects etc. – ask children to watch and see if it counts accurately. Opportunity for children to see errors in counting. Split the children into ability groups and then the adult working with them can explain what the activity is.

Main activity (15 mins): *Lower group activity:* Teacher to continue to work with this group at the table setting up various role play situations involving counting and adding numbers 1–5 (e.g. fruit shop, bus stop). Practical activity using both 'counting all' and 'counting on' methods.	*Middle group activity:* Working with teaching assistant children to complete worksheet on addition. Involves adding numbers 1–10 together by counting all of the pictures. Children to record their answer by drawing the total number of objects for each question.	*Higher group activity:* Working with teaching assistant on independent activity. Children have to roll two dice and add the numbers on each die together to get the answers up to 12 using the 'counting all' strategy. Record results on blank page in a pictorial form.
Extension: If appropriate for this group extend the activities to include numbers up to 10.	*Extension:* Children to add written numerals next to their pictures – refer to number line for help.	*Extension:* Children to add written numerals next to their pictures.

Review:
Children to return to the carpet area and reinforce points made in the introduction to the main activity. Show a few examples of questions – ask children what they would do to work out the answer.

Assessment opportunities:
Can the lower ability group count up to 5 objects and add numbers between 1 and 5 together?
Can the middle ability group work out addition problems accurately using 'count all' and 'count on' methods appropriately?
Can the higher ability group work independently on addition problems using numbers 1–12?
Assessment will take place during main activity with the help of EAs in the room.

Teacher's role: During main activity to work with the lower ability group.	Use of classroom support: During main activity to explain to and support up to 10 children in their work.

Figure 3.6 Trainee's plans for Reception lesson in numeracy

Date	Class/Year/Group/Set: Sherbourne yr4 3

Previous lesson's work, and errors and misconceptions that need to be addressed:

Recalling multiplication facts and arrays

EYFS-PSRN NC references: Ma 2, 1g, 2c, 3d, 4a Level descriptors: between 2-5, approx level 3	Learning objectives: Place value and multiplying integers by 10, 100 or 1000

Resources: Mental/oral: Place value cards and list Main activity: White board worksheets Plenary:	Mathematical language: multiply, times, columns, abacus diagram, thousands, hundreds, tens, units

Mental/oral starter: Activity and questions to ask: Play the place value circle game using 27 cards with two to four digit numbers on.	Assessment: Can the pupils? Recognise the place value properties of 2-4 digit integers.

Introduction to main activity: Teacher: Using the 100 square and white board with laminated number cards, demonstrate what happens when we multiply by 10, using the place value abacus diagram. → Then discuss place value for integers multiplied by 100 and 1000.	Pupils: Listening on the carpet Discuss and answer questions. Demonstrate the numerous methods being taught th h t u = 462

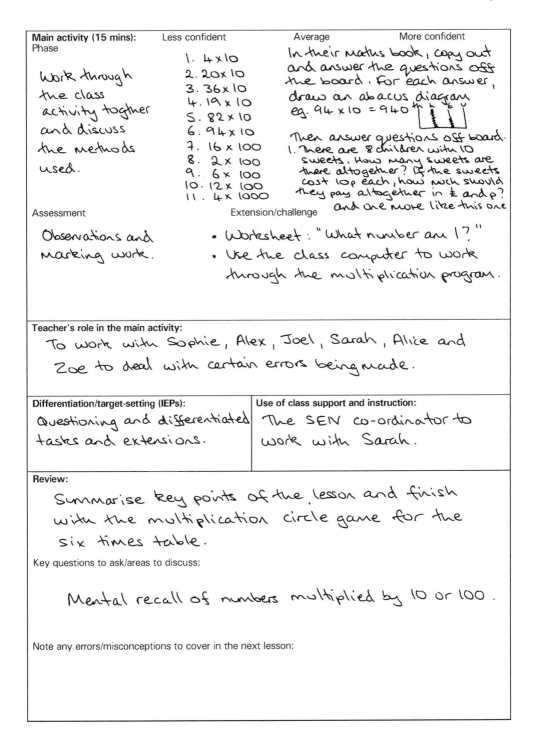

Main activity (15 mins): Phase	Less confident	Average	More confident

Work through the class activity togther and discuss the methods used.

1. 4 × 10
2. 20 × 10
3. 36 × 10
4. 19 × 10
5. 82 × 10
6. 94 × 10
7. 16 × 100
8. 2 × 100
9. 6 × 100
10. 12 × 100
11. 4 × 1000

In their maths book, copy out and answer the questions off the board. For each answer, draw an abacus diagram eg. 94 × 10 = 940

Then answer questions off board.
1. There are 8 children with 10 sweets. How many sweets are there altogether? If the sweets cost 10p each, how much should they pay altogether in £ and p? and one more like this one

Assessment

Observations and marking work.

Extension/challenge

- Worksheet : "What number am I?"
- Use the class computer to work through the multiplication program.

Teacher's role in the main activity:

To work with Sophie, Alex, Joel, Sarah, Alice and Zoe to deal with certain errors being made.

Differentiation/target-setting (IEPs):

Questioning and differentiated tasks and extensions.

Use of class support and instruction:

The SEN co-ordinator to work with Sarah.

Review:

Summarise key points of the lesson and finish with the multiplication circle game for the six times table.

Key questions to ask/areas to discuss:

Mental recall of numbers multiplied by 10 or 100.

Note any errors/misconceptions to cover in the next lesson:

Figure 3.7 Trainee's lesson plan for numeracy Year 4

may only be in the wording of the instructions, not in the content of the task. This is an important aspect to remember as it helps to break down the barriers to learning.

Differentiation can be achieved through the following.

- *Task.* This is where the task changes. An obvious example in mathematics is keeping to the main objective but changing the range of numbers being used. For example, an objective focusing on subtraction might involve three levels of differentiation with numbers up to 10, numbers up to 50 and numbers up to 100 for each of the different groups. It might also mean that the nature of the task changes from a sheet of calculations to an investigation using previous knowledge. Differentiation is not just about catering for the least able but should be seen in terms of inclusion – meeting the needs of all.
- *Teaching.* Setting different questions in the mental/oral phase, who you ask to demonstrate specific examples in the main activity and how you decide on the support are all examples of differentiation through teaching.
- *Interest.* Particularly for groups who might have potential barriers to learning, setting mathematics in a context that has 'real' meaning for children can help to motivate and support their learning. A common example would be to focus on gender and, say, use sport to motivate a class that had a large number of boys as opposed to girls. Traveller children or those who have recently moved to the country can need support in feeling that even in mathematics care is taken of their needs and interests.
- *Outcome.* All children can be given the same task but with different expectations of how far or how much they will achieve in the task set.
- *Adult support.* The same task may be set for all children but the differentiation would be supported by the adult input to ensure that all children have equal access to the task set. This support could be you as the teacher or it might be additional adult support in the classroom. The crucial aspect of this is that you need to plan how you envisage this support will enhance the learning and ensure that you convey that to the adult support.

For more on assessment, see Chapter 5.

- *Resource support.* This can take a variety of forms but can be an effective way of supporting children. If the lesson has a focus on multiplication a resource might be a table square, which allows some children to engage with the same level of work as the rest of the class and at the same pace.
- *Technology.* You might have the support of computer programs which are designed for children to work on individually. Alternatively you might decide that the use of a calculator could support children working with larger numbers than they might be able to manage without such support. For more able groups, it could allow them to focus more on the patterns in investigative work than on the calculations involved.
- *Grouping.* Not always grouping according to ability can provide a different approach to differentiation. Mixed ability groupings can provide peer support in tasks.
- *Recording.* Asking children to record in different ways can provide support and add challenge. Sometimes asking them to record without words can be a challenge. Not recording everything but asking children to record their favourite number sentence or the most difficult question they may have been asked and why can also be alternatives for differentiation.
- *Role within group.* Children need to be 'trained' to work in groups rather than just sitting together, but when they are, they can be assigned different roles in the group, which again either support their strengths or challenge them to do things they usually avoid. Clearly you do need to know the children well to work in this way and they need to be familiar with this approach. Don't assume that you can walk into a class and immediately make this run smoothly – any class will need time to build up to this approach.

It is important when planning the group work for the main activity that you don't assume that when the lower attaining group finish their work they can go on to the middle group's work and they in turn can go on to the higher attaining group's work. The result of this may only be one group for whom to plan extension work, but it may not meet the needs of children for extension and challenge. The ability range of the groups may be close, but they could also be quite far apart. This would result in a mismatch between the learners in the groups and the work given as extension. Extension and challenge require as much preparation and thought as every other part of the children's work.

Special note

In teaching mathematics, teachers (and trainees) are required to have due regard for inclusion (providing effective learning opportunities for all children). Certain aspects of inclusion (e.g. the educational needs of looked-after children, children with long-term medical conditions and children with physical and mental disabilities, significantly low attaining children, children for whom English is a second or additional language, travelling children and refugees) lie beyond the scope of this text.

PRACTICAL TASK PRACTICAL TASK **PRACTICAL TASK** PRACTICAL TASK

Select a task, worksheet or other activity and look at how you can make it easier or harder, and how you could add support to the activities to enable you to offer different versions of the same task to different children.

Choosing the right activities

A difficult area when you start teaching can be the selection of what are the most appropriate activities to use with children. You will want to start to collect a bank of good activities for use during your placements. The most versatile activities have a practical starting point. The following list of questions about what makes a good activity might help you make the decision about the choice of task.

Does the intended task allow:

- access for all;
- possibility for extension;
- possibility for narrowing or simplifying;
- enjoyment (this can often be forgotten in the routine of day-to-day activities);
- appropriate levels of challenge?

Does it offer/present:

- a practical starting point;
- stimuli for visual, auditory and kinaesthetic learners;
- stimuli and opportunities for mathematical discussion using mathematical language rather than just incidental chat;
- stimuli and opportunities and reasons for children to work and talk together (this will support auditory learners);

- reasons for children to record their ideas from mathematical mark-making in EYFS to developing algebraic thinking in Key Stage 2;
- clarity of underlying mathematics – as the teacher you will need to make this explicit when you introduce the activity;
- opportunities for repetition without becoming meaningless, both for teachers and children? (adapted from Briggs, 2000)

PRACTICAL TASK PRACTICAL TASK **PRACTICAL TASK** PRACTICAL TASK

Choose a number of activities from different sources and decide if they are 'good' activities using the previous lists of criteria to make your judgements. Keep those that meet the criteria and start to collect a file of ideas for your mathematics teaching organised under either topics or age groups.

Resources

In order to look at resources you need to think about the resources that you will use to teach and the resources that the children will use, as separate parts of your preparation for teaching. The preparation of resources can directly affect how a lesson will go both in terms of the learning and in terms of the organisation and control of any class.

Resources for the teacher to use

You need to ask yourself some questions before deciding on appropriate resources for your teaching.

- What do I need to demonstrate and which is the best way to do this?
- How can I offer a range of different images to support children's learning of mathematics?

The following are some suggestions.

Arrow cards

Large arrow cards can help to demonstrate place value and how reading numbers differs from writing numbers. So 800 and 70 and 3 are condensed when we write 873.

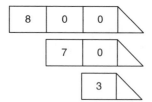

The three arrow cards on the left combine to give the one on the right.

In terms of planning for their use, first have you or the school got a set of arrow cards? Check their condition and the number and size. Resources have to look right so that they can be clearly read; not faded or too small for the whole class to see. If you only have one set, then you can't, for instance, make more than one number requiring the same digits. While this might appear obvious, it is easy to grab resources at the last minute without checking and find yourself in difficulties with the questions you have planned because you haven't checked. You might decide that if you are going to use these then the children all need access to the same resources for follow-up activities – in which case again you need to check availability.

Counting stick

These are very popular with teachers as they provide a focus for children's attention when counting. They also provide one way of helping to visualise the pattern of numbers along an unmarked number line. You can make numbers to attach to the number line and, depending on what it is made of, you also need to experiment with what will keep numbers attached to it during a teaching session.

Number lines and tracks

These are quite different things – in a number track the numbers appear in the spaces whereas in a number line the numbers are on a line.

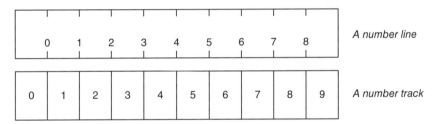

A number line

A number track

One of the biggest problems with planning to use these as resources is where to put them. Many schools do not have a long enough wall to put up a continuous number line from 1 to 100. Alternatives need careful planning and preparation but do not always provide the same image for children or the same opportunities for teaching. For example, it is far easier to model the difference between two numbers by attaching pegs or something similar to a number line that is standing proud from the wall than it is with a flat number line. You can make a number line to stand in a wooden base that could be moved into an appropriate position for teaching in the classroom and then put away again.

The other issue to be planned in terms of number lines is the range of numbers that the line covers. For younger children a short number line can give the impression that counting stops at, say, 10 or 20. These also don't give children an opportunity to look at the patterns within our number system.

Number squares

If space is an issue another way of exploring number patterns is by using a number square, preferably as a permanent display. This can either be on a display board or as part of one of the freestanding boards many schools have. Some of these have pockets for numbers so you can move the numbers around or remove them; some have disks that can do the same. Others are on write-on wipe-off material. With the latter it is important to plan that you have the right kind of pens that will wipe off rather than damage the board by grabbing a pen at the last minute. All these can be used for modelling aspects of the number system, number patterns, odds and evens and place value.

1	2	3	4	5	6	7	8	9	10
11	12	13	14	15	16	17	18	19	20
21	22	23	24	25	26	27	28	29	30
31	32	33	34	35	36	37	38	39	40
41	42	43	44	45	46	47	48	49	50
51	52	53	54	55	56	57	58	59	60
61	62	63	64	65	66	67	68	69	70
71	72	73	74	75	76	77	78	79	80
81	82	83	84	85	86	87	88	89	90
91	92	93	94	95	96	97	98	99	100

Whiteboard/chalk board

Although these are in common use in most classrooms they still need to be considered when planning. First, make sure that you have either sufficient chalk or markers that are appropriate to the surface and the work and are a colour that can easily be seen from anywhere in the classroom. You also need to plan either that all children sitting at their tables can see the board and/or there is enough space in front of the board for the whole class to sit comfortably during whole-class teaching time.

It is easy to think of a board to write on and display examples but if you want to use the board several times during the lesson you need to plan ahead. The following example of this is from a student's lesson. The lesson was about angles and the student wanted to draw angles with a board protractor to demonstrate its use. The board was small and therefore these initial illustrations had to be rubbed off in order that the board could be used again. A useful piece of planning would have been to pre-draw some angles on a large sheet of paper/card. These could have been measured in the lesson and removed from the board during times when this was needed for other illustrations of work but still kept available as a resource during the rest of the lesson.

There is also a real skill in organising the data on your board so that children can easily follow the instructions, etc., particularly for children with dyslexia, who require structure in order to follow work on boards. Planning the space on your board can be a helpful part of lesson preparation: displaying the date and the lesson objectives and sectioning off part of the board for notes and setting tasks. If using an OHP you also need to think about these aspects in relation to projecting any images during the lesson. Check how much space the OHP will need and maybe mark it out.

Using the same resources every day can make lessons dull and uninspiring. If children are not sure what you might use in each lesson it adds to interest and motivation and can assist with classroom control, as they want to behave in order to see what you will offer next. It also makes it much easier to move away from worksheets in the main activity if you have plenty of practical resources as starting points for activities. It is also easier to plan specific and appropriate extension activities for groups that end up being less time-consuming once you have the resources available.

Resources for the children to use

Small individual chalk or white boards
These can be an alternative to number cards and paddles so that everyone can show an answer and be involved, particularly in the mental/oral phase, though they can also be used in the rest of the lesson. First, availability and the right kinds of pens need to be planned for. Then you need to think about what the learning objectives are and how using the boards will assist you in achieving them. If, for example, one of the objectives is writing numbers either in digits or words then this can be a good way of practising these skills and of spotting children who have difficulties with numeral formation, recording numbers involving place value or writing number names correctly.

Digit cards
These can have limitations if the children only have 0–9 digit cards, as you can't show some two-digit numbers like 22 or three-digit numbers. This means that, when planning your questions, you need to take this into consideration. Some two- and three-digit numbers, though not all, can be shown if children work in pairs. Alternatively you need to plan for more digit cards to be available for each child if using them in the mental/oral phase. Cards with words like 'odd' and 'even', 'less than', 'more than' can be used instead of just digit cards in the same way. There are also commercially produced cards for money, fractions and decimals, which you could consider planning to use.

Arrow cards
As described above, these can assist children in understanding place value and how to read and write numbers from ten. When teaching using arrow cards, it can be helpful for children to have the same resources to repeat your modelling for reinforcement.

Fans or paddles
Lots of different types of these are now available including those which show decimals, money, shapes and fractions as well as digits. They can be limiting for the same reason as the digit cards. Some of the money ones only have one coin of each denomination in a set. This clearly limits the questions you might plan to ask children if only one set is available.

Individual number lines
These can be on strips of paper/card or attached to table tops to assist children in calculating during any part of the lesson. A quick alternative would be to use metre rulers if available though you do have to make sure they will be kept on the tables and not used for sword fights!

Individual counting sticks

Again these enable children to remodel what you are doing on a counting stick at the front for themselves on one of their own. They could also be used to support activities where the children might look at patterns of multiples by attaching small numbers to their sticks, possibly as a means of differentiating the task through the support of resources.

Mathematics dictionaries

The last of the practical resources here for you to think about is a mathematics dictionary. We think about making dictionaries available in English lessons more often than mathematics ones, but they can be a useful planning tool for extension work. You can set challenges for children to find out about a topic or a definition and report back to the rest of the class. Children could produce a poster to explain a concept either to the rest of the class or possibly for a younger age group, though you need to look at the dictionary before planning the challenge/task. Alternatively a class might aim to make its own dictionary of terms and definitions over the length of your school placement. In addition, dictionaries are very useful for checking that you have the right definition of terms as there is a lot of content to remember. If children ask questions that you are unsure of then looking it up together can help you if you are not confident about your answer. Therefore, having one available in the classroom when you are teaching can be a support to you as well as the children.

Different starting points for planning

The *Independent Review of the Primary Curriculum* carried out by Jim Rose (2008) suggested at the interim stage a more cross-curricular approach to the primary curriculum while keeping elements of mathematics, English, ICT and modern foreign languages separate. This section begins to look at different kinds of planning for mathematics, linking it to other subjects in the curriculum and also thinking outside the National Curriculum. There are different ways of thinking about planning mathematics, and the following are examples. They are not specifically aimed at a particular age group; they are examples of how to think about each of the starting points. Each one contains ideas that could be used with a variety of different age groups across the Early Years and primary years. The first uses a book as the stimulus for planning across the curriculum (see Figure 3.8). You will notice that not all areas of the curriculum are covered. The reason for this is that it is possible to make strong links for some subject areas, whereas others would only be tenuous and, as a result, you need to decide which subjects it is possible to cover with cross-curricular planning. It is better to concentrate on the strong links and to ensure coverage across a number of planned topics rather than squeeze in all areas from one starting point. The tenuous links make it more difficult for teachers to assist children in making the connections between subjects and activities. Both the examples, the storybook and the mathematical topic as a starting point (see Figure 3.9), do not detail all the possible activities but offer a starting point for you to think about your planning from a different perspective.

PRACTICAL TASK PRACTICAL TASK **PRACTICAL TASK** PRACTICAL TASK

Take a topic and try a plan like the examples in Figure 3.8 and 3.9 for a short period of your teaching. Discuss with your class teacher/mentor the opportunities to try out your plans as part of your teaching placement.

THE BIGGER PICTURE ~~THE BIGGER PICTURE~~ THE BIGGER PICTURE

When you are planning for mathematics, you need to plan suitable activities that will include all children and ensure that every child makes progress. You are likely to have children in your class or group who have additional and special educational needs. You may also have in the same group or class children who are mathematically able, gifted and talented. Talk to class teacher colleagues, take advice from the inclusion leader or teacher responsible for children with special needs and discuss the children with any teaching or learning support assistants who know them well to see what they suggest will help. See also *Teaching Primary Special Educational Needs* (Learning Matters, 2010).

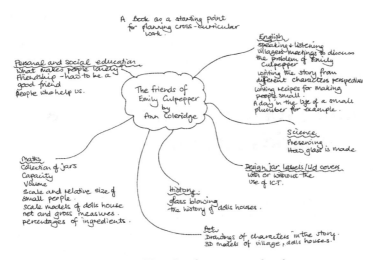

Figure 3.8 Planning from a storybook

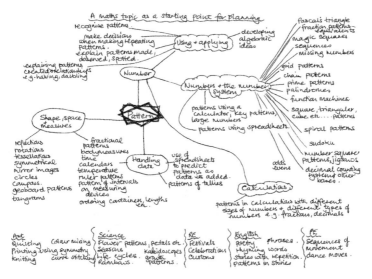

Figure 3.9 Planning for a mathematics topic

The computing curriculum and mathematics

The introduction of the National Curriculum programme of study for computing aims to ensure that all pupils:

- *can understand and apply the fundamental principles and concepts of computer science, including abstraction, logic, algorithms and data representation*

- *can analyse problems in computational terms, and have repeated practical experience of writing computer programs in order to solve such problems*

- *can evaluate and apply information technology, including new or unfamiliar technologies, analytically to solve problems*

- *are responsible, competent, confident and creative users of information and communication technology.*

(DfE, 2013b)

Although a programme of study in its own right, there are many overlaps with mathematical thinking and the symbiosis between computing and mathematics should be considered in your planning.

Planning for the use of ICT in a mathematics lesson

Computers

This is the most obvious use of ICT and can be the most difficult for you to think about in terms of planning. The first issue is preparation and, with computers, this means being familiar with the software and hardware available. You do need to think through the kinds of software or packages that you will use and why. Table 3.1 provides an introduction to the kinds of items that are available in most schools with some examples.

For more on the use of ICT, see Turvey et al. (2014) Primary ICT and Computing Knowledge, Understanding and Practice, from Learning Matters.

Category	Examples
Drill and practice	*Hooray for Maths* *The Number Works* *Mighty Maths* Also a number of programs that are part of commercial maths schemes
Integrated Learning Systems (ILS)	*Success Maker* *Global Learning Systems*
Logo	*Logo*, screen turtle and *Roamer world* With links to programmable robots like *Roamer/pips/pixies*
Number specific	*ATM Developing number* *Counting machine*
Algebra	*DragonBox*, a mobile application for tablets
Data handling	*Black Cat* software *Excel* Databases, e.g. *Find it* *Junior View Point*

Miscellaneous small software	*My World* *Fun School Maths* *Maths Explorer*
Websites: some of these have activities that you can use in maths lessons	ATM (www.atm.org.uk/) NRICH (http://nrich.maths.org/frontpage) BBC Schools (www.bbc.co.uk/schools/websites/4_11/site/numeracy.shtml)
Interactive whiteboard	A number of resources available, search for 'IWB maths resources' in your browser

Table 3.1 Classifications of ICT

EMBEDDING ICT EMBEDDING ICT **EMBEDDING ICT** EMBEDDING ICT

Use the categories in Table 3.1 as a starting point to begin to collect together resources for various types of activity in the different aspects of mathematics. The internet is a great source of interactive resources, downloadable programs and modelling software. Use a reliable search engine to find these and then examine them carefully to find the examples that suit the needs of your children and that best fit in with your planning. Ask the mathematics subject leader and your class teacher colleagues what software is already available in school and try to gain access to the school's virtual learning environment (VLE) as well. The following two books in this series will help you: Barber *et al.* (2007) *Learning and Teaching with IWBs: Primary and Early Years,* and Gillespie *et al.* (2007) *Learning and Teaching with Virtual Learning Environments.* (Both are from Learning Matters.)

Once you have decided to use computers you then need to plan the organisation. This will be different according to the topic and the availability of machines. If you have a class set of mobile tablets, for example, then you may plan for whole-class work or independent/paired work using appropriate applications (apps).

If you have only one computer you may feel that demonstrating the use of the software to the whole class may be the most useful method. Each group in turn then works on the computer with you or with other adult support during a single lesson, or maybe over a sequence of lessons, depending on the content of the program.

Planning for working in a suite of computers is quite a different prospect. You obviously need to check the software available and find out how it works, as sometimes the software can operate much more slowly on a network. The other issue in terms of planning for teaching in a suite is the organisation of the room and how you will gain children's attention at specific times during the lesson. This might sound very basic but control of children in front of computer screens can be problematic. You need to agree ground rules and establish a signal, for example, for when you want children to stop work and give you their attention.

If working in a suite where you have projection facilities, or even facilities for looking in on their screens, then you can check on what each child or small group of children is doing. In these circumstances the software you choose to work on needs to be accessible by all of the children. If there are issues about the ability of the children to read instructions on the screen, you might consider mixed-ability groupings or paired work to allow access to all. Children working at a terminal on their own are obviously not discussing the mathematics and any strategies they are using. If this is the case you may want to plan in times when you ask children to join together and discuss their work either within the suite time or in a following session, using printouts of work completed.

Having children working individually through drill and practice exercises is not the most productive use of suite time which might only be available to the class on a limited basis, particularly during numeracy lessons.

The advantage of the computer suite is that all of the children can be introduced to and make initial explorations with programs that you might then use with groups in the classroom when fewer machines are available. So ICT can form part of the strategy for an individual lesson or for a sequence of lessons where you are planning to develop the children's mathematical skills. A good example of this would be Logo, which could be introduced in the context of a suite and followed up with differentiated challenges in the classroom.

Suggested activities for a mathematics lesson in a suite

The following is a very brief overview of some ideas for working in a suite. It is necessarily general, as the idea is to show the potential rather than a specific plan for an age group. The intention is to get you thinking about how you could use computers effectively in mathematics if the opportunities are available, and what this means for planning a lesson.

Introduction

1. With the whole class, use a counting machine which you can set to count in different sized steps. Stop the count and ask for predictions of the next number. You might try one or two of these and then show the class how to change the steps. In pairs/small groups they could challenge each other to find the rules predicting what the next number will be in the sequence.
2. With the whole class, if children have a machine each, you could choose a table from the ATM Developing Number software to complete within a time limit. This task could be given to pairs or small groups working against the clock where one person is inputting the answers.

Main activity

Using the Complements part of the ATM Developing Number software package, look at complements of numbers that are appropriate for the year group. Demonstrate different ways of working out the complements of the given number. Ask children for strategies they would use, e.g. bridging through ten, counting up or using known facts. Then set them a challenge to use the same strategies to solve complements for different numbers. Here you could differentiate with the size of number but still use the same strategies.

Review

Here you could use the Developing Number software again and go over some of the questions that have been answered by a range of children. Pick up on any errors and misconceptions. Then take the children on further, introducing larger numbers where the same strategies could apply, hence extending their learning.

Interactive whiteboards

IWBs are commonplace in classrooms. The following is an example of a 1–100 grid that can be used to show patterns of multiples, in this case 6.

1	2	3	4	5	6	7	8	9	10
11	12	13	14	15	16	17	18	19	20
21	22	23	24	25	26	27	28	29	30
31	32	33	34	35	36	37	38	39	40
41	42	43	44	45	46	47	48	49	50
51	52	53	54	55	56	57	58	59	60
61	62	63	64	65	66	67	68	69	70
71	72	73	74	75	76	77	78	79	80
81	82	83	84	85	86	87	88	89	90
91	92	93	94	95	96	97	98	99	100

The board can be set up so that the colours of the squares will change if touched with a marker or with a finger.

PRACTICAL TASK PRACTICAL TASK **PRACTICAL TASK** PRACTICAL TASK

Find out about the IWBs in your placement school. Go to the following website and select a resource for Key Stage 1 or Key Stage 2 that you can incorporate into your planning: www.tes.co.uk

Digital cameras

Digital cameras can provide opportunities to focus on patterns in the environment, symmetry and, when rescaling images, ratio and proportion. The planning stage of using a camera might have to be spread over several sessions as you have to plan time for children to take the photographs before being able to work with them in a numeracy lesson. Pictures taken with ordinary cameras can also assist children in looking at patterns and shapes, though again time needs to be spent collecting the images.

Photocopiers

These can be a useful resource for enlarging worksheets displayed for a class/group to work from if an IWB or OHP is not available. It can also be used for demonstrating enlargements, ratio and proportion. If images of different sizes are copied before the lesson then they can be given to groups to investigate the relationships between the images as part of one of the activities, say in the main activity phase of the lesson. Or you could plan part of a lesson for children to work with an adult to produce images of particular sizes.

Calculators

There are two strands to planning for using calculators in the lesson. The first is the use of a calculator and the second is using it effectively as a tool to support more open-ended activities. This is where the focus of the activity is looking for the pattern or the methods of solving a problem rather than the arithmetic which, if not completed with a calculator, would get in the way of extending the children's mathematical thinking.

Calculators come in different kinds, though most modern ones are all scientific. Check that all the calculators operate in the same way and that there are sufficient for the whole class. If you can, use an IWB calculator that is the same as the pupils' to demonstrate procedures.

Evaluating the teaching and learning

Lesson evaluations

An evaluation should be completed as soon as possible after each lesson. The two main areas to focus on are the children's learning and your teaching. In the area of the children's learning, you will want to note those children who did not achieve the objectives for the lesson and why you think they had difficulties, made specific errors and experienced misconceptions that did not allow them to achieve. You will also want to know if children have exceeded your expectations and specifically what they demonstrated in terms of their understanding during the lesson that could be used to take them further. This will be part of your assessment evidence that you will later transfer to records of progress and attainment.

You will also need to consider your own performance in the lesson. The danger here is to dwell on things that go wrong and not think about the positive aspects of the lesson you have just taught. A good strategy is to consider the positive aspects first and note two or three things that were good and that you will continue to include in your teaching. Then turn to thinking about those aspects which you want to improve. You do not need to give a blow-by-blow account of what has occurred in the lesson. Again try to select two or three things that you are going to work on in the next lesson or series of lessons. In this way you are using your evaluation like the formative assessment you carry out in relation to the children's learning and alter the next lesson as a result.

Children not reaching objectives:	Children exceeding the objectives:
Notes for next day/week focusing on teaching	
Good aspects for development:	Areas:

Weekly evaluations

Since you are also planning on a weekly basis, it is useful to evaluate the week as well, drawing on your individual lesson evaluations in order to feed into the next weekly plan.

Objectives attained:	Objectives not attained:
Children not reaching objectives covered: Target:	Children exceeding objectives covered: Target:
Action for next week/half term:	
Teacher's targets:	

A SUMMARY OF **KEY POINTS**

➢ Planning effective learning for mathematics takes place on four levels:

  – long-term planning is often constructed by the whole school and so is not usually an activity that trainees are involved in;

  – medium-term planning is often constructed by teams of year group teachers or individual class teachers and is again not usually an activity that trainees are involved in;

  – weekly planning is constructed by all teachers from the medium-term plans;

  – daily lesson plans are not always constructed by classroom teachers, except when being observed, but are usually expected of trainee teachers.

➢ The long- and medium-term plans may merge in some schools or settings, particularly in the EYFS.

➢ Careful planning for lessons can assist you in delivering effective mathematics lessons where there is clear progression in children's learning, and its importance cannot be overestimated.

➢ Planning should always focus on the learning first, through clear objectives.

➢ Key elements in a lesson plan include:

  – a clear structure, usually with a mental/oral starter, main activity and plenary/review phase;

  – use of appropriate mathematical vocabulary;

  – effective use of questioning and opportunities for mathematical discussion;

  – making explicit connections between aspects of mathematics for the children;

  – direct teaching throughout the lesson to the whole class, groups and individuals;

  – effective use of resources;

  – clear differentiation to meet the diversity of children's needs;

  – appropriate choice of activities to match the mathematical content and children's age and needs;

  – assessment of and for learning;

  – evaluation of teaching;

  – targets set for the future in terms of learning and teaching.

M-LEVEL EXTENSION > > > > M-LEVEL EXTENSION > > > >

When you have the opportunity to observe your class teacher or other colleagues, ask to look at their planning and discuss how they set about planning the lesson you saw and the series of lessons that it was a part of. Ask how they planned the differentiation that you observed. After reflecting on your discussion, decide how you would differentiate this activity for children of differing levels of ability. What about those children with specific learning difficulties or particular needs, for example children with English as an additional language? Would they require any particular support or additional resources? Remember that you may also have in the same group or class children who are able, gifted and talented in mathematics. When you have made your decisions, discuss your notes with your mentor/class teacher and ask for feedback specifically on planning when a colleague observes you teaching.

REFERENCES REFERENCES **REFERENCES** REFERENCES REFERENCES

Briggs, M. (2000) 'Feel free to be flexible'. *Special Children*, pp. 1–8.

DfE (2011) Teachers' Standards. Available at www.gov.uk/government/publications/teachers-standards (accessed 13/4/14).

DfE (2013a) *The National Curriculum in England: Key Stages 1 and 2 framework document* London: DfE. Available at: www.gov.uk/government/uploads/system/uploads/attachment_data/file/260481/PRIMARY_National_Curriculum_11-9-13_2.pdf (accessed 13/4/14).

DfE (2013b) *Computing Programmes of Study: Key Stages 1 and 2.* London: DfE. Available at: www.gov.uk/government/uploads/system/uploads/attachment_data/file/239033/PRIMARY_National_Curriculum_-_Computing.pdf (accessed 13/4/14).

Rose, J. (2008) *Independent Review of the Primary Curriculum: Interim Report.* Nottingham: DCSF Publications.

Williams, P. (2008) *Independent Review of Mathematics Teaching in Early Years Settings and Primary Schools.* Nottingham: DCSF Publications.

FURTHER READING FURTHER READING FURTHER READING

Briggs, M. and Davis, S. (2008) *Creative Teaching: Mathematics in the Early Years and Primary Classrooms.* London: David Fulton Routledge.

Briggs, M. and Pritchard, A. (2002) *Using ICT in Primary Mathematics Teaching.* Exeter: Learning Matters.

DfES (2001) *Guidance to Support Pupils with Specific Needs in the Daily Maths Lesson.* London: DfES.

Fox, B., Montague-Smith, A. and Wilkes, S. (2000) *Using ICT in Primary Mathematics: Practices and Possibilities.* London: David Fulton.

Jacques, K. and Hyland, R. (eds) (2007) *Professional Studies: Primary and Early Years.* Exeter: Learning Matters.

Ofsted (2009) *Mathematics: Understanding the Score.* London: Ofsted.

Turvey, K., Allen, J., Potter, J., and Sharp, J. (2014) *Primary ICT and Computing Knowledge, Understanding and Practice.* London: Sage/Learning Matters.

4
The mathematics lesson

Introduction

This chapter will discuss mathematics lessons, consider how the typical daily lesson form came about and the implications for, and management of, teaching mathematics in primary schools.

The publication of the Cockcroft Report in 1982 marked the beginning of change in the way mathematics was taught in primary schools. Among its recommendations were:

- the need to acquire mental strategies without moving too quickly into written calculations so encouraging children to develop their own calculation methods;
- the use of whole-class teaching;
- the integration of problem-solving into the curriculum.

The eventual outcome of the report was the content of the mathematics part of the National Curriculum (NC), introduced in 1989. The NC had the intention that all schools would have a nationally standardised syllabus to follow, designed to develop knowledge, skills and understanding progressively. Schools were given guidance on the proportion of the teaching time in the week that was to be given to each subject, including mathematics (Dearing, 1993), and from that the timetable for each day was determined.

The Cockcroft Report included the statement: *The ability to solve problems is at the heart of mathematics* (Cockcroft, 1982, p. 249), which was taken as a recommendation for a necessary part of the NC entitled 'Using and Applying'. Initially this was written as a programme of study (PoS) stated separately from the other PoS, but the 2000 NC incorporated the using and applying of mathematics into the other PoS, although it still exists as an attainment target and has to be assessed. One of the Ofsted (2008) recommendations was that separate reporting of pupil attainment in using and applying mathematics should be reintroduced into statutory end of key stage assessments. At the time of writing there was no further indication of the DfE's plans in relation to this.

Children often experience difficulties in transference, meaning that the more the curriculum is separated into discrete areas, the less likely it is that children will be able to transfer knowledge, skills and understanding from one area to another, both within and outside mathematically specific work. Ofsted (2008) recommended that schools give more attention to developing children's understanding with a wide range of opportunities to use and apply mathematics. Consideration of integrating using and applying with the teaching of knowledge, skills and understanding should improve transference.

However, it became evident that, while the NC gave clear directives on content and progression, there were weaknesses that needed to be addressed.

> *In particular, there were concerns about the level of basic calculation skills, including mental mathematics, overuse of commercial schemes that promoted standard calculation methods and teachers managing rather than teaching.*

> (Straker, cited in Thompson 1999)

> *In addition, the emphasis on differentiation had resulted in a tendency for children to work individually through schemes with a consequent loss of cohesion through common strands.*

> (Brown, cited in Thompson 1999)

The outcome of this was that too many children were not achieving the standard they possibly could. In 1996 the National Numeracy Project (NNP) was launched. From this arose the non-statutory National Numeracy Strategy (NNS), implemented in schools from September 1999, which gave a framework for teaching mathematics that promoted both equity and equality of teaching (Brown *et al.,* 2000).

The recommendation from the NNP for a daily mathematics lesson was, in many schools, in place prior to the implementation of the NNS. There was, at this time, no nationally recommended structure to the daily mathematics lesson, but with the introduction of the National Literacy Strategy (NLS) in 1998, schools anticipated and so applied the advisory structure that would be given in the NNS. With the advent of the PNS (2006), the strategies for teaching literacy and numeracy were reviewed, with numeracy reverting to the title of mathematics. A new National Curriculum in England came into force in September 2014 (DfE, 2013a). Schools were given permission by the DfE to plan mathematics as they wished, removing the need for a three-part structured lesson and encouraging a more creative, flexible approach to learning. The Ofsted handbook also changed to reflect this expectation of schools.

How mathematics lessons can be structured

Daily mathematics lessons were introduced as part of the first national strategies, and continued under the PNS. Although the requirement to have regard for the primary national strategies has been discontinued, you may find that schools and individual teachers you work with are still using elements of them, including the three-part mathematics lesson, which included a mental maths starter, main teaching activities, often with group or individual work, and a plenary review.

Schoenfeld (2006, p. 335) asserted that, *Mathematics is a living subject which seeks to understand patterns that permeate both the world around us and the mind within us*. He stated that it is the responsibility of teachers to give children: *opportunities to study mathematics as an exploratory, dynamic, evolving discipline rather than as a rigid, absolute, closed body of laws*. They need to be able to: *use mathematics in practical ways, from simple applications ... to complex ... so that they are: flexible thinkers with a broad repertoire of techniques and perspectives for dealing with novel problems and situations*. They will then become: *analytical, both in thinking through issues themselves and in examining the arguments put forth by others*.

Ofsted (2008, p.16) noted that in weaker lessons, *pupils simply completed exercises in textbooks or worksheets, replicating the steps necessary to answer questions to National Curriculum tests or external examinations. Success too often depended on pupils remembering what to do rather than having a secure understanding*.

Denvir and Askew (2001) observed that:

- *whilst children are willing to, wanting to and almost always taking part, many are frequently not engaged in mathematical thinking;*
- *children frequently copy from each other with some never doing the work for themselves, becoming adept at convincing the teachers they are good workers and thinkers. In general copying is not regarded by the children as being wrong.*

Mental mathematics

Despite the recommendations of the Cockcroft Report (1982) it was found by the National Numeracy Project (NNP) that children (and teaching) were still too reliant on written or technological calculations, becoming too inflexible in their methods and thinking. As a result, one of the most significant areas for attention became mental mathematics, leading to the introduction of daily mental mathematics sessions. These teach children to:

- remember and instantly recall number facts;
- use known facts to derive new facts;
- select and combine strategies to solve problems.

The recommendation was that the first five to ten minutes of the daily mathematics lesson should be concerned with mental mathematics and, where possible, the content should be linked to the subject being covered in the main lesson. This encourages children to realise that mental mathematics is a desirable and often convenient way of approaching calculation.

Sometimes there is no directly related mental mathematics possible and, rather than force artificially created links, you should consider using discrete alternatives. These sessions may be taught at the beginning of the daily mathematics lesson, where they provide a valuable mental 'warm-up', or may be placed at a different time of the day if you consider this more appropriate or useful. For example, ten minutes before lunch could be used for working on some mental multiplication, or ten minutes after break might offer the opportunity for some mental work on equivalent fractions. Of course you can always use such times as registration or lining up for assembly for some number work related to dinner numbers or absent children.

Main teaching

Most of the rest of the time in the daily mathematics lesson is usually used for teaching and practice of the planned area of mathematics. You can decide each day the appropriate division of time between whole-class teaching and individual or group work.

For example, when introducing a new concept, you will need to spend time revisiting previously related concepts, and ascertaining existing knowledge, skills and understanding, before the new (or developmental) concept is broached. You could manage this preliminary mathematics work through a variety of strategies including whole-class questioning, group tasks or individual assessment work. It may take ten minutes at the start of the lesson (including mental mathematics) or may take the whole lesson. The means by which you achieve this will depend on a variety of factors which will be unique to that particular situation, such as:

- the age of the children;
- the ability of the children;
- the time since the concept was previously visited; and
- the complexity of the concept.

From that stage, the introduction of the new concept may take up much of the teaching time for the first day with whole-class teaching, while a few days on your whole-class input may be minimal, serving merely to ensure that all are comfortable with the ongoing work before continuing with previous work in groups or individually.

Regardless of how the time is divided for this part of the lesson, what is important is that you, the teacher, are teaching throughout. The visual imagery that is developing through the mental and oral work needs concrete and visual models to help strengthen the children's understanding. The consequent improved flexibility of transference both within and outside mathematics lessons will in turn provide the basis and incentive for further expansion in both confidence and cognition. Whether you are teaching groups or individuals or even the whole class, you need to *sequence learning carefully,* help the children to *make links to related areas of mathematics, use visual aids and demonstrate ways of thinking* to ensure that the children *understand the methods they are learning* (Ofsted, 2008, p. 12) and you will need to take time for planning the teaching materials, including resources to achieve this.

The integration of problem-solving and investigations, previously noted as being weak, into this part of the lesson can build on the mental and oral work done. Through this, you will encourage your children to use and apply their knowledge and skills with reasoning and logical organisation and to learn and use the correct mathematical vocabulary to provide clarity to their explanations.

Your children's recording of progression through their work does not have to be written but it must be clear and evident. Talking through their work not only helps their peers but also helps the children themselves clarify their thoughts and therefore their processing and understanding of concepts.

Review

Each lesson needs to be finished effectively. Even if the work is to be continued the following day, a review of five to ten minutes gives the opportunity to:

- revisit daily and longer-term objectives so establishing progress;
- pick up on any errors and misconceptions;
- celebrate children's successes;
- allow children to practise communicating their thoughts and processes;
- note any areas that may need revisiting or reinforcing before moving on (possibly achieved in part by setting relevant homework).

(Adapted from Ofsted, 2000)

The review can be led by you or the children but you need to take care to ensure that it has a purpose related to the lesson and is therefore of value.

Aspects of mathematics lessons

Most schools teach one dedicated mathematics lesson each day, but there are alternatives such as 'maths weeks' and mathematics topics where mathematics permeates a whole unit of work (often for half a term) across the curriculum. This section focuses on the considerations that you should take into account when planning for dedicated mathematics lessons. Some aspects are mentioned here as an introduction and are covered in detail in other chapters.

Time of day

Most schools timetable English and mathematics lessons for the morning, with what remains of the morning and the afternoon set aside for all other curriculum areas. It is not, of course, necessary to have the daily mathematics lesson in the morning and schools need to make their own decisions about how to organise the day. Neither is it necessary for you to have a whole mathematics lesson all in one go (especially with the younger children), although a predominance of this structure during the week helps develop continuity and links between mental, oral and written mathematics. Opportunities for both planned and unplanned mathematics, especially to practise and develop mental strategies, can occur at any time during the day and you should be alert to possibilities.

The role of language

Developing knowledge and use of the appropriate mathematical vocabulary is crucial, but it is up to you to decide how you manage this.

RESEARCH SUMMARY RESEARCH SUMMARY **RESEARCH SUMMARY**

Mayow (2000, p. 17) states that *it is clearly important to introduce mathematical vocabulary as it is needed, but not to the point of obscuring the child's ability to understand.* She goes on to say that *meaning is crucial in bridging the gap in mathematical understanding, and therefore language and number are intrinsically linked.* Turner and McCullouch (2004, pp. 2–3) develop this, stating that *[l]anguage is the means by which we describe our mathematical experiences. It involves the use of* both *mathematical terminology and terminology that is associated with explanation and instruction. A teacher therefore needs to ensure that the language used has a shared meaning – without shared meaning children are likely to develop misconceptions by making* false *connections or not being able to access explanations.* This means being aware of language that is firstly ambiguous. Teaching needs to take misconceptions associated with language into consideration and planning that includes identification of possible ambiguity in the language that is to be used will help you with this. You then need to devise teaching strategies that take such language into account.

Ofsted (2008, p. 12) confirms that *in such circumstances, pupils become confident learners as they develop skills in articulating their thinking about mathematics.*

Resources

Many commercial companies have developed ranges of resources for mathematics lessons, such as number lines, 100 squares and digit cards. When planning, you need to decide:

- which resources will enhance teaching and learning;
- when it is appropriate to use them;
- how to progress learning from concrete representations to abstract understanding;
- how to determine the appropriate application of concepts and so be discriminating in their use.

Differentiation

RESEARCH SUMMARY RESEARCH SUMMARY **RESEARCH SUMMARY**

Ofsted (2008, p. 13) found that *the best teaching seen concentrated on ensuring that every pupil was challenged throughout the lesson. This approach went beyond providing different work for groups and might be best described as pupil-centred or personalised.*

The PNS (DCSF, 2008) advised that for children working significantly below the level of their class or group, learning objectives related to the aspect on which the whole class is working *should be chosen as much as possible. However, they should be right for each child at each stage of their learning and development.*

The PNS continued, saying that *planning for individual children or groups of children based on informed observation and assessment for learning will be informed by knowledge of their priorities. For the majority of the time it will be appropriate for children to work on objectives that are similar and related to those for the whole class. However, at other times you will also have to consider whether the children have other priority needs that are central to their learning, for example a need to concentrate on some key skills.*

The best work for each child is that which provides both success and challenge, and this particular dilemma of providing effective differentiation in whole-class teaching exercises experienced teachers as well as student teachers. Therefore you need to plan specifically. Our own childhood memories of anticipating the possibility of being asked something we cannot answer and the subsequent humiliation (real or perceived) is sufficient evidence that the need for us as teachers to avoid this situation and promote self-esteem in the children is a high priority.

After all, as many children with high mathematical ability dread being wrong (often as expectations of them are high) as do average or lower ability children. Questioning that is differentiated and effectively directed can engage all at their own level. Ofsted (2008, p.14) acknowledges that one of the challenges *is to find quick ways of checking on the progress of pupils working independently while focusing intensively on a particular group. This was done most successfully when good planning wove in key questions which allowed the teachers, as they moved around the class, to pinpoint quickly any misconceptions or errors.*

The use of teaching assistants for individuals or groups can provide you with valuable support throughout a mathematics lesson. The involvement of teaching assistants in planning and the preparation of resources, including ICT, helps to ensure that both teacher and assistants are working towards the same goals without any confusion that could arise through lack of communication.

While many schools have chosen to place children into sets for mathematics lessons this does not remove the need to differentiate. It is just the range that has narrowed and it is important to remember that differentiation is still necessary.

THE BIGGER PICTURE ~~THE BIGGER PICTURE~~ THE BIGGER PICTURE

When you are planning differentiation as part of your duty to ensure the inclusion of all children, remember that there are sources of advice within your school (class teachers and teaching or learning support assistants who work with the children, and the inclusion leader or special educational needs co-ordinator) and from local authority services (such as those for children with additional and special educational needs, for those with English as an additional language and for traveller and minority ethnic children, and a 'virtual head-teacher' with responsibility for looked-after children).

Early Years Foundation Stage

For more on mathematics in the EYFS, see Chapter 6.

You can undertake planning for children in the EYFS in very much the same way as for older children, from the basis of learning objectives. However, the structure of the primary mathematics lesson needs to be interpreted to ensure that Reception children are being taught in ways suited to their age and maturity. This may mean that you teach mathematics in much smaller time frames or in a form that integrates it with the rest of the day's work. A useful gauge is to work towards introducing the discrete mathematics lesson by the third term for most children, with perhaps just the very youngest not meeting it until the start of Year 1.

Mixed-age classes

Many schools, whether through choice or not, have more than one year group in each class. The mathematics lesson allows you to teach all children at their own level, taking account of their social, emotional, cognitive and chronological development. Some mathematical topics can be taught to all children at the same time and others lend themselves better to separate taught sessions, but the development work can be planned in the same way as other differentiation.

Assessment

The inherent flexibility of mathematics lessons, being objective-led rather than task led, allows both for assessment to take place and for that assessment to directly influence the lessons which follow. While working with the whole class or with groups or individuals, you have many opportunities to evaluate children's progress against the learning objectives.

For more on assessment, see Chapter 5.

Throughout mathematics lessons you can monitor children's responses to the teaching either through general observations or through more specifically directed questions or tasks, built into the planning. Regular formative assessment allows you to develop a comprehensive picture of the progress of the class and enables the adjustment of teaching to suit the requirements of each child. Through this routine assessment, the early detection of errors, misconceptions or lack of understanding in the children, or of poorly determined differentiation, can enable effective progress to be maintained and frustration or boredom in the children to be avoided.

In addition to the routine, everyday formative assessment, mathematics lessons can be used, in whole or in part, for more formal, summative assessment. It has already been mentioned that it is usually a good idea at the start of a new area of mathematics to establish the current status of the children's knowledge, skills and understanding. Therefore, it is clearly valuable to ascertain how much has been added to this state during the course of the work. This assessment will then, in turn, inform the next stage of planning.

Information and communication technology (ICT)

For more on using ICT, see Chapters 2 and 3.

ICT has a role to play in the effectiveness of mathematics lessons. The phrase 'information and communication technology' encompasses many resources including video/DVD, audio tape/CD recorders, calculators, interactive whiteboards (IWBs) and computers.

RESEARCH SUMMARY RESEARCH SUMMARY **RESEARCH SUMMARY**

Ofsted (2008, p.18) noted a reduction in the effective use of ICT as a tool for problem solving, also saying *the potential of ICT to enhance the learning of mathematics is too rarely realised*. They also commented that the use of IWBs brings *positives and negatives to teaching and learning* and particularly note that *too often teachers used them simply for PowerPoint presentations with no interaction by the pupils*. They were concerned that this extended to a *reduction in pupils' use of practical equipment.*

Computers can be organised either into suites serving either all or some of the school, or can be sited in each classroom. Computers can be used for whole-class teaching as well as for group and individual work. It is important, however, that you choose software and internet access to complement the learning objectives and that children are taught how to use these programs. Effectively integrated computer work can help children to practise and apply skills and knowledge through exciting, interactive adventure programs, pursue investigations using spreadsheets or expand understanding, use and application through internet challenges. The range of available, suitable material is expanding rapidly and the time you spend working through a program or website during the planning stages of the mathematics lesson is essential to ensure that the content matches the learning objectives and is appropriate for the age and abilities of the children who will use it.

EMBEDDING ICT EMBEDDING ICT **EMBEDDING ICT** EMBEDDING ICT

The calculator provides a valuable resource for removing the unnecessary tedium of extensive or repetitive calculations. If a child understands the underlying mathematical concept of the calculation and is engaged in applying it to a problem or investigation, then the use of a calculator is appropriate. Of course, despite being relieved of the mechanics of calculation, children need to know how to use the calculator correctly and to be able to estimate the answer to each stage of the calculation so they are able to judge the reasonableness of the solution found. Teaching calculator skills is as important as teaching how to use any mathematical resource and should be integrated into planning.

Teachers' subject knowledge

If mathematics lessons are to be of maximum benefit to children, it is necessary for you to be fully competent and confident about your own mathematical subject knowledge, skills and understanding. Weaknesses in this area have long been identified as significant in the quality and effectiveness of mathematics teaching (Ofsted, 2000). The implementation of the Professional Standards for Teachers (TDA, 2008) and Skills Tests for entry into initial teacher training were intended to address this issue. However, all teachers with all levels of subject knowledge, and whatever their experience, need to address this.

RESEARCH SUMMARY RESEARCH SUMMARY

RESEARCH SUMMARY RESEARCH SUMMARY

Ofsted (2008, p.15) findings showed that many lessons were characterised by *the teacher doing most of the talking, emphasising rules and procedures rather than concepts.* They noted that they, especially the older children, *listened attentively but passively* with their role *confined to watching the teacher.*

Millett et al. (2004, p. 202) found that although there had been a step up in the teaching of mathematics, progress was still limited. However, attitudes had improved and teachers *who feel more confident, more enthusiastic and who are getting more enjoyment from their mathematics teaching* will undertake continuing professional development *with interest, rather than with fear.*

However, a teacher who has had to work and think hard to overcome their own lack of understanding and mathematical self-esteem can often prove to be a more empathetic teacher than one who has rarely had to question their own mathematical understanding. You have a professional obligation to be the best you can for your children, and focus on direct, interactive teaching in mathematics lessons, thus providing an impetus for improved subject knowledge.

To improve your own subject knowledge on placements, you can seek advice from your class teacher, mentor, mathematics subject leader or the Mathematics Specialist Teacher (MaST) in your school.

If you are concerned about any aspect of your subject knowledge, see the companion title in this series, Primary Mathematics: Knowledge and Understanding *(Learning Matters, 2014).*

Flexibility

You need to exercise your professional skills to make constructive, creative use of the time while still adhering to the good practice principles of direct, interactive teaching in mental, oral and written mathematics. This allows you to plan for a variety of different approaches to teaching and learning mathematics determined by the nature of the particular aspect of mathematics being studied. After all, *mathematics is a creative discipline* (DfEE/QCA, 1999, p. 60). For example, lessons can be prepared to meet objectives that might focus sharply on skills development or provide practice of varied strategies to improve depth and breadth of knowledge and understanding or to undertake extended investigations. If the mathematics lesson is to benefit children, it must engage, motivate, stimulate, excite, inspire, encourage, fulfil, challenge and satisfy.

A SUMMARY OF **KEY POINTS**

➢ **Most schools offer a dedicated three-part mathematics lesson every day.**

➢ **You need to consider a range of aspects when planning your mathematics lessons, including the time of day when the lesson is taught, the resources that are appropriate, including the use of ICT, and how the time can be used flexibly, including for assessment.**

> ➤ It is important to differentiate the lessons, including for mixed-age classes, in order that all children are included.
> ➤ The role of language and the development of vocabulary are crucial aspects of teaching and learning mathematics within this structure.
> ➤ The role of the teacher in direct teaching results in a clear requirement for confident and accurate mathematics subject knowledge.

M-LEVEL EXTENSION > > > > M-LEVEL EXTENSION > > > >

Start a collection of discrete mental mathematics activities for use in different lessons and situations as and when these are appropriate, for example in PE or just before you go to assembly. Use the research summaries and ideas for further reading and then try out some of the examples suggested in this chapter and in your own wider reading. As you get to know the children who you are working with better, you will start to perceive patterns in how they work and any commonly held beliefs or misconceptions as you have opportunities to explore the children's ideas in more detail. How will you challenge any misconceptions that they may hold without losing their trust or discouraging them from engaging with mathematics? Can a seemingly simple activity such as a mental mathematics session help to address some of these issues and dispel the misconceptions?

REFERENCES REFERENCES **REFERENCES** REFERENCES REFERENCES

Brown, M., Millett, A., Bibby, T. and Johnson, D. (2000) Turning our attention from the what to the how: The National Numeracy Strategy. *British Educational Research Journal,* 26(4): 457–71.

Cockcroft, W. H. (1982) *Mathematics Counts.* London: HMSO 4/98.

Dearing, R. (1993) *Interim Report on the National Curriculum and its Assessments*. London: DfEE.

Denvir, H. and Askew, M. (2001) *Pupil Participation in 'Interactive Whole Class Teaching'.* Unpublished paper delivered at British Society for Research into Learning Mathematics day conference, 3 March.

DCSF (2008) *Primary National Strategy.* London: DCSF.

DfE (2011) *Teachers' Standards.* Available at: www.gov.uk/government/publications/teachers-standards (accessed 13/4/14).

DfE (2013) *The National Curriculum in England: Key Stages 1 and 2 framework document*. London: DfE. Available at: www.gov.uk/government/uploads/system/uploads/attachment_data/file/260481/PRIMARY_National_Curriculum_11-9-13_2.pdf (accessed 13/4/14).

DfEE/QCA (1999) *The National Curriculum for England.* London: HMSO.

Mayow, I. (2000) Teaching number: does the Numeracy Strategy hold the answers? *Mathematics Teaching,* 170, 16–17.

Millett, A., Askew, M. and Brown, M. (2004) The Impact of the National Numeracy Strategy in Year 4 (II): Teaching. *Research in Mathematics Education*, vol 6.

Ofsted (2000) *The National Numeracy Strategy: The First Year.* London: Ofsted.

Ofsted (2008) *Mathematics; Understanding the Score.* London: Ofsted.

Schoenfeld, A. (2006) 'Learning to think mathematically: Problem solving, metacognition and sense making in mathematics', in Grouws, D. (ed.) (2006) *Handbook of Research on Mathematics,* pp. 334–70. NCTM.

TDA (2008) *Professional Standards for Qualified Teacher Status and Requirements for Initial Teacher Training.* London: TDA.

Thompson, I. (ed.) (1999) *Issues in Teaching Numeracy in Primary Schools.* Buckingham: Open University Press.

Turner, S. and McCullouch, J. (2004) *Making Connections in Primary Mathematics.* London: David Fulton.

FURTHER READING FURTHER READING FURTHER READING

Barber, D., Cooper, L. and Meeson, G. (2007) *Learning and Teaching with IWBs: Primary and Early Years.* Exeter: Learning Matters.

DfES (2000) *Mathematical Vocabulary.* London: DfES.

Gillespie, H., Boulton, H., Hramiak, A. J. and Williamson, R. (2007) *Learning and Teaching with Virtual Learning Environments.* Exeter: Learning Matters.

Haylock, D. (2010) (4th edn) *Mathematics Explained for Primary Teachers.* London: Sage.

Mason, J., Burton, L. and Stacey, K. (2010) (Revised edn) *Thinking Mathematically.* Harlow: Pearson Education Limited.

Ofsted (2009) *Mathematics: Understanding the Score. Improving practice in mathematics teaching at primary level.* London: Ofsted.

Thompson, I. (2010) (2nd edn) *Issues in Teaching Numeracy in Primary Schools.* Buckingham: Open University Press.

Williams, P. (2008) *Independent Review of Mathematics Teaching in Early Years Settings and Primary Schools.* Nottingham: DCSF.

5
Assessment, recording and reporting

Introduction

One of the first things to establish when looking at assessment is the terminology used. You need to be clear about what each of the terms means. You will see that although each term has a specific meaning, some of the terms can be applied to the same kinds of assessment activities, i.e. more than one term may apply to a specific assessment situation.

- Assessment for learning (AfL) – Assessment completed to inform the planning of future learning and teaching. This involves the teacher and the child in a process of continual review of the progress of learning. This is sometimes described as formative assessment.

- Assessment of learning – Assessment which provides a summary of assessment to date. This is sometimes described as summative assessment.
- Assessment as learning – this has developed from the personalised learning agenda with the increased awareness of the learner's role in their own assessment and application of different learning styles to the teaching process. This aspect focuses on reflecting on evidence of learning. This is the part of the assessment cycle where learners and teachers set learning goals, share learning intentions and success criteria and evaluate their learning through a dialogue including self- and peer-assessment.

Further terms relating to assessment are presented in the following table.

Ipsative	Identifies performance in relation to previous experience. An example of this would be a portfolio of a child's work where the child and you as the teacher could identify progress over time.
Norm referenced	Assessment designed to enable comparisons to be made between learners in relation to a normal distribution.
Criterion referenced	Identifies performance against statements of criteria.
Diagnostic	Conducted by teachers or other professionals to discover the precise nature of a learner's difficulties. It can be seen as formative assessment, though formative assessment may not give you the specific level of detail about difficulties and whether they are errors or misconceptions. A very useful example of diagnostic assessment is a clinical interview (Ginsburg, 1981). This might sound a daunting challenge for a trainee but what it means in practice is getting an individual to do some mathematics and talk to you while they are completing the task, allowing you a dialogue to explore their understanding. You would need to record the dialogue either by taking notes and/or making an audio recording.
Teacher assessment	Carried out by teachers and built into schemes of work.
Continuous assessment	Assessment formed over a period of time based on observation and records of achievement.
End-of-Key-Stage 2	Externally set tests completed by all children in Year 6.
QCA tests	Optional tests in Years 3, 4 and 5.
Self-assessment	A child's own judgement of the quality of their work.
Foundation Stage profile	Assessment at the end of Reception year.
Target setting	Setting specific learning objectives for an individual, group, class, year group or school.
Evaluation	Judgements made about the effectiveness of activities and/or lessons and/or teaching.
APP	Assessing pupil's progress.

Personalised learning

Associated with assessment is the move to develop a personalising learning agenda, the key components of which are as follows.

Component	Features
Learning how to learn	Giving learners skills, strategies and procedures to enable them to become metacognitive and self-managing learners.
Assessment for learning	Developing a wide range of assessment strategies, which place the emphasis on formative rather than summative approaches by engaging the learner in the assessment process.
Teaching and learning strategies	Providing learners with a wide variety of appropriate options to enable them to learn in the most effective way for them to experience the full range of teaching and learning strategies.
Curriculum choice	This involves changing the curriculum experience from the 'set meal' to the à la carte' menu. Pupils are given increasing choice of what they study and when they study it.
Mentoring and coaching	The one-to-one relationship is central to any model of personalising learning – it is the most powerful expression of a commitment to the learning of the individual. Mentoring may be used to monitor academic progress, support metacognition and provide focused support for aspects of the curriculum.

The first two and the final elements of this agenda are particularly helpful in relation to developing your understanding of current assessment practices. This shifts the focus of assessment from an activity which is 'done to' children to one which is done with children.

Assessment for learning

RESEARCH SUMMARY RESEARCH SUMMARY **RESEARCH SUMMARY**

The Assessment Reform Group (2002) developed the following principles for assessment for learning from their research, including Black and Wiliam's (1998) *Inside the Black Box*, to guide classroom practice. This will involve all the adults working with children in schools and Early Years settings.

Principles for assessment for learning to guide classroom practice: 10 principles

Assessment for learning should:

1. be part of effective planning for teaching and learning;

2. focus on how pupils learn;

3. be recognised as central to classroom practice;

4. be regarded as a key professional skill for teachers;

5. be sensitive and constructive because any assessment has an emotional impact;

6. take account of the importance of learner motivation;

7. promote commitment to learning goals and a shared understanding of the criteria by which pupils will be assessed;

8. provide constructive guidance for learners about how to improve;

9. develop learners' capacity for self-assessment and recognising their next steps and how to take them;

10. recognise the full range of achievement of all learners.

The reason why you will be assessing children's learning of mathematics is to plan effective teaching and learning for the future for all children. Assessment must also provide feedback to them in order to motivate them and target their learning. Children must be aware of what the focus of any assessment will be for each piece of work and who will be assessing their work.

PRACTICAL TASK PRACTICAL TASK **PRACTICAL TASK** PRACTICAL TASK

Review the assessment you undertook on your previous placement in light of the ten principles above. To what extent did your assessment reflect the principles? How can you make your assessments more effective next time?

Remember that more detail is expected from your assessment and record-keeping than from an experienced teacher. In your placements towards the end of your course you will be required to keep records of the whole class's progress and attainment in mathematics. Clearly, you will not be able to build up the kind of detailed picture that the class teacher has, simply because your placements will not be long enough to enable you to identify every feature of a child's mathematical ability. However, you will be able to work with some aspects of answering problems orally, calculation strategies, their written methods, known facts and areas of error or misconception. On earlier placements in your course you will have kept records for mathematics of the children with whom you have been working. This may have started with a small group and worked towards records for the whole class. In this way you will have been building up your experience of using ways of assessing children's number work and methods of recording that provide you with sufficient information in order to make judgements about their progress and attainment.

One major issue of assessment is the difference between identifying the work that an individual, group, class or set has covered and their attainment and progress. You will need to be able to keep a check on both these aspects. Coverage, however, is not sufficient alone for assessment purposes, though it is essential for monitoring children's access to the curriculum.

You will be making judgements about children's work through marking and by considering responses to questions posed all the time in the classroom. What you will need to do is to think about ways to record this information to assist future planning and/or discussions with the class teacher/your mentor about teaching and learning in mathematics.

Cowie (2005) suggested that assessment for learning is different from other forms of assessment as it aims to enhance the learning rather than measure it. Children and all adults involved in their learning share the criteria by which they are being judged and include opportunities for their self-monitoring in the process in order that assessment for learning can be successful. A key part of this article is the focus on the barriers to success of the assessment, linking to the aim of breaking down the barriers to learning.

Are there any barriers to success with assessment for learning? This type of assessment practice relies on teachers developing in their children an orientation towards 'learning' as distinct from 'performance'. The study also highlighted the further complication that children are motivated by social goals (such as establishing relationships with teachers and peers) as well as academic goals. Cowie suggested that child dispositions are not fixed and can be changed by, for example, the way teachers give feedback and the type of feedback given.

The following techniques will provide you with information about assessments for learning.

Assessment during the lesson

During the main activity or sustained work period of the daily mathematics lesson you could be working with a group and choose to assess specific skills, knowledge and/or understanding of the topic taught. One trainee achieved this by developing her own sheet on which she recorded the information to assist her in future planning.

Date	Group
Objectives Learning Outcomes	
Notes including specific barriers to learning – attitudes, behaviour as well as match of work to the children's needs	
Objective(s) achieved	
Targets	
Review	

Design a lesson plan to sit with a group to carry out in-depth assessment in the main activity phase of the lesson. Listen carefully to what each child says. Watch carefully the actions of each child on whom you are focusing.

Assessment at the end of the lesson

One way to assess a number of children at the same time is to map out the progression expected in order that you can identify specific difficulties. Figure 5.1 is a blank template that you could use to begin this process. Figure 5.2 is one that is already filled out for a specific objective.

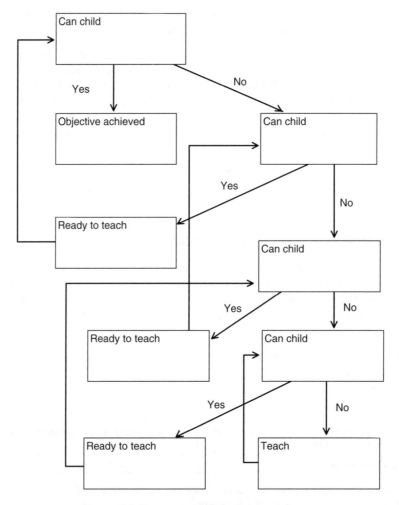

Figure 5.1 Assessment flowchart pro forma

PRACTICAL TASK PRACTICAL TASK **PRACTICAL TASK** PRACTICAL TASK

Produce your own flowchart for an objective you will be teaching, which will help you assess children's progress. Then use the information to plan the next lesson.

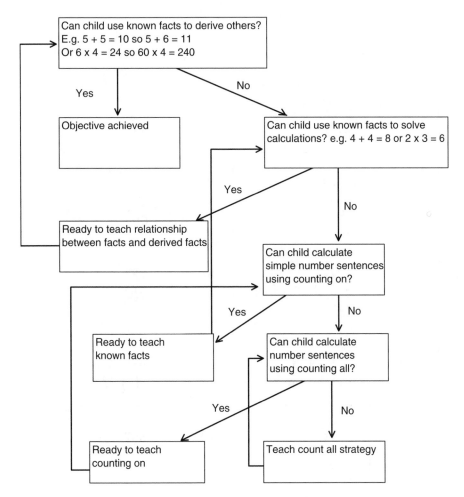

Figure 5.2 Completed assessment flowchart – using known facts to derive others

Marking

Schools often have clear policies on marking, or at least guidance in relation to the style of marking, and it is worth asking your class teacher/mentor about your place-ment school's views on this issue. The following focuses on some general issues about marking for you to consider alongside school-specific guidance.

Try to mark the work by John shown overleaf and, as you do so, think about what you can tell from it.

At this stage there are no specific comments about this example of John's work. The idea is to get you to think about what kinds of assumption you are making about the work as you mark.

John Y3

1.	30 + 57 **87**	6.	21 - 15 14
2.	47 + 15 7⁶1	7.	82 - 24 82
3.	12⁵74 + 159 13⁶112	8.	29⁸3 - 185 108
4.	5 + 135 648	9.	438 - 21 417
5.	11 + 696 29	10.	687 - 47 640

- Before children are asked to hand in work they should know that you will be marking this specific task rather than it being self-marked or peer-marked.
- Children should know what you will be focusing on when marking and it should relate to individual targets set where appropriate. Many schools have adopted the WILF acronym of 'What am I Looking For' in each piece of work so children know what is expected of them.
- Children should have been reminded about any layout or presentation issues.
- When receiving the work you will want to look for successes as well as aspects that will need to be developed and may well form some future targets for the individual.
- Indicate which answers are correct and which are not. Do not mark a whole page of work wrong but see the child separately. Make sure that you indicate if there are any corrections to be completed and why.
- Try to write comments that inform the child and that are in legible handwriting; try to avoid writing 'good' or 'well done' on their own – say why a piece of work is good.
- Set children between one and three targets as a result of marking this piece of work.
- Choose a colour of pen that is in contrast to the child's work. There may be a school policy about the colour(s) to use.

- If you are not sure what is going on when you look at a child's work, do not mark it. Set aside time to talk to the child individually. We can make assumptions about difficulties based on the recording we see and that can lead us to plan intervention that is not appropriate.
- This type of marking can assist you as a teacher in collecting evidence of children's progress and attainment. You can use this as formative assessment, which will inform the next stage of planning. It will give you and others an indication of the amount of help needed to complete a task if this information is added to your comments on the work, e.g. 'Robert worked with Majid on this problem' or 'Amy used a calculator for this work'. You can use it as the basis of pupil conferences and it will assist you in compiling summative reports for parents. Table 5.1 will help you think about the type of feedback that you give when marking.

Positive feedback	Type A Rewarding	Type B Approving	Type C Specifying attainment	Type D Constructing achievement	Achievement feedback
	Rewards	Positive personal expression Warm expression of feeling General praise Positive non-verbal feedback	Specific acknowledgement of attainment/ use of criteria in relation to work/ behaviour Teacher models More specific praise	Mutual articulation of achievement Additional use of emerging criteria Child role in presentation Praise integral to description	
Negative feedback	Punishing	Disapproving	Specifying improvement	Constructing the way forward	Improvement feedback
	Punishments	Negative personal expression Reprimands Negative generalisations Negative non-verbal feedback	Correction of errors More practice given Training in self-checking	Mutual critical appraisal	

Table 5.1 Feedback from marking strategies

Source: Adapted from Gipps (1997), cited in Conner (1999)

The key features of written feedback are to:

- show success;
- indicate where improvement is needed;
- give an improvement suggestion;
- give space for the child to act on the feedback.

The following are examples of assessment and recording, including target-setting, for children. They are designed to be used in conjunction with your school's marking and

MARRA policies (monitoring, assessment, recording, reporting, accountability) and also provide you with some potential strategies if the school has not fully developed this area yet.

From Cowie's (2005) research in relation to assessment for learning it is important to note that children did not find comments like 'very good' helpful and preferred feedback in the form of suggestions of what to do next. They also found it helpful if teachers used a language that they understood and if teachers revisited ideas and explanation in the class time as well as giving individual feedback. Black and Wiliam (1998) pick out specific issues that relate to marking and giving feedback which you need to consider as you mark children's mathematics work. They found that teachers:

- valued quantity and presentation rather than the quality of learning;
- lowered the self-esteem of children by over-concentrating on judgements rather than advice for improvement;
- demoralised children by comparing them negatively and repeatedly with more successful learners;
- gave feedback that serves social and managerial purposes rather than helping children to learn more effectively;
- worked with an incomplete picture of children's learning needs.

Oral feedback

There are two different kinds of oral feedback: they are the planned and the responsive. With the planned feedback you will have time to consider how you phrase the feedback for an individual, group or whole class so it is likely to be based on marking a class set of books or the teacher's reflection on a previous lesson. This may include general feedback on strengths and areas for development against the objectives and this can help model feedback for children to use in peer- or self-assessment situations. The responsive feedback is usually in the form of the comments that the teacher will make during the lesson to individuals, groups and to the class depending on the specific activity that is being undertaken. For a trainee teacher this can be very daunting as it is part of thinking on your feet while teaching. If you are not sure, it is worth saying directly to the individual, group or class that you want to take away the information and to think about it before you give feedback rather than feeling uncomfortable about the position in which you find yourself. This strategy shows that you have listened and/or observed what is going on and that you are responding. You can then plan a more considered response but you must make sure you follow through with the response and give feedback. It may be an issue that you wish to discuss with your mentor/class teacher before talking again to the children involved. Don't forget to ensure that all children get some oral feedback, including children with additional needs. For this group you may want to plan your feedback very carefully if it is to be public. For any child negative feedback in a public arena could damage their self-esteem and their attitude to mathematics.

PRACTICAL TASK PRACTICAL TASK **PRACTICAL TASK** PRACTICAL TASK

From the last mathematics session/lesson you taught, plan feedback for individuals/a group or the class and ask your mentor/class teacher to observe you doing this to gain some specific feedback on your performance in this area.

Monitoring the development of mental calculation strategies

Below are lists of the mental calculation strategies you might expect children to use, against which you can check their achievement and progress. If you add dates to this form of assessment record you can begin to identify progress over time. Often this is the most difficult area for trainees as the length of some placements can be quite short. The examples are of specific records focusing on the mental/oral strategies but you may wish to adapt something like this to fit more closely your needs for recording attainment and progress of a specific class. A completed grid is also included (see Figure 5.4).

An example of a student's work using this type of grid is shown overleaf.

Observing an individual/group working

Figure 5.3 is an example of the observations made of a child's working and annotated work.

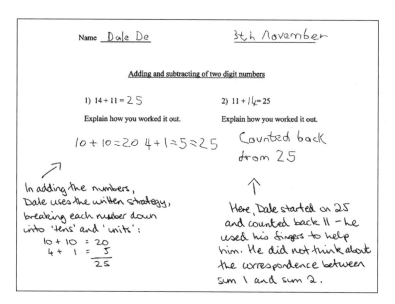

Figure 5.3 Observations of an individual's working

Early Years Foundation Stage strategies	Y/N	Notes	EYFS-PSRN ref.
Can repeat a number rhyme accurately with appropriate actions			
Recites the number names in the correct order (say up to what number)			
Counts accurately objects using one-to-one correspondence (say up to what number)			

Finds a specific digit and says what it is (e.g. asked to find a number 5 can do so)			
Finds a number of objects to match a numeral or carries out an action a number of times (e.g. asked to find four objects can do so, or can hop five times)			
Uses count all to find total of small numbers of objects			
Uses count on from either number in a calculation			
Uses count on from the largest number			
Knows how many in small numbers of objects without counting (from the pattern of objects, e.g. :•: is five)			
Has some known facts (note what they are like, e.g. 1 +1 = 2)			

Key Stage 1 strategies	Y/N	Notes	NC level
Can count on or back in 10s or 1s (say how far)			
Finds a small difference by counting up from the smaller number to largest			
Reorders numbers in calculation			
Adds 3/4 small numbers by putting largest number first			
Finding pairs that total 9, 10, 11			
Bridges through a multiple of 10 then adjusts			
Uses knowledge of number facts and PV to add/ subtract pairs of numbers			
Partitions into 5 and a bit when adding 6, 7, 8, 9			
Adds/subtracts a near multiple of 10 to or from a two-digit number			
Identifies near doubles			
Uses patterns of similar calculations			
Says a subtraction statement corresponding to a given addition statement			
Multiplies a number by 10/100 shifting its digits one/ two places to the left			
Uses knowledge of number facts and PV to multiply or divide by 2, 5, 10, 100			
Uses doubling or halving			
Says a division statement corresponding to a given multiplication statement			

Key Stage 2 strategies	Y/N	Notes	NC level
Counts on or back in 10s or 1s or 100s.			
Counts using decimals and fractions			
Counts from any number in whole numbers and decimals steps extending beyond zero			
Finds a small difference by counting up from the smaller number to largest			
Counts up through the next multiple of 10, 100, 1000			
Reorders numbers in calculation			
Adds 3 or 4 small numbers, finding pairs that total 9, 10, 11			
Bridges through a multiple of 10 then adjusts			
Partitions into tens, units and hundreds, adding tens first			
Bridges through 100			
Uses knowledge of number facts and PV to add/subtract pairs of numbers			
Partitions into 5 and a bit when adding 6, 7, 8, 9			
Adds/subtracts a near multiple of 10 to or from a two-digit number			
Identifies near doubles			
Uses patterns of similar calculations			
Says a subtraction statement corresponding to a given addition statement			
Multiplies a number by 10/100 shifting its digits one/two places to the left			
Uses knowledge of number facts and PV to multiply or divide by 2, 5, 10, 100			
Uses doubling or halving single digits			
Uses doubling and halving of two-digit numbers			
Says a division statement corresponding to a given multiplication statement			
Uses known facts and PV to multiply or divide by 10 and then 100			
Partitions to carry out multiplication			

An example of students' work using a similar grid is shown overleaf.

Key objectives Year 5	Anthony (Low ability →)	Rachel	Adam	Ashley (High ability)
Count on or back in units, tens or hundreds.	✓	✓	✓	✓
Explain the value of each digit in a four-digit number.	not really. After prompting, not confident	✓	✓	✓
Write in figures numbers like fifty-six thousand and nine.	X	✓	✓ ok...	✓
Order a set of decimals with the same number of decimal places: all positive numbers.	✓	✓	✓	✓
...With negative numbers and zero.	not zero–did not include X	✓	✓	✓
Round a number to the nearest integer. 10s, 100s, 1000s	✓	✓	✓	✓
Mentally add or subtract any pair of two-digit numbers.	weak	✓	✓	✓
Double two-digit numbers. Halve numbers	✓ weaker on halving	✓	✓	✓
Add several small numbers – reordering numbers to make calculations easier.	yes–needed prompting to reorder	✓	✓	✓
Find a small difference by counting up from the smaller to larger number.	✓	✓	✓	✓
Work out how many to make the next 100 (e.g. 651 + □ = 700)	X	X	✓	✓
Work out how many to make the next 1000.	X N/A	X	✓	✓
Use a written method to add or subtract three or four-digit numbers, explain it...	+ –evidence in wk bk – weak, issues with ev	✓	✓	✓
...and check by approximating.	X	X	not tested	not yet
Say a subtraction statement corresponding to a given addition statement (the 4 facts).	yes– evidence in work book	✓	✓	✓

Figure 5.4 Identifying children's mental strategies in mathematics

The same can be done for written strategies. The following pro forma has been devised in a different way to demonstrate the variety of possible formats for different purposes, in this case to show progress in written strategies from Reception to Year 6.

	Written recording and calculation strategies	Y/N	Notes
R	Records in the context of play, e.g. marks, stamps, physical objects		
Yr 1	Records in the context of practical activities and when solving simple number problems, e.g. number sentences		
Yr 2	Develops recording in the context of practical work and explaining how problems were solved, e.g. how much money there would be if there are 5 coins in a box		
	Uses the symbols +, –, ×, – and = to record and interpret number sentences involving all four operations. Calculate the value of an unknown in a number sequence (□+ 2 = 6 and 30 – □ = 24)		
Yr 3	Uses informal paper and pencil methods to support, record and explain mental addition and subtraction of number to 1,000, e.g. using an empty number line to show how 301 – 45 was calculated		
	Begins to use column addition and subtraction, using expanded form, e.g. 456 + 63: 400 +50 +6 +60+3 400 + 110 +9 =519		
Y r4	Refines and uses efficient written methods +/–2-digit and 3-digit whole numbers and £p.		
	Develops and refines written methods for TU × U and TU ÷ U including division with remainders		
	Chooses and uses appropriate ways of calculating (mental, mental with jottings, pencil and paper) to solve problems		
Yr 5	Extends written methods to column addition and subtraction of 2 integers less than 1,000 and decimals with up to 2 decimal places e.g. 456 + 362		
	Completes short multiplication of HTU by U		
	Completes long multiplication of TU by TU		
	Short division of HTU by U		
	Chooses and uses appropriate ways of calculating (mental, mental with jottings, written methods, calculator)		
	Explains methods and reasoning in writing		
Yr 6	Uses efficient written methods to add and subtract integers and decimals, and x and divide integers and decimals by 1-digit integers and to multiply 2-digit and 3-digit integers by a 2-digit number		

(Continued)

	In solving mathematical problems and problems involving 'real life', explains methods and reasoning in writing		
	Begins to develop from explaining a generalised relationship in words to expressing it in a formula using letters and symbols		

PRACTICAL TASK PRACTICAL TASK **PRACTICAL TASK** PRACTICAL TASK

Make notes of what is happening when a group is working, and think about what you gain from doing this. What are the difficulties/disadvantages of trying to assess children in this way?

To assist you in observing in classrooms you may find it useful to read Wragg (1999). Observation is often used as a technique in the Early Years where children may be in play or less structured situations than a mathematics lesson in Key Stages 1 or 2. If you have the opportunity you may be able to observe in an Early Years setting. If you are able to observe in both situations you will be able to reflect on the relative appropriateness of the technique in each situation.

Remember to note verbal and non-verbal behaviours that may give you more information about barriers to learning.

Concept mapping

An alternative way of finding out about children's understanding is to use a technique more often associated with science teaching, which is to ask children to construct concept maps. These can range from simple labelled diagrams and drawings to more

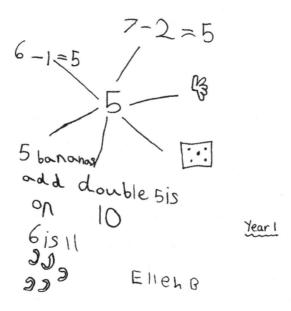

complex maps, which involve asking children how they connect a wider range of words. Arrows can be added to show the direction of the relationship between items.

A simple example of this technique from a Year 1 child is shown opposite. She was asked to think about 5 and what she thought of when she saw the numeral 5. As you can see, her thoughts range from the face of a die to thinking about 5 as the answer for number sentences. You would need to know the context and prior experience of the child to know whether or not she is making connections from what she has been taught or new connections by herself.

In the second example below, a Year 6 child was asked to think about fractions and what they meant to him. Although he started with drawing the cake which is often the first image that people think of when asked about fractions he moves on to see the connection between sharing a cake and decimals and percentages.

For more on concept mapping in science, see Chapter 9 of **Primary Science, Teaching Theory and Practice** *(Learning Matters, 2014).*

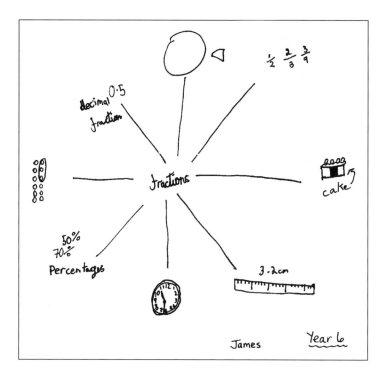

PRACTICAL TASK PRACTICAL TASK **PRACTICAL TASK** PRACTICAL TASK

Before you start to teach a topic, ask the class to spend a few minutes constructing a concept map. You can use this to see any obvious errors and misconceptions about the topic. This will be valuable information on which to base your planning.

The other thing you can do is to ask the children to draw a concept map at the end of the series of lessons on the topic, then compare the items included and the connections between them.

Probing questions

Teachers can use probing questions as part of their direct teaching of the objective in order to:

- get children to think about the new learning;
- make links and so develop a more secure understanding;
- explore whether children have any misconceptions which can then be addressed at the beginning of the main activity part of the lesson.

Probing questions may also be used as part of the plenary/review in order to:

- collect evidence of children's understanding to inform effective planning of future lessons;
- identify and rectify misconceptions.

An example of probing questions for a Year 4 class is as follows:

Key objective: find remainders after division

> Do all your divisions have remainders?
>
> Make up some division questions that have a remainder of 1, etc.
>
> How did you get your answer?
>
> Make up some division questions that have no remainder.
>
> How did you do this? Why won't they have a remainder?
>
> Tell me a number that has no remainder when you divide it by 2, 3 or 5.
>
> Are there any others?

Target setting

The context for the following example is a specifically targeted task during which the teacher makes notes about a group of children:

Name	Comments/notes
Joe	Shows good understanding of four rules for two-digit numbers in all cases – confident.
Laura	Makes careless mistakes – often masking her lack of understanding. Focuses on the procedures for calculating rather than using knowledge of numbers.
Jenny	Lacks knowledge of odd numbers – this was apparent in lesson on halving and identifying numbers that could not be halved into two equal groups of whole numbers.
Lee	Some work needed on the operation of division – does not see division as sharing.
Shakira	Reasonable awareness – some confusion over place value. Need to spend time with her while she calculates in order to find out exactly what the problems are.
Leon	Not sure of multiplication facts – needs support with different ways to help him learn facts.

This will give the teacher notes about the children's achievement during a specific task and will often include comments about attitudes. How easy would someone else find it to interpret these records? What do you think might be the next step for each of these children? How might you change these records to make them easily interpreted by another teacher?

Assessment conference with an individual child

PRACTICAL TASK PRACTICAL TASK **PRACTICAL TASK** PRACTICAL TASK

Plan to spend 10 minutes with a child to talk about their mathematics, review their progress and together set targets for the next few weeks' work. In setting targets you need to choose ones that are achievable both in quality and in content. Concentrate on one area at a time so the child doesn't feel swamped. Always pick out things the child has achieved as well so the conference doesn't dwell on negative issues alone – praise success. Remember this process is not just for children with special needs but for all and target setting can be a good way of raising expectations for the higher attaining children. Set a time by which you will review these targets. The main purpose of this conferencing and target setting is to give children goals to aim for against which they can measure their own success. It may be possible for some children to conference in small groups but there will be others for whom it is better to work on an individual basis.

You will need to keep a record of targets set, for example:

Child's name:	Year:
Term:	Class:
Date of assessment:	Date of review:
Targets set:	Comment on achievement:
1.	
2.	
3.	

Diagnostic assessment

Below is an example of closed diagnostic assessment for errors in subtraction. This form of assessment is often used when you can see that a child has a problem but perhaps can't identify exactly what is going wrong. It can take the form of setting a child/group specific questions and observing how they tackle these and/or

1. 326   542   2. 6$\overset{9}{\cancel{0}}$2   8$\overset{9}{\cancel{0}}$2
    - 117   - 387   - 437   - 396
    ─────   ─────   ─────   ─────
      211   245   265   506

3. $\overset{s}{\cancel{6}}$02 $\overset{7}{\cancel{8}}$04   4. 70$_\cdot$3   60$_\cdot$4
    - 327   - 456   - 678   387
    ─────   ─────   ─────   ─────
      225   308   175   307

5. $\overset{6}{\cancel{9}}$02   '$\bar{2}$05   6. 326   54$^\cdot$2
       368   - 9   - 117   - 389
    ─────   ─────   ─────   ─────
      344   1106   210   200

7. 702   - 508
    - 3$\cancel{6}$8   4$\cancel{7}$7
    ─────   ─────
      454   109

Source: Resnick (1982) (adapted from Brown and Burton 1978), quoted in Dickson *et al.* 1984.

asking children to talk you through their method of working on questions. This commonly occurs when children are using algorithms without understanding. They do not remember the method sufficiently to succeed at answering the questions and errors are the result. The examples above are of errors in subtraction. Try to identify the error in each case.

What does each example represent in relation to the children's understanding of the method and how would you rectify it?

Here is the analysis of what is happening:

1. The child has subtracted the smaller digit from the larger digit regardless of which is on top.
2. The child has 'exchanged' from zero (that is, has not continued the 'exchanging' from the column to the left of the zero).
3. The child has missed out the column with the zero and 'exchanged' instead from the next column, disregarding the middle column.
4. The child has 'exchanged' but has not decremented either column.
5. The child has 'exchanged' from the correct column and decremented that column but not the column containing the zero. Zero has then been subtracted from 12 instead of 1.
6. The child has written 0 as the answer in any column in which the bottom digit is larger than the top.
7. The top digit in the column being 'exchanged' from is zero, so the child has 'borrowed' from the bottom digit instead.

These errors all indicate a misunderstanding of the subtraction algorithm and aspects of place value.

PRACTICAL TASK PRACTICAL TASK **PRACTICAL TASK** PRACTICAL TASK

Try observing one child or a group using a formal algorithm. What does the children's writing tell you about their understanding?

Ask a child to explain how he/she did one of the questions. What assessment can you make of his/her understanding?

Assessing pupil's progress (APP)

This is the tracking of progress using diagnostic information about individuals' strengths and weaknesses. In order to make a judgement about children's work, you will need to follow the steps in the following diagram. (Source: DCSF, 2010, p. 30)

Collect together:
- children's work that demonstrates independence and choice
- any other evidence, plans and notes
- assessment guidance materials
  - level judgement flowchart
  - assessment guidelines to be completed.

→ Identify level borderline for attainment target

Look through the work for each assessment focus and highlight applicable AF criteria

Consider which level offers the 'best fit' and tick the appropriate level-related box for each AF

Make an overall level judgement

PRACTICAL TASK PRACTICAL TASK **PRACTICAL TASK** PRACTICAL TASK

Read the APP handbook (DCSF, 2010). Then use the following steps to assess the child's mathematics and make a judgement about their level of attainment.

You will need:

- evidence of the child's mathematics that shows most independence, for example from work in other subjects as well as in mathematics session/lesson;

- other evidence about the child as a mathematician, for example notes on plans, the child's own reflections, your own recollections of classroom interactions and oral answers given during mental starters;

- a copy of the assessment guidelines for the level borderline that is your starting point.

Discuss your results with your mentor/class teacher before giving any feedback to the child involved.

Using observation in the EYFS

Observation is a key skill to develop as part of your teaching skills. You may be asked by your tutors and school-based staff to be aware of what is going on all around the classroom at all times, so that you notice if a child goes out of the class without asking or interactions between children become heated. This is quite a different observational skill from that needed to make assessments of children. You will not be able to keep track of everything in detail but you will be able to note significant events that will assist all of those working with children to make judgements about progress and achievement in their learning. Early Years teachers and other adults use observation much more than those working with older children because of the kinds of activities in which the children are engaged. Observation can be very helpful with older learners as you can pick up more about ways of working and attitudes as they work, so even if you are not planning to work in EYFS, developing observational skills is useful to all teachers. Practitioners should:

- make systematic observations and assessments of each child's achievements, interests and learning styles;
- use these observations and assessments to identify learning priorities and plan relevant and motivating learning experiences for each child;
- match their observations to the expectations of the early learning goals.

By observing children in play situations you may see them using their mathematical knowledge of one-to-one correspondence, counting, matching or talking about their knowledge of shapes; for example, 'Let's use the cylinders 'cos they will roll'. All the adults working with children in the EYFS will contribute to these observations that will be used to compile the profile at the end of the EYFS. There will be two kinds of observations of young children. The first will be planned observations which you may plan with the team of adults working in the class and include activities outside as well as indoors, and the second will be the spontaneous noticing of significant learning that you will wish to record.

Observation can be used with older learners but, although it will give you a wealth of information about their learning and approaches to tasks, it is time-consuming. As a consequence, observation is used less with older learners but it is still worth practising as part of your assessment skills as a teacher. You may also find this a helpful method of assessment if looking at the use of mathematical skills, knowledge and application when teaching using a cross-curricular approach. You may find a sheet like the one below is a helpful initial guide to your observations.

Date		Observer		Child/Group	
Context Related objective and learning outcomes					
Unaided task		Aided task		Practical task	
Notes					
Reference to any recording by child/group					
Objective achieved		Objective partially achieved		Objective not achieved	
Notes		Notes		Notes	
Targets set as a result of observation			Review date		

PRACTICAL TASK PRACTICAL TASK **PRACTICAL TASK** PRACTICAL TASK

Plan to observe a child or a small group while they are completing a mathematics task. Discuss your notes and reflection with your mentor/class teacher. Consider how you might redesign your pro forma for future observations. Consider also any planning issues that arose, which will assist you in planning time for future observations. Again discuss these with your mentor/class teacher and include discussion about the setting's or school's approach to observation of children's mathematical learning.

Keeping records

There are many useful pro formas to support your recording of assessment.

Year group records

Many schools use year group records at the end of a half term or term, with a 'traffic lights' system to highlight the objectives that children have achieved in green, those that some have had difficulties with in orange and those not achieved or not addressed in red. These are then used to plan the next half term/ term's objectives. This process gives an overview of achievement within a set or class (see Tables 5.2 and 5.3).

Objectives Year 2														
Count in steps of 2, 3, and 5 from 0, and in tens from any number, forward and backward														
Recognise the place value of each digit in a two-digit number (tens, ones)														
Identify, represent and estimate numbers using different representations, including the number line														
Compare and order numbers from 0 up to 100; use <, > and = signs														
Read and write numbers to at least 100 in numerals and in words														
Use place value and number facts to solve problems														
Solve problems with addition and subtraction: • using concrete objects and pictorial representations, including those involving numbers, quantities and measures • applying increasing knowledge of mental and written methods														
Recall and use addition and subtraction facts to 20 fluently, and derive and use related facts up to 100														
Add and subtract numbers using concrete objects, pictorial representations, and mentally, including: • a two-digit number and ones • a two-digit number and tens • two two-digit numbers • adding three one-digit numbers														
Show that addition of two numbers can be done in any order (commutative) and subtraction of one number from another cannot														
Recognise and use the inverse relationship between addition and subtraction and use this to check calculations and solve missing number problems														
Recall and use multiplication and division facts for the 2, 5 and 10 multiplication tables, including recognising odd and even numbers														

Calculate mathematical statements for multiplication and division within the multiplication tables and write them using the multiplication (×), division (÷) and equals (=) signs

Show that multiplication of two numbers can be done in any order (commutative) and division of one number by another cannot

Solve problems involving multiplication and division, using materials, arrays, repeated addition, mental methods, and multiplication and division facts, including problems in contexts

Recognise, find, name and write fractions $\frac{1}{3}$, $\frac{1}{4}$, $\frac{2}{4}$ and $\frac{3}{4}$ of a length, shape, set of objects or quantity

Write simple fractions for example, $\frac{1}{2}$ of 6 = 3 and recognise the equivalence of $\frac{2}{4}$ and $\frac{1}{2}$.

Choose and use appropriate standard units to estimate and measure length/height in any direction (m/cm); mass (kg/g); temperature (°C); capacity (litres/ml) to the nearest appropriate unit, using rulers, scales, thermometers and measuring vessels

Compare and order lengths, mass, volume/capacity and record the results using >, < and =

Recognise and use symbols for pounds (£) and pence (p); combine amounts to make a particular value

Find different combinations of coins that equal the same amounts of money

Solve simple problems in a practical context involving addition and subtraction of money of the same unit, including giving change

Compare and sequence intervals of time

Tell and write the time to five minutes, including quarter past/to the hour and draw the hands on a clock face to show these times

Know the number of minutes in an hour and the number of hours in a day

Identify and describe the properties of 2-D shapes, including the number of sides and line symmetry in a vertical line

(Continued)

(Continued)

Identify and describe the properties of 3-D shapes, including the number of edges, vertices and faces																					
Identify 2-D shapes on the surface of 3-D shapes [for example, a circle on a cylinder and a triangle on a pyramid]																					
Compare and sort common 2-D and 3-D shapes and everyday objects																					
Order and arrange combinations of mathematical objects in patterns and sequences																					
Use mathematical vocabulary to describe position, direction and movement, including movement in a straight line and distinguishing between rotation as a turn and in terms of right angles for quarter, half and three-quarter turns (clockwise and anti-clockwise)																					
Interpret and construct simple pictograms, tally charts, block diagrams and simple tables																					
Ask and answer simple questions by counting the number of objects in each category and sorting the categories by quantity																					
Ask and answer questions about totalling and comparing categorical data																					

Table 5.2 Year group record sheet for a Year 2 class

Number and Place Value — Name

Year 3	Year 4	Year 5	Year 6
Count from 0 in multiples of 4, 8, 50 and 100; find 10 or 100 more or less than a given number	Count in multiples of 6, 7, 9, 25 and 1000	Read, write, order and compare numbers to at least 1 000 000 and determine the value of each digit	Read, write, order and compare numbers up to 10 000 000 and determine the value of each digit
	Find 1000 more or less than a given number	Count forwards or backwards in steps of powers of 10 for any given number up to 1 000 000	
	Count backwards through zero to include negative numbers	Interpret negative numbers in context, count forwards and backwards with positive and negative whole numbers, including through zero	Use negative numbers in context, and calculate intervals across zero
Recognise the place value of each digit in a three-digit number (hundreds, tens, ones)	Recognise the place value of each digit in a four-digit number (thousands, hundreds, tens, and ones)		
Compare and order numbers up to 1000	Order and compare numbers beyond 1000		
Identify, represent and estimate numbers using different representations	Identify, represent and estimate numbers using different representations		
Round any number to the nearest 10, 100 or 1000	Round any number to the nearest 10, 100 or 1000	Round any number up to 1 000 000 to the nearest 10, 100, 1000, 10 000 and 100 000	Round any whole number to a required degree of accuracy
Read and write numbers up to 1000 in numerals and in words	Read Roman numerals to 100 (I to C) and know that over time, the numeral system changed to include the concept of zero and place value	Read Roman numerals to 1000 (M) and recognise years written in Roman numerals	
Solve number problems and practical problems involving these ideas	Solve number and practical problems that involve all of the above and with increasingly large positive numbers	Solve number problems and practical problems that involve all of the above	Solve number and practical problems that involve all of the above

Table 5.3 Years 3–6 record sheet for individual child

Records for a group/class

These are blank record sheets, which can be used for a group/class. The idea is that you write in your learning objectives for the lesson and then assess whether the children have achieved them. Where children have specific difficulties, these are recorded in greater detail (see Tables 5.4 to 5.8).

NAME	ATTENDANCE REGISTER												TARGETS ACHIEVED									
	☑= PRESENT 0 = ABSENT												1	2	3	4	5	6	7	8	9	10

A = ACHIEVED HD = HAD DIFFICULTY WITH NA = NEEDS ATTENTION U = UNFINISHED
TARGET 1-
TARGET 2-
TARGET 3-
TARGET 4-
TARGET 5-
TARGET 6-
TARGET 7-
TARGET 8-
TARGET 9-
TARGET 10-

Table 5.4 Blank evaluation and assessment record sheet for use after each lesson

Assessment:- Needs Attention
Name: Subject: Date:
Objectives of lesson:
Problem(s):
What needs to be done:
Evaluation:

Table 5.5 More detailed assessment sheet for a specific individual

These are designed to give an overview. You will want to supplement them with daily and weekly notes on individuals/groups as a result of observation and marking to provide information for diagnostic purposes, to enrich reports to parents and to assist in individual target-setting:

Topic: Calculations – pencil and paper procedures Week Commencing: 20th November 2000
addition/subtraction

Name	20.11	21.11	22.11	23.11	24.11	Additional Notes, including overall grasp of topic.
	1	2	3	3	4	
Anthony						
Scott						
Morgan						
Chelsey						
Liam						
Natalie						
Emma						
Nicola H						
Nicola T						
Becky						
Mellissa						
Ashley						
Harleen						
Ben						
Thomas						
Lauren						
Jody						
Hannah						
Hollie						
Sonia						
Tannia						
Stacey						
Laura						
James						
Rachel						
Natasha						

Key

*	Achieved target - firm understanding of concepts.
+	Struggled with a few aspects, would benefit from further practice.
=	Had difficulty with, needs reinforcement.
-	Needs attention, understands some elements.
.	Has not understood key concepts.
o	Absent.

Target

1	Calculate additions in columns, including setting them out correctly in HTU columns – awareness of place value.
2	Adding numbers with 1 or 2 decimal points.
3	Calculate subtractions in columns, including setting them out correctly in HTU columns - awareness of place value.
4	Subtracting numbers with 1 or 2 decimal points.

Table 5.6 Supplementary daily/weekly record sheet

School

Mathematics record Sheet

Key Objectives Year 1

Key Objectives	VICTORIA	CARLA	SHANNON	LEAH	NORINA	HOLLIE	ALEX	ANDREW F.	SOPHIE	KATIE	SARAH	MATTHEW	STEVEN	DANIEL	TASHYAN	FAY	STEFAN	ABIGAIL T.	ABIGAIL G.	JASPREET	NISHA	ANDREW B.	CHRISTOPHER	JOSHUA	JACK	ADAM	KAMRAAN	RAVINDER
Count reliably at least 20 objects.																												
Count on and back in ones, twos, fives from any small number, and in tens from and back to zero.	△	△	△✓	✓	✓						✓		✓	△	✓	✓	△	△	△	✓	✓	✓	✓	✓	✓	✓	✓	✓
Read, write and order numbers from 0 to at least 20; understand and use the vocabulary of comparing and ordering these numbers.	△	△	△✓	✓	✓	△	△	△	△	△✓	✓	△	✓	△	✓	✓	△	△	△✓	✓	✓	✓	✓	✓	✓	✓	✓	✓
Within the range 0 to 30, say the number that is 1 or 10 more or less than any given number.																												
Understand the operation of addition, and of subtraction (as 'take away' or 'difference'), and use the related vocabulary.	△	△	△✓	△	△		△	△	△	△	✓	△	✓	△	✓	✓	✓	△	△✓	✓	✓	✓	✓	✓	✓		✓	✓
Know by heart all pairs of numbers with a total of 10.	△	△	△✓	△	△	△	△	△	△	△	✓✓	△✓	✓	△	✓	✓	✓	△	△✓	✓	✓	✓	✓	✓	✓	✓	✓	✓
Use mental strategies to solve simple problems using counting, addition, subtraction, doubling and halving, explaining methods and reasoning orally.	△	△	△	△	△	△	△	△	△	△	✓✓	✓✓	✓	△	✓	✓	✓	✓	✓✓	✓	✓	✓	✓	✓	✓	✓	✓	✓
Compare two lengths, masses or capacities by direct comparison.	△	△	△	△	△	△	△	△	△	△	✓✓	△	✓	△	△	△	△	△	△✓	✓	✓	✓	✓	✓	✓	✓	✓	✓
Suggest suitable standard or uniform non-standard units and measuring equipment to estimate, then measure a length, mass or capacity.	△	△	△	△	△	△	△	△	△	△	✓✓	△	✓	△	△	✓	✓	✓	✓	✓	✓	✓	✓	✓	✓	✓	✓	✓
Use everyday language to describe features of familiar 3-D and 2-D shapes.	△	△	△	△	△	△	△	△	△	△	✓✓	△	△	△	△	△	✓	✓	✓	✓	✓	✓	✓	✓	✓	✓	✓	✓

Table 5.7 Year 1 class record sheet

MATHS

	NAME	ATTENDANCE REGISTER ☑ = PRESENT O = ABSENT										TARGETS ACHIEVED									
													1	2	3	4	5	6	7	8	9	10
RED	BILLY	✓	✓	✓	✓	✓	✓	✓	✓	✓	✓	A+	HD	HD	A	HD	A	A	HD	A	A
	FAIZ	✓	✓	✓	✓	✓	✓	✓	✓	✓	✓	A	A+	A+	A	HD	A	HD	NA	A	A
	JANINE	✓	✓	✓	✓	✓	✓	✓	✓	✓	✓	HD	A	HD	A	HD	A	A	HD	U	A
	KATRINA	✓	✓	✓	✓	✓	✓	✓	✓	✓	✓	A	A	A	A	HD	A	A	HD	A	HD
	TOM	✓		✓	✓	✓	✓	✓	✓	✓	✓	A	A	HD	A	HD	A	A	A	A	A
	KIRAN	✓	✓	✓	✓	✓	✓	✓	✓	✓	✓	A	A	A	A	A	A	A	HD	A	A
BLUE	SOPHIE	✓	✓	✓	✓	✓	✓	✓	✓	✓		A	A	A	A-	A	A	A	A	A	A
	LIAM	✓	✓	✓	✓	✓	✓	✓	✓	✓		A	A+	A	A	A	A	A	A	A	A+
	LIAM	✓	✓	✓	✓	✓	✓	✓	✓	✓		HD	HD	A	A	AU	HD	A+	A	A	A+
	LYDIA	✓	✓	✓	✓	✓	✓	✓	✓	✓		A	HD	A	A	A	A	A	NA	A	A
	MOLLY	✓	✓	✓	✓	✓	O	✓	✓	✓		A	HD	A	A	A	✗	A	A	A	A
	FIONA	✓	✓	✓	✓	✓	✓	✓	✓	✓		A	A	A	A	A	A	A	A	A	A
	LAUREN	✓	✓	✓	O	✓	✓	O	O	O		A	A	A	✗	A	A	A	✗	✗	✗
	SARAH	✓	✓	✓	✓	✓	✓	✓	✓	✓		A	HD	HD	A	AU	A	A	A	A	A
GREEN	FAHMIDA	✓	O	✓	✓	✓	✓	✓	✓	✓	✓	A	✗	AU	A	A	A	A	A	HD	A
	JASKAREN	✓	✓	✓	✓	✓	✓	✓	✓	✓	✓	A	A	A	A	A	A	A	A	A	A
	DANNY	✓	✓	✓	✓	✓	✓	✓	✓	✓		HD	A	HD	A	HD	A	A	A	A	A
	ALEX	✓	✓	✓	✓	✓	✓	✓	✓	✓		A	A	HD	A	A	A	A+	A	A	A+
	NEEL	✓	✓	✓	✓	✓	✓	✓	✓	✓		A	A	A	HD	A	A	A	A	A	A
	HANNAH	✓	✓	✓	✓	✓	✓	✓	✓	✓	✓	A	A	HD	A	A	A	A	HD	A	A
YELLOW	HANNAH	✓	✓	✓	✓	✓	✓	✓	✓	✓		A	A	A	A	A	A	A	A	A	A
	HANEESH	✓	✓	✓	✓	✓	✓	✓	✓	✓		A	A+	A	A	A	A	A	A	A	HD
	DAYLION	✓		✓	✓	✓	✓	✓	✓	✓		A	A	A	A	A	U	A	A	A	A
	CHARLOTTE	✓	✓	✓	✓	✓	✓	✓	✓	✓		A	HD	A	A	A	A	A	A	A	A
	SAM	✓	✓	✓	✓	✓	✓					U	A	NA	A	AU	A	A	HD	A	A
	LIA	✓	✓	✓	✓	✓	✓	✓	✓	✓		U	HD	A	A	A	O	A	NA	A	HD
	NIKHOLAS	✓	✓	✓	✓	✓	✓	✓	✓	✓		U	U	A	HD	AU	U	A	NA	A	A
	SAGE	✓	✓	O	✓	✓	✓	✓	✓	✓		U	HD	✗	A	A	HD	A	NA	A	A

A = ACHIEVED   HD = HAD DIFFICULTY WITH   NA = NEEDS ATTENTION   U = UNFINISHED

20/11/	**TARGET 1** - TOP: ABLE TO DO SUBTRACTION WITH MONEY MIDDLE: ABLE TO DO SUBTRACTION *beginning with money* BOTTOM: *ABLE TO DO* SUBTRACTION
21/11/	**TARGET 2** - TOP: ABLE TO MAKE UP VALUES AND WRITE A SUM NAME MIDDLE: MAKE UP VALUES BOTTOM: COUNT VALUES
27/11/	**TARGET 3** - TOP: MIDDLE: MAKE UP VALUES WITH A SET NUMBER OF COINS BOTTOM: COUNT VALUES
28/11/	**TARGET 4** - COMPLETE P97 + 8 IN NHM BOOK 1 CORRECTLY
29/11/	**TARGET 5** - MEASURE OBJECTS USING HANDS, FEET OR CUBES
30/11/	**TARGET 6** - MEASURE OBJECT USING WHICHEVER METHOD APPROPRIATE ACCURATELY
4/12/	**TARGET 7** - COMPARE TWO OBJECTS WEIGHTS USING BALANCE SCALES
4/12/	**TARGET 8** - CHOOSE CRITERIA FOR TWO SETS
7/12/	**TARGET 9** - PUT OBJECTS INTO TWO SETS
	TARGET 10 - ABLE TO USE THE COMPUTER EFFICIENTLY TO PRACTICE + and −

Table 5.8 Completed evaluation sheet for a series of lessons

One of the difficulties about these types of record is the key that is used to differentiate achievement against the objectives. A clear key can make the records accessible to all but sometimes the key could be interpreted in a range of ways. Look at the examples of students' records shown in Tables 5.7 and 5.8. Which is clearer to understand and why?

EMBEDDING ICT EMBEDDING ICT EMBEDDING ICT EMBEDDING ICT

ICT can be used not only as a direct support to children's learning through planned activities, but it can also help teachers with their ongoing assessment for learning, their regular record-keeping and in reporting on children's progress to their parents. There are commercially available programs to support all of these applications, but many local authority admin systems now have data-handling functions to track individual pupils' progress, their attainment as measured through summative assessments, and other important data such as attendance records. You may find that your school has pro formas that it uses as part of its assessment procedures and these may be available on the school's intranet or virtual learning environment (VLE). Ensure that you are familiar with the assessment policy and any forms used, and that you understand how they are used. Before using any of them, discuss them with your mentor/class teacher or the assessment co-ordinator.

Summative assessment or assessment of learning in mathematics

Profile for the end of the Early Years Foundation Stage

Since 2008, the assessment at the end of the Early Years Foundation Stage has been the EYFS Profile, which is based on detailed observation of the children throughout the EYFS aged 3–5. In 2012 a revised EYFS profile came into effect. The EYFS profile summarises and describes children's attainment at the end of the EYFS. It is based on ongoing observation and assessment in the three prime and four specific areas of learning, and the three learning characteristics. A completed profile consists of 20 items of information: the attainment of each child assessed in relation to the 17 early learning goal (ELG) descriptors, together with a short narrative describing the child's three learning characteristics.

National Curriculum tests

At the end of Key Stage 1 the use of the tests is under the control of teachers who can decide when to use them with their children and there is a greater emphasis on teacher assessment. This does mean that if you are teaching in Key Stage 1 you will need to keep detailed notes about the children in order to make judgements about their learning and report this as part of the statutory assessment and to parents and carers.

During Key Stage 2 some schools use optional tests for Years 3, 4 and 5 to monitor progress before the statutory assessments in Year 6. The optional tests were designed to aid target setting and decide which children would benefit from the use of booster materials or other interventions in order to reduce the barriers to learning and achievement at nationally expected levels. The optional tests were discontinued in July 2014 and schools still using them will draw upon their own stock.

At the time of publication, The Standards and Testing Agency was reviewing all future National Curriculum Tests in mathematics to *ensure that they remain accessible to all pupils, and that they are primarily tests of mathematics rather than reading* (DfE, 2011b, p.10). It was envisaged that new end of Key Stage assessments would be introduced in summer 2016 and that these would be of a *higher and more ambitious expected standard* (DfE, 2013, p. 7) than existing tests. At the time of publication there were two level 3–5 papers, normally sat on consecutive days. Since 2014 calculators were not allowed to be used in the tests. There were also two level 6 papers, often sat on the same day. Calculators were allowed in these.

RESEARCH SUMMARY RESEARCH SUMMARY **RESEARCH SUMMARY**

Cooper and Dunne (2000) researched the National Curriculum Test questions for mathematics at Key Stages 2 and 3. Their focus was that some of the questions selected for use in the tests produced unintended difficulties for pupils as a result of the ways in which mathematical operations were embedded in textually represented 'realistic' contexts. Understanding the 'rules of the game' could be the reason why some groups of pupils performed poorly on this type of question. In test items with 'realistic' elements pupils are required to draw on their everyday experiences as well as their previous knowledge and understanding of mathematics. At the end of Key Stage 2 working-class and intermediate-class pupils perform less well than service-class pupils on 'realistic' items and the effect is large enough to make a considerable difference to pupils' futures. Differences between the genders are similar though smaller. Cooper and Dunne's research suggests that, as teachers, we need to be aware of the predisposition and effects of prior knowledge of our pupils when they respond to test items that have 'realistic' elements.

Reporting to parents

Reports cover the whole of the primary curriculum and the report for mathematics is only a very small section of what should be communicated to parents.

When writing reports to parents you need to remember who the audience is and what they expect to read about their child. Written reports should be supportive and meaningful (i.e. not full of education jargon), and should include positive remarks, but also they should not hide any difficulties. They should include aspects of knowledge, skills, understanding and application. Sometimes it is appropriate to mention presentation and/or attention to tasks by some children.

Reports can come in different formats. They can be computerised and generated from a bank of suggested phrases or they can be tick sheets, full written reports or any combination of these. Computerisation can lead to quite impersonal reports though it can save time. Written reports usually include targets for the next term/year. They are also usually written when the teacher has had the class for a considerable part of the year so they know the children well.

Consider this example of a child's mathematics report:

> I am delighted in Sam's progress this year. He has worked hard, always concentrates well and seems to have gained in confidence. He is now happy to work independently and has been imaginative and thoughtful in his approach to investigative work.

This particular report could have been about any subject and for any child. It is not specific, and it does not really tell you what the pupil can and cannot do.

Now consider this second example:

Mathematics

Sarah understands place value and can read, write and order whole numbers. She is beginning to have more confidence in developing her own strategies for solving problems. She has a good grasp of the four rules and with help can use inverse operation. She needs to become more independent in this aspect. She is competent in using decimal notation for money and measurement, and can relate simple fractions with whole numbers. She needs to speed up her mental recall of tables and number bonds. She can construct and interpret information from graphs and use the computer to represent her data. She enjoys the practical aspects of mathematics and can work equally well as a member of a group or as an individual and is presenting her work in a neater and more orderly fashion. She needs to have more confidence in her own ability.

This report is much clearer. It could only be referring to mathematics and there are clear statements of what the child can and cannot do and what she needs to do to improve.

THE BIGGER PICTURE   THE BIGGER PICTURE   THE BIGGER PICTURE

When you are planning how to assess the children with whom you are working, choose a sample of them and ask if you can have permission to look at the assessment records kept for each child over time, which may include seeking parental permission in some cases. Note the types of assessment that have been undertaken on each child and whether there any differences between the range of assessments carried out on children of different abilities, or on particular groups such as able, gifted and talented children, those with additional and special educational needs, children learning English as an additional language or looked-after children. Reflect on the different ways in which assessment is being used to monitor and promote children's learning.

A SUMMARY OF **KEY POINTS**

> Assessment is an integral part of the teaching and learning process.
> Assessment for learning or formative assessment is used to plan effective teaching and learning of mathematics.
> A variety of different techniques can be used to collect information on which to base judgements about progress and attainment.
> Marking children's work requires careful planning and must include feedback to the children.

> ➤ Teachers need to be making judgements about progress in mathematical learning and targeting next steps for learning and teaching.
>
> ➤ Record-keeping is a summary of other assessment information that you will have as the teacher.
>
> ➤ Reporting to parents needs to be informative and accurate, and to set targets for future learning.

M-LEVEL EXTENSION > > > > M-LEVEL EXTENSION > > > >

Find out more about personalised learning and the one-to-one tuition initiative. How will these affect your planning for mathematics and the types of assessment that you undertake? What implications are there for recording and for reporting to parents?

REFERENCES REFERENCES **REFERENCES** REFERENCES REFERENCES

Assessment Reform Group (2002) *Principles of Assessment for Learning: 10 Principles.* Cambridge: Cambridge University of Cambridge, Faculty of Education.

Black, P. and Wiliam, D. (1998) *Inside the Black Box: Raising Standards through Classroom Assessment.* London: King's College, London.

Conner, C. (ed.) (1999) *Assessment in Action in the Primary School.* London: Falmer Press.

Cooper, B. and Dunne, M. (2000) *Assessing Children's Mathematical Knowledge: Social Class, Sex and Problem Solving.* Buckingham: Open University Press.

Cowie, B. (2005) Pupil commentary on assessment for learning. *The Curriculum Journal,* 16 (2): 137–61.

DCSF (2010) *Assessing Pupils' Progress.* London: DCSF.

DfE (2011) *Teachers' Standards.* Available at www.gov.uk/government/publications/teachers-standards (accessed 13/4/14).

DfE (2011b) *Independent Review of Key Stage 2 Testing, Assessment and Accountability: Government Response.* London: DfE.

DfE (2013b) *Primary Assessment and Accountability under the New National Curriculum.* London: DfE. Available at: www.gov.uk/government/uploads/system/uploads/attachment_data/file/298568/Primary_assessment_and_accountability_under_the_new_curriculum_consultation_document.pdf (accessed 13/4/14).

Ginsburg, H. (1981) The clinical interview in psychological research on mathematical thinking: aims, rationales, and techniques. *For the Learning of Mathematics*, 1 (3): 4–10.

Gipps, C. (1997) *Assessment in Primary Schools: Past, Present and Future.* London: British Curriculum Foundation.

Resnick, L. B. (1982) (adapted from Brown and Burton, 1978) quoted in Dickson, L., Brown, M. and Gibson, O. (1984) *Children Learning Maths: A Teacher Guide to Recent Research.* London: Holt, Rinehart & Winston.

Wragg, E. C. (1999) (2nd edn) *An Introduction to Classroom Observation.* London: Routledge.

FURTHER READING FURTHER READING FURTHER READING

Briggs, M., Woodfield, A., Martin, C. and Swatton, P. (2008) *Assessment for Learning and Teaching in Primary Schools.* Exeter: Learning Matters.

Clarke, S. and Atkinson, S. (1996) *Tracking Significant Achievement in Primary Mathematics.* London: Hodder & Stoughton.

Jacques, K. and Hyland, R. (eds) (2007) *Professional Studies: Primary and Early Years.* Exeter: Learning Matters.

Torrance, H. and Pryor, J. (1998*) Investigating Formative Assessment: Teaching, Learning and Assessment in the Classroom.* Buckingham: Open University Press.

6
Mathematics in the Early Years Foundation Stage

Introduction

Before children arrive in school they will have had a range of experiences which introduce them to, and require them to use, mathematical concepts. Some are quite overtly mathematical, such as singing number rhymes or creating patterns with objects; others involve mathematical concepts more subtly, such as sorting the washing or laying the table. As teachers it is important to acknowledge and extend the pre-school experiences of the children within the classroom. Maths 'talk' needs to be developed from the Early Years, so that children are confident to share and discuss their methods and outcomes rather than silently internalising the language of maths. Mathematics is a subject where there is a great danger of rapidly moving towards the silent approach, producing pages of written work and formal algorithms from a young age. It is important that classroom practice reflects a far more active approach. The mathematical experiences of young children should be active, multisensory, challenging, practical and relevant.

RESEARCH SUMMARY RESEARCH SUMMARY **RESEARCH SUMMARY**

Anderson *et al.* (2007) summarise much of the recent research into pre-school mathematics. They conclude that pre-school children evidence a strong capacity to deal with number and therefore the emphasis on pre-number activities may be inappropriate for many children in Early Years settings in school. They also highlight the important role parents and carers play in mediating mathematics learning opportunities with their children. Informal learning opportunities need to be encouraged and modelled within daily routines and play. They summarise some fascinating and challenging results of Ginsburg's work in day care settings observing children at play. He observed that these pre-school children were able to engage in relatively advanced mathematical explorations, which would imply we should be offering a more conceptually rich environment within our Early Years classrooms. This finding supports their earlier conclusion regarding pre-number activities.

All of these findings offer us challenges as mathematics teachers of Early Years children. We need to know that we are addressing their learning needs, scaffolding and supporting as needed but also not underestimating their capacity to engage with mathematics at an appropriately challenging level.

The Statutory Framework for the Early Years Foundation Stage (EYFS) came into force from September 2014. The EYFS is a single framework for care, learning and development for children in all Early Years settings from birth to the August after their fifth birthday. This means that teachers in Foundation Stage settings within schools need to ensure they enable their children to meet the goals laid out. The EYFS sets the standards that all early years providers must meet to ensure that children learn and develop well and are kept healthy and safe. It promotes teaching and learning to ensure children's 'school readiness' and gives children the broad range of knowledge and skills that provide the right foundation for good future progress through school and life.

One area of learning and development identified within the EYFS is mathematics:

> *Mathematics involves providing children with opportunities to develop and improve their skills in counting, understanding and using numbers, calculating simple addition and subtraction problems; and to describe shapes, spaces, and measures.*

Play

One of the key ways children learn in the Foundation Stage is through play. The EYFS identifies play and exploration as one of the commitments to learning and development. This commitment includes opportunities for learning through experience, adult involvement and plenty of space and time to play outdoors and indoors. Table 6.1 links these opportunities to possible mathematical situations or outcomes.

The range of mathematical play activities children should experience might include: telling, listening to and creating stories; listening to, singing and adding actions to songs; games and imaginative play, including role-play; construction activities; and communicating mathematical information to others, e.g. producing labels for the 'class shop', menus for the 'class café'. These activities will give children the opportunity to use, explore and experiment with numbers, patterns, shapes and measures.

The EYFS rightly describes the role of the practitioner as crucial in play. It suggests that:

- practitioners plan and resource a challenging environment where children's play can be supported and extended;
- practitioners can extend and develop children's language and communication in their play through sensitive observation and appropriate intervention.

Through play and exploration, within an appropriate context for learning and with effective adult involvement, children can:	Possible mathematical context or outcome:
• experience play physically and emotionally	The physical exploration of mathematics is vitally important for children. Maths need not be something that is solely undertaken sitting in a group, but it should be something that involves active engagement through very physical play situations as children explore and solve problems with numbers, patterns and shapes.
• play alone or with others	Mathematics is an activity that is frequently undertaken individually. However, working collaboratively to construct, explain and extend new learning is a vital context for mathematics.
• use the experiences they have and extend them to build up ideas, concepts and skills	Consolidation and practice are frequently used within mathematics teaching. These, together with productive discussions that challenge the children to discuss maths and engage in 'maths-talk' and frequent, appropriate use of practical manipulatives, will support the children as they further extend their conceptual understanding.
• express fears and relive anxious experiences	Mathematics anxiety is a well-documented reality for some children in school. Being able to articulate this and express fears within a supportive context should help ensure mathematics anxiety occurs less often for children.
• try things out, solve problems and be creative	Mathematics can be, and should be, an extremely creative and imaginative subject that conjures up ideas and images to be used or explored further.
• take risks and use trial and error to find things out	Investigating and problem-solving in mathematics involve a great deal of risk-taking and learning from your mistakes. Being confident to take risks and learn from mistakes is an important part of a child's mathematical development.

Table 6.1 Linking play and the teaching of mathematics

These areas will be developed further in this chapter as we look more at teaching and learning mathematics in the Foundation Stage.

Teaching

In order to become an effective mathematics teacher in the Foundation Stage you need to consider all aspects of your practice. You need to think about how you are encouraging the children to see themselves as mathematicians. Young children thoroughly enjoy using new words, so engage them with appropriate mathematical vocabulary, encourage them to see themselves, and describe themselves, as mathematicians. From the outset this fosters the development of positive attitudes towards their mathematics learning. Maintain this positive attitude in the children by planning a varied range of mathematical opportunities. Encourage emergent recording as the children start to record their mathematics and try not to stifle their enthusiasm by negatively affecting their confidence just at the point that they start to record their mathematics. Talk to them and take an interest in how they achieved their answer, not just in the answer itself. This further encourages the children to view themselves as mathematicians. Make sure you give the children access to a wide variety of resources to manipulate within their mathematics learning. The children need to be able actively to construct understanding by engaging practically with tasks. Think when it is appropriate to ask for some recording of mathematics – it should not become purely a paper-chasing exercise for the children!

Beyond this there are many other implications for us as teachers. First, let us consider the children as they arrive in school. Young children are innately curious and come to school with a great deal of knowledge and understanding in a range of mathematical areas. Their interaction with their physical environment and with other people, as well as the conclusions they have drawn and the ideas they have established from these interactions, form the starting point as they enter the classroom. Their enthusiasm is boundless and their capacity to enjoy new experiences offers teachers a wonderful opportunity to continue the children's mathematical development in a very positive and stimulating manner.

THE BIGGER PICTURE   THE BIGGER PICTURE   THE BIGGER PICTURE

When you are planning topics in the Early Years, think about planning across all of the areas of learning rather than just for problem-solving, reasoning and numeracy. Think about how mathematical concepts might fit into a wider topic or unit of work. For example, comparing eye and hair colour and measuring heights might fit in with the theme of 'Ourselves' and investigating patterns and tessellations might form part of a half-term's focus on 'Buildings'. Collecting data on favourite foods or numbers of different types of animal might both be included in a cross-area plan based on 'Food and farming'.

Clear scaffolding to ensure children feel supported as they learn is vital; using real-life contexts and not letting children feel exposed or vulnerable is also crucial. This has clear implications for planning, monitoring, assessment and recording. Knowing exactly where each child is, and what they know, understand and can do is clearly vital if we are to plan meaningful activities that support and extend the children's mathematical learning. This is a very big task for any teacher. It is important to remember that you do not have to do all of this on your own. In Early Years classrooms, teachers should have the help and support of an Early Years assistant. There are currently many initiatives to support the training and development of the role of Early Years assistants and these professional colleagues play a vital role in any Early Years classroom. They can be used to record observations and assessments of children's learning to support your planning for further development. It is important to remember that it is your responsibility as the teacher to ensure your assistant knows the intended outcomes for the children when engaging in activities. It is also your responsibility to ensure they know how, when and where to record their observations. Using classroom support in this way is invaluable in ensuring you have a full and detailed picture of the children's knowledge and understanding of mathematics.

Mathematical 'talk' is also vital in ensuring children continue to develop a precise and accurate understanding of the technical mathematical vocabulary. Capitalise on every opportunity throughout the day, as part of the classroom or playground organisation and during play activities, as well as clearly planning opportunities to develop the full range of mathematical vocabulary through specific activities.

In order to be able to achieve all this as a Foundation Stage teacher, you need to be confident in your understanding of mathematics. The demands of a Foundation Stage classroom are such that you need to be able to respond flexibly to any situation and capitalise on every learning opportunity. In the same way that you want to develop a positive attitude towards mathematics in the children, you need to view yourself as a mathematician. What does this actually mean for you as a practitioner? What it means is that you are confident in your own mathematical ability; you know you have a sufficient understanding of mathematical concepts to understand the links between different areas of mathematics in order effectively to support your teaching.

For more teaching strategies, planning and assessing in the Foundation Stage, see Chapters 2, 3 and 5.

PRACTICAL TASK PRACTICAL TASK **PRACTICAL TASK** PRACTICAL TASK

When you are in school in a Nursery or Reception class, watch the class teacher when they are engaged in interactive oral work. What strategies do they use to:

- involve the children?
- ensure a brisk pace?
- monitor the learning of children?
- tackle errors and misconceptions?
- Think back to the features of effective teaching detailed above. How are these features evidenced within the strategies you have observed?

Learning

For more on using resources in the EYFS, see Chapters 2 and 3.

You can effectively help to support the learning of mathematics by the children in your Foundation Stage class by ensuring the learning is purposeful. Using contexts that are enjoyable for the children also promotes learning, for example play activities and games; also allow for child-initiated activities. Encourage the children to be active, confident and enthusiastic as they join in with mathematics activities and mathematics talk.

So, how do you achieve all this?

Capitalise on the children's enthusiasm and curiosity and ensure the environment allows for children to initiate activities that will extend their mathematical learning. Make sure children have access to things such as coins, tills, calculators, different objects and shapes, numbers, different-sized containers and rules, stacking toys, wooden bricks and construction toys, paper, card, labels, pencils, pens and crayons. All of these resources allow children to initiate activities that can promote their learning of mathematics. Having pencils and paper freely available allows children to record, if they wish, in a way that is meaningful for them. They are far more likely to record if they understand the purpose of the record, and if it is self-initiated there is no question that they understand the purpose.

For an example of using a book as a starting point for mathematics, see Chapter 2.

Children will see themselves as mathematicians if they are encouraged to develop positive attitudes, grow in confidence and enjoy their mathematical experiences. It is the role of the teacher to ensure that this happens.

For more information on using ICT in your teaching, see Chapters 2 and 3.

One strategy that can develop these positive attitudes, confidence and enjoyment is the use of children's fiction as a stimulus for work in mathematics. Books such as *Kipper's Toy Box* by Mick Inkpen are good for counting, or use *I Don't Want To Go To Bed* by Julie Sykes, which is good for ordinal number. Lots of books offer the opportunity to discuss comparatives in size: *Guess How Much I Love You* by Sam McBratney, *Thud!* by Nick Butterworth or the *Large Family* books by Jill Murphy (e.g. *Five Minutes' Peace* or *A Piece of Cake)* are just a few. There are some lovely stories that introduce children to the passing of time and the sequencing of events: *We're Going on a Bear Hunt* retold by Michael Rosen (sequencing events), *The Very Hungry Caterpillar* by Eric Carle (days of the week) and *The Bad Tempered Ladybird* also by Eric Carle (o'clock time). Take the opportunity to capitalise on the children's enjoyment of books and stories and use them as a stimulus for mathematical activity.

By utilising a range of strategies appropriate to the subject content and children being taught, you will be able both to sustain and develop the enthusiasm, curiosity and confidence of the children as they learn mathematics.

EMBEDDING ICT EMBEDDING ICT **EMBEDDING ICT** EMBEDDING ICT

When teaching children in the Early Years, remember to build on their high levels of engagement by giving them opportunities to interact with a wide range of media and technologies. When you are developing a dramatic play area, remember to make these as realistic and up to date as possible by including a range of information and communication technologies. In the hairdressing salon or boarding kennel, include a laptop or mobile tablet so that the children can take bookings and make appointments. In a coffee shop or restaurant, include a calculator to add up the bills. In a hotel reception area, include the computer so that the children can print out customers' accounts. Include an electronic till, a basic calculator and an up-to-date looking telephone or mobile in the shop or cafe role-play area. When planning guided play activities, include the choice of both mathematical mark-making and recording the outcomes of problem-solving tasks on the laptop or PC, and ensure that all children have a turn at completing programs on the computer, for example to practise their shape or number recognition. Photocopy or scan and print out the children's work to include in a class book or to be sent home to share with parents.

Parents and carers as partners

A good relationship with parents and carers with everyone working together has a very positive impact on the children. Children need to feel secure and confident. Where they recognise that there is consistency and mutual respect between home and school, this is most successful. An open and ongoing sharing of information from home to school and vice versa is vital to a successful partnership. It is important that parents are kept informed about the mathematics that their children will be studying. A display about the curriculum for the term/half-term/week can be very useful, but do not forget working parents who may rarely be able to visit the school and see the board. Make sure there are sufficient written communications to keep them suitably informed about, and involved in, the mathematics their child is studying. A mathematics evening can be a useful event, especially at the beginning of the year, when you can outline the curriculum for mathematics and share together the expectations that you have.

THE BIGGER PICTURE   THE BIGGER PICTURE   THE BIGGER PICTURE

When you are planning homework activities, they must, of course, be purposeful and either extend children's knowledge or understanding or consolidate a skill already learnt in school. You can involve parents in supporting even very young children's learning by sharing in advance the topics or aspects of mathematics that you plan to study. Many Nursery and Reception classes and other Early Years settings have regular newsletters for parents and you could ask to put in a short article. This is helpful for parents, especially if you are asking children to undertake 'finding out' tasks as they might plan a trip to their local library or want to supervise children's safe use of the internet. As many adults perceive themselves not to be good at mathematics, or are lacking in confidence, it is helpful to include a list of simple practical maths activities for families to do together, and they will enjoy collecting empty packaging and comparing the different shapes and sizes.

Parents and carers need to feel welcome in the classroom and, as a teacher, you need to acknowledge the expertise and skills of the parents and utilise them to support the children. Parents are often very willing to be involved with supporting in class. In order to ensure you make best use of them, plan for their involvement. An activity where children are exploring, maybe using different sized containers in water play and sand play, is enhanced dramatically by appropriate intervention to question and challenge the children's thinking. It is not always possible for you, the teacher, to be there; you may be working with another guided group at this time. If you know you are going to have a parent in the class, share the intended outcomes of the session with the parent and use him or her to support this independent group.

Equally there may be parents who are very concerned about their own level of mathematical understanding and worried about further supporting their child's mathematical development. Some schools have found it useful to run mathematics evenings for parents which focus more on the subject content in order to enable the parents to support their children successfully. These evenings work when there is a relationship of mutual respect and trust.

In any Foundation Stage setting it is important to recognise the important role parents and carers have played in the child's mathematical development before arriving at school. It is equally important explicitly to encourage this role in the future to ensure you really are working together in partnership to develop the child's mathematical learning.

Chapters 7–12 detail a progression in mathematics areas throughout Key Stages 1 and 2. This chapter will now move on to consider the progression throughout the Foundation Stage before children enter Key Stage 1 as they work to attain the early learning goals set out in the EYFS document (2014).

Although the EYFS Guidance is reviewed and updated regularly, the progression that follows remains appropriate for all children developing mathematical understanding regardless of the statutory documentation in place when you are reading this.

Progression in aspects of mathematics

Counting

In a Reception class a teacher is considering the counting strategies of the class. Tom is asked to count the number of crayons on his table.

He clearly counts out loud, 'One, two, three'. When asked by the teacher, 'So, how many crayons are there?' he immediately starts to count out loud again, 'One, two, three'. Straightaway, this tells the teacher a great deal about Tom's understanding of counting and the experiences he needs to extend and support his development.

REFLECTIVE TASK

What do you know about Tom's understanding of counting? What do you think is the next step in his learning? How might you enable him to achieve this?

Counting is something that we, as adults, do without thinking. It is a completely internalised and automatic action. Yet for children there are three clear prerequisites before they can start to count meaningfully.

First, they need to know the number names in order. Before they arrive at school many children will have learnt quite a range of number names, some consistent and

accurate, others less so. Being able to recite the names consistently in order is sometimes referred to as the 'stable-order principle'. The use of songs and rhymes encourages the learning of the number names in order within an enjoyable and appropriate context. *1, 2, 3, 4, 5, once I caught a fish alive* and *1, 2 buckle my shoe,* along with many other rhymes, encourage learning the number names in ascending order, whereas other rhymes such as *5 little speckled frogs* and *10 fat sausages* encourage descending order. Children can show the numbers on their fingers while singing or reciting the songs and rhymes.

Second, they need to have an understanding of matching one-to-one (also called one-to-one correspondence). When children can do this they point to, or touch, an object as they count, to show that they have included it. They say one name for each item counted, making sure they count all objects and don't count any more than once. Children who cannot yet match one-to-one may well point or touch; however, their pointing and the reciting of the number names do not coincide, leading to inaccuracies.

Finally, children need to understand that the last number spoken in the count represents the number of elements in the set. This is the cardinal aspect of number. This is the aspect of counting that Tom does not yet understand. He repeats his count every time he is asked how many there are and is unable to state that the last number, i.e. 3, is equivalent to the number of crayons he has counted.

As an extension to these fundamentals for counting, Gelman and Gallistell (1978) (cited in Cockburn, 1999) outline two further principles which are a part of our counting skills. The first of these is the 'order irrelevance principle'. This basically means that we don't have to count left to right. We could count right to left or start in the middle; the sequence is irrelevant to the number in the count. This might seem so obvious that it does not seem necessary to state it. However, consider children's reading: p-a-t and t-a-p are two very different things, so here the order is extremely relevant. Children are rarely told that in some situations the order is vital and yet they still manage to learn when it is the case.

The other principle of Gelman and Gallistell is the 'abstraction principle'. It has been claimed that children can only count objects that are perceptually similar, so in order to be able to count they must first be able to sort. Gelman and Gallistell suggest that children are not this limited in their counting and can in fact count groups of 'things'. The extension of this principle allows counting of unseen objects, e.g. how many people live in your house?

What experiences do you need to provide to develop counting skills?

- Rhymes and stories that encourage counting in sequence.
- Games that involve counting, e.g. clapping games.
- Counting the number of children present today, the lunch numbers, etc.
- Playing dominoes or board games, e.g. snakes and ladders.
- Sets of counting materials, e.g. in the role-play shop.
- An accessible number line/frieze.
- In the playground, e.g. counting the number of skips with a skipping rope or the number of bounces with a ball.
- Hopscotch – the number names in order.

Number

There are three areas that require consideration under this heading: the reading and writing of number, the manipulation of number, and calculating.

First, we will consider the reading and writing of number. Many children enter school able to recognise some written digits. It may be the number that represents their age or their house number. In order to be able to progress within written number work, children eventually need to be able to identify and write the digits from zero to nine. The starting point for many children will be the use of their own symbols or tallies to 'label'. For example, they might write their own price labels in the class shop, or label how many of a particular object are in each box. In order to move from this towards writing numbers children need lots of opportunity to encounter and recreate the digits. Here you might use cut-out digits that you can place different textures behind for them to trace with their fingers, e.g. fur, sandpaper, etc.; you might write in the air tracing the shape of the digit together (remember if you are facing the children you will need to 'mirror write!'); you can encourage the children to make the digits in a range of different media, e.g. play dough, salt dough, paint, traced in sand, etc. All of this encourages greater familiarity with the digits. As children start to recognise the digits you can ask them to match the number to the set, play games with number cards and produce their own number lines.

As children learn to recognise and record number, it is important that they become confident with the manipulation of number. This will support the development of a 'number sense', an understanding of the size of a number and where it fits in our number system. This will be invaluable as the children become more and more confident with calculations and develop a range of effective and efficient strategies. To encourage this from the Foundation Stage upwards children can be presented with number lines with missing numbers to find, with jumbled numbers to sort into consecutive numbers, then jumbled numbers to sort into order but not containing consecutive numbers. These activities will encourage children to explore, investigate and discuss: greater than or less than; before, after, between; largest, smallest; and so on.

Whether or not children can recognise written numbers when they arrive in school, many children can engage in simple calculations. If given a number problem within a real-life context, a significant number of children have already developed strategies to solve the problem. For example, if you have a teddy and you give him two sweets, then you tell the child the teddy actually wants three sweets, many children are able to give the teddy one more sweet and solve the problem. They can respond with similar success to simple subtraction, multiplication and division problems. In teaching calculation strategies you need to move the children on from their level of understanding on entry to the class. One of the first calculation strategies children will employ is a counting strategy. Many children will be dependent on this strategy for a great number of years throughout Key Stages 1 and 2. Children begin by 'counting all' when combining, i.e. adding, two or more sets. This is extended to a 'counting on' strategy, where the second set is counted on from the last number in the first set. For example, there are four sweets in the bag, if I add three more how many are there all together? The child then counts on from the 4, saying 5, 6, 7.

Similarly for subtraction, children develop counting strategies to enable them to calculate. They can partition a set of objects and take some away; they then count how many are left to achieve an answer. This is extended to a 'counting back' strategy, which is the inverse of 'counting on'. For example, there are seven sweets in the bag, I eat two, how many are left? Counting back from the 7, the child says 6, 5.

What experiences do you need to provide to develop an understanding of number?

- Number labels in classroom, both numerals and child written.
- A range of media in which to create digits.
- Number card games.
- Board games, e.g. snakes and ladders.
- An accessible number line/frieze.
- Sets of counting materials, e.g. in the role-play shop, to count and label.

Shape and space

REFLECTIVE TASK

There is an interesting debate associated with early spatial development. It centres on whether children should be taught about 2-D or 3-D shapes first. Before reading on, think about this and try to decide what you feel the advantages and disadvantages are of 2-D first or 3-D first.

The argument for 3-D shapes is as follows: as children live in a 3-D world and have therefore encountered a great number of 3-D shapes, these shapes are realistic. 3-D shapes also allow children to consider more than one property at a time, thus improving their knowledge and understanding of the properties of shapes and also leading them to consider the shape of individual faces, and thus to a study of 2-D shape. However, children also encounter plenty of 2-D shapes, often as patterns, for example bonding patterns in brick work, panes of glass in windows, wallpaper, tiling patterns and so forth. In society today, with much increased access to technology, many children entering school will be very used to 2-D representations on computer screens and games machines. This means that 2-D shape is also a realistic context for young children. Some people might argue that resourcing 2-D shape is cheaper and easier; others would argue that there are plenty of 3-D shapes in every home, including cylinders, cubes, cuboids, prisms, spheres, etc. What is clear from this is that encountering and exploring both 2-D and 3-D shapes is very important for children in the Foundation Stage.

Free practical exploration is an important part of the process of children learning about the properties of shapes. Using wooden blocks allows them to explore which will stack, which will roll, which have flat faces, which have curved faces, and so on. This can lead to sorting shapes and thus to early classification activities.

PRACTICAL TASK PRACTICAL TASK PRACTICAL TASK PRACTICAL TASK

Gather together some 3-D shapes (about 20 if you can) – packaging boxes are usually very good. How many different ways can you sort them? Do not immediately go for the obvious mathematical criteria. Try to think how you might classify them if you were a child, for example shapes I like, shapes I've seen before, and so on. Record the criteria you have used for your sorting. Try this activity with some children in a Foundation Stage setting if you get the opportunity. Observe their discussions and interactions as they make their decisions.

Shapes can be used appropriately to begin to develop the idea of pattern in mathematics. Mathematically patterns repeat; this might not always be the case socially. Children need to have the opportunity to talk about, recreate and extend patterns. This can be done using both 2-D and 3-D shapes. For example:

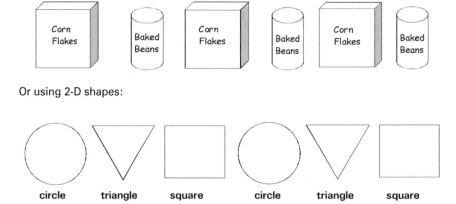

Or using 2-D shapes:

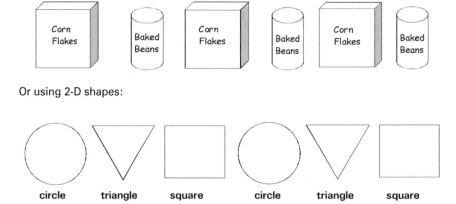

circle   triangle   square   circle   triangle   square

When introducing patterns to children do not launch straight in with specific 'mathematical' resources, e.g. multilink, but start by using objects which are familiar to the children, for example the boxes in the diagram above. Gradually refine the experience until children become confident in extending and creating patterns within a mathematical context.

Equally important is the opportunity to describe shapes. This gives children the chance to use everyday language alongside their developing mathematical vocabulary. 'Feely bags' are a very useful resource here, allowing children the opportunity to feel what is in the bag and describe it to someone else to see if they can recognise it. Another useful activity is to put a range of shapes in front of the child and ask them to close their eyes. You can then describe one of the shapes, and when the child opens their eyes they see if they can pick out the shape you were describing. These activities support the progression from using everyday language towards using precise mathematical vocabulary.

A further important aspect of spatial work is that of position. In the Foundation Stage children can begin to develop their understanding of where something is located in space alongside their understanding of prepositions. For example, you might choose to set up an 'assault course' with the PE apparatus. You can then give instructions for the children to follow, e.g. 'Jess, I want you to go under the bench, over the box and sit on the mat'. The children can then give instructions to one another. This development of prepositional language is fundamental to children developing an understanding of location in space, and ultimately to the use of Cartesian co-ordinates to describe transformations.

What experiences do you need to provide to develop spatial understanding?

- Construction, e.g. building bricks and blocks.
- Sorting both 2-D and 3-D shapes, by their own chosen properties.
- Sets of shapes to explore and compare.

- Describing shapes, e.g. using feely bags.
- Developing prepositional language, e.g. in PE or the playground.

Measures

In the Foundation Stage children will use a great deal of comparative language when working with measures. They will explore to see if something is longer than or shorter than, heavier than or lighter than, or holds more than or less than. Initially with direct comparison the children will need to compare just two things, for example the length of two pencils, the mass of two teddies, the capacity of two bottles. They can then move on to a comparison of three things. They also need the opportunity to apply their understanding of comparison to find something which is longer than..., wider than..., lighter than..., and so on.

The development of appropriate and accurate language is crucial in all mathematical areas. In the study of measures there is a great deal of language to be developed right from the Foundation Stage. Use of 'social' language can lead to confusion as children develop an understanding of more and more measurement concepts. For example, 'bigger' can mean a multitude of things: in length – longer, wider, thicker; in mass – heavier; in capacity – holds more; and so on. The implication of this is the need for detailed planning of activities and structured play situations to ensure the introduction and development of accurate and meaningful language.

In the study of time children need to start with a consideration of the passing of time. They can make a class 'timeline' of the day, each morning when the register is taken. This 'timeline' can be located on a board at child height and they can put pictures and word labels on it to detail the progression in activities throughout the day. At different times throughout the day you can refer the children back to the timeline to explain that 'before' play we did music, 'after' lunch we will do PE, and so forth. This understanding of the passing of time needs to include an introduction to the days of the week. There are songs that can be sung to help children learn the names in order, just like the counting songs which aid learning the number names in order. The Foundation Stage is the ideal time to start considering the passing of time and the ordering of events as these are vital underpinnings in learning to tell the time. As children move from the Foundation Stage into Year 1 they will be expected to start telling the time to the hour and half-hour.

What experiences do you need to provide to develop an understanding of measurement concepts?

- Rhymes and stories in which children encounter measurement concepts.
- Opportunities to develop comparative language.
- Focused sand and water play to compare capacities.
- Balances and sets of objects to balance.
- Pieces of string, laces, dowel, etc., some of the same length, some different, for comparing within the set and against other objects.
- A class timeline.
- 'Cog' clocks to explore telling the time on an analogue clock.

A SUMMARY OF **KEY POINTS**

➤ In order to support the mathematical development of children throughout the Foundation Stage, it is important to ensure that positive and productive relationships are developed with parents and carers.

➤ You need to have a good personal subject knowledge of mathematics in order to understand the links between different areas and also to respond flexibly to situations.

➤ It is important to undertake careful monitoring, assessment and recording of progress to inform clear and appropriate planning for learning.

➤ Children must have access to well-planned and structured play opportunities with appropriate adult intervention.

➤ It is vital that 'maths talk' forms part of the normal daily routine.

➤ There should be opportunities for children to initiate activities that promote mathematical learning.

➤ It is crucial that children are given the opportunity to develop positive attitudes and increase their confidence in mathematics from a secure and positive environment and role model for mathematics learning.

➤ You must capitalise on the boundless enthusiasm of children and their capacity to enjoy new experiences.

M-LEVEL EXTENSION > > > > M-LEVEL EXTENSION > > > >

The development of the EYFS has resulted in many new documents and resources being published. Talk to your university tutors and/or colleagues in school to ensure you can keep as up to date as possible. The Children's Workforce Development Council, Sure Start and the British Association for Early Childhood Education are all useful organisations involved in the care and education of young children. Use their websites to find out what is available in terms of recent research in this area.

Also consider speaking to the subject leader responsible for mathematics within the Foundation Stage. He/she will be able to support you by giving you ideas or pointing you in the direction of additional resources. Consider how PSRN can be promoted through links to the other areas of learning. Are there particular topics/themes that are suited to such a cross-curricular approach?

REFERENCES REFERENCES **REFERENCES** REFERENCES REFERENCES

Anderson, A., Anderson, J. and Thauberger, C. (2007) 'Mathematics learning and teaching in the Early Years', in Saracho, O. N. and Spodek, B. (eds) (2007) *Contemporary Perspectives on Mathematics in Early Childhood Education.* Charlotte: IAP.

Cockburn, A. D. (1999) *Teaching Mathematics with Insight.* London: Falmer Press.

DfE (2014) *Statutory Framework for the Early Years Foundation Stage: Setting the standards for learning, development and care for children from birth to five.* London: DfE. Available at: http://www.gov.uk/government/uploads/system/attachment_data/file/299391/DfE-00337-2014.pdf (accessed 23/4/14).

DfE (2011) *Teachers' Standards.* Available at: www.gov.uk/government/publications/teachers-standards (accessed 13/4/14).

FURTHER READING FURTHER READING FURTHER READING

Carruthers, E. and Worthington, M. (2006) *Children's Mathematics: Making Marks, Making Meaning.* London: Sage.

Montague-Smith, A. (2002) *Mathematics in Nursery Education*. London: David Fulton.

Pound, L. (2006) *Supporting Mathematical Development in the Early Years.* Buckingham: Open University Press.

Pound, L. (2008) *Thinking and Learning About Maths in the Early Years*. Oxford: Routledge.

Skinner, C. (2005) *Maths Outdoors.* Cheltenham: BEAM.

Thompson, I. (ed.) (2008) *Teaching and Learning Early Number*. Buckingham: Open University Press.

Tucker, K. (2005) *Mathematics Through Play in the Early Years: Activities and Ideas.* London: Paul Chapman.

7
Number

Introduction

Children need to become numerate in order to confidently tackle mathematical problems independently. In order to achieve this, they should have a sense of the size of a number and where it fits into the number system. Developing this 'number sense' is crucial if children are going to move on to become effective and efficient at calculating, both mentally and using pencil and paper methods. A clear progression in the development of concepts is important for children to enable them to fully understand the structure of our number system, how to represent numbers and how numbers relate to one another. This chapter will identify the progression, continuing from and extending that already identified in Chapter 6.

In order to develop functional numeracy, children need to progress in the areas of:

- number and place value;
- addition, subtraction, multiplication and division;
- fractions (including decimals and percentages);
- ratio and proportion;
- algebra.

Progression in aspects of number

Counting

The principles of counting and learning to count have been clearly detailed in Chapter 6. However, in considering the progression in counting it is important to remember that counting does not solely involve counting on in ones, i.e. 0, 1, 2, 3, 4, 5, 6, ... but can, and frequently does, involve counting in steps of different size, e.g. counting on in twos – 0, 2, 4, 6, 8, 10, 12, ...; starting from a number other than zero, e.g. counting on in twos – 7, 9, 11, 13, 15, 17, ...; and counting back, e.g. counting back in 0.5s – 2, 1.5, 1, 0.5, 0, –0.5, –1, ... By practising and becoming familiar with counting on and back in steps of different sizes, children will acquire a knowledge and understanding that will support them significantly in developing their calculation and problem-solving skills.

The National Curriculum's progression in counting is identified below. It is important to note that the progression in counting involves the introduction of negative numbers and fractions. Counting is extended through zero to negative numbers and counting in fractional or decimal parts is introduced.

- Count to and across 100, forwards and backwards, beginning with 0 or 1, or from any given number.
- Count, read and write numbers to 100 in numerals; count in multiples of twos, fives and tens.
- Count in steps of 2, 3, and 5 from 0, and in tens from any number, forward and backward.
- Count from 0 in multiples of 4, 8, 50 and 100; find 10 or 100 more or less than a given number.
- Count up and down in tenths; recognise that tenths arise from dividing an object into 10 equal parts and in dividing one-digit numbers or quantities by 10.
- Count in multiples of 6, 7, 9, 25 and 1000.
- Count backwards through zero to include negative numbers.
- Count up and down in hundredths; recognise that hundredths arise when dividing an object by one hundred and dividing tenths by ten.
- Count forwards or backwards in steps of powers of 10 for any given number up to 1 000 000

The value of counting should not be underestimated. Many children will use counting as their main calculation strategy for a significant period of time whether adding, subtracting, multiplying or dividing. Indeed Effie Maclellan (1997, p. 40) goes further in stating, *There is now little doubt that children's understanding of number is rooted in counting.*

THE BIGGER PICTURE   THE BIGGER PICTURE   THE BIGGER PICTURE

When you are planning number work, it is helpful to incorporate practical activities into real-life situations around school and in the community. For example, many schools take part in charity and fundraising events, such as sponsored walks or silences, and end of term or summer fairs that are open to parents, friends and other members of the community. There are lots of opportunities for older Key Stage 2 children to get involved in organising these. Think of the mathematics in drawing a plan to show where the stalls will go, making up a 'float' of change for each stall holder, serving customers and making change, and counting the takings at the end of the fair and then working out the profit after the floats and any expenditure on purchasing refreshments for sale have been deducted.

Properties of numbers and number sequences

Odd and even numbers

Besides counting in ones and steps of different size, one of the first properties of number that children are introduced to is that of 'odd' and 'even'. This is often introduced as an extension of counting in twos from zero and one. Practical resources or pairing up groups of children can be used to demonstrate divisibility by two.

Once children can recognise odd and even numbers they can start to consider some of the properties of combining these numbers in different ways. What happens when two even numbers are added? Two odd numbers? An odd and an even number?

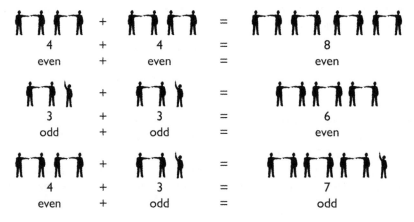

Exploration of subtraction of odd and even numbers will reveal the pattern in their differences. At the top end of Key Stage 2 children can investigate patterns in the products of odd and even numbers.

Multiples

A further property of numbers which children will start to investigate during Key Stage 1 is recognising multiples.

A multiple is a number which is the product (i.e. achieved by multiplication) of an integer with a given number, e.g. some multiples of 3 are 6 (3×2), 15 (3×5) and 24 (3×8).

A discussion of children's proof of this can be found in Chapter 7 of **Primary Mathematics: Knowledge and Understanding** *(2014) from Learning Matters.*

Children will start by recognising multiples of 2 (even numbers) and multiples of 10, as they will experience counting in tens from quite a young age. Here again is evidence of the importance of counting. They will then start to recognise multiples of 5, 100 and 50 as they increase their counting and calculation repertoire. By the end of Key Stage 2, they should recognise all multiples up to 10×10.

As numbers get bigger it is harder to spot immediately if a number is a multiple of a certain integer. In order to assist this there are certain tests of divisibility which children in upper Key Stage 2 quite enjoy applying – and if they are enjoying their mathematics learning they are developing a positive attitude towards it.

Two

For an integer to be divisible by 2, it must have either 0, 2, 4, 6 or 8 as the last digit, i.e. it is an even number.

Three

For an integer to be divisible by 3, the sum of its digits must also be divisible by 3. For example, is 312 divisible by 3? The sum of the digits is $3 + 1 + 2 = 6$, 6 is divisible by 3 and therefore 312 is divisible by 3, in fact $312 \div 3 = 104$. What about 32,451? The sum of the digits is $3 + 2 + 4 + 5 + 1 = 15$, 15 is divisible by 3 and therefore 32,451 is divisible by 3; $32,451 \div 3 = 10,817$.

Four

For an integer to be divisible by 4, the last two digits must be divisible by 4. For example, is 348 divisible by 4? 48 is divisible by 4 ($48 \div 4 = 12$) and therefore 348 is divisible by 4; in fact $348 \div 4 = 87$. What about 35,260? 60 is divisible by 4 ($60 \div 4 = 15$) and therefore 35,260 is divisible by 4; $35,260 \div 4 = 8,815$.

Five

For an integer to be divisible by 5, it must have either 0 or 5 as the last digit.

Six

For an integer to be divisible by 6, it must be an even number which satisfies the rule for divisibility by 3.

Eight

For an integer to be divisible by 8, when halved it must satisfy the rule for divisibility by 4. For example, is 432 divisible by 8? First halve the number 432 which gives 216, now check to see if 216 is divisible by 4. 16 is divisible by 4, hence 216 is divisible by 4, and 432 is divisible by 8; in fact $432 \div 8 = 54$.

Nine

For an integer to be divisible by 9, the sum of its digits must be divisible by 9. For example, is 792 divisible by 9? The sum of the digits is $7 + 9 + 2 = 18$, 18 is divisible by 9 and therefore 792 is divisible by 9; in fact $792 \div 9 = 88$. What about 42,453? The sum of the digits is $4 + 2 + 4 + 5 + 3 = 18$, 18 is divisible by 9 and therefore 42,453 is divisible by 9; $42,453 \div 9 = 4,717$.

Ten

For an integer to be divisible by 10, it must have 0 as the last digit.

PRACTICAL TASK PRACTICAL TASK **PRACTICAL TASK** PRACTICAL TASK

Look at the following numbers and decide if they are multiples of (i.e. are they divisible by) 2, 3, 4, 5, 6, 8, 9 or 10. They may be multiples of more than one number.

| 5,472 | 3,564 | 4,215 | 2,340 | 72,432 |

Factors

A factor can be defined as any number that divides into another number exactly, e.g. 8 is a factor of 32, but 5 is not. Children can use their knowledge of multiplication tables to find factors of numbers. Factors are usually found as pairs, the exception being square numbers.

For example, factors of 24:

24 = 1 × 24	24 = 2 × 12	24 = 3 × 8	24 = 4 × 6
24 = 24 × 1	24 = 12 × 2	24 = 8 × 3	24 = 6 × 4

So the factors of 24 are: 1, 2, 3, 4, 6, 8, 12, 24.

Square numbers

A square number is the product of two equal factors, i.e. a number multiplied by itself, e.g. 2 × 2 = 4. It can be written as $2^2 = 4$ (i.e. 2 to the power 2). In learning their multiplication tables, children will have already encountered square numbers.

Square numbers can be represented as squares (hence the name!):

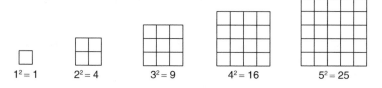

$1^2 = 1$ $2^2 = 4$ $3^2 = 9$ $4^2 = 16$ $5^2 = 25$

For more on indices, see Chapter 2 of **Primary Mathematics: Knowledge and Understanding** *(2014) from Learning Matters.*

Children should also know that square numbers have an odd number of factors, because one factor (i.e. the square root) is multiplied by itself to obtain the answer, e.g.

1	has the factor 1	(one factor)
4	has the factors 1, 2, 4	(three factors)
9	has the factors 1, 3, 9	(three factors)
16	has the factors 1, 2, 4, 8, 16	(five factors)

Numbers that are not square have an even number of factors, e.g.

2	has the factors 1, 2	(two factors)
6	has the factors 1, 2, 3, 6	(four factors)
18	has the factors 1, 2, 3, 6, 9, 18	(six factors)

Another interesting set of numbers, which children can be introduced to as well as square numbers, is the set of triangle numbers. In the same way that square numbers form squares, triangle numbers form triangles.

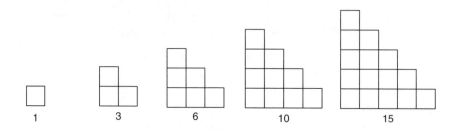

1   3   6   10   15

An interesting feature of triangle numbers that children may notice is that if two successive triangle numbers are added the sum is a square number, e.g.

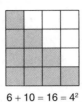 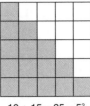

$1 + 3 = 4 = 2^2$	$3 + 6 = 9 = 3^2$	$6 + 10 = 16 = 4^2$	$10 + 15 = 25 = 5^2$

Some numbers are both square and triangular although they are quite rare. Obviously the first number this applies to is 1, the second is 36 (6^2), the next 1,225 (35^2), the next 41,616 (204^2) and the next 1,413,721 ($1,189^2$) getting further and further apart. Children find exploration of 'big' numbers quite fascinating.

Prime numbers

A prime number can be defined as a number that has only two factors, 1 and itself. This means that 1 is not a prime number, as it only has one factor, itself. There are some fascinating ways for children to explore prime numbers.

For more on Eratosthenes' work, see Chapter 10.

One person they might be introduced to is Eratosthenes (c. 276–194 BC). He was a Greek mathematician and a librarian at the University of Alexandria. He used a rather ingenious method for calculating the circumference of the Earth and was also very interested in prime numbers. He worked out a method of finding prime numbers which became known as the Sieve of Eratosthenes. If all the prime numbers up to 150 need to be established, Eratosthenes worked out that it was only necessary to consider multiples of every number up to 13. He knew this because any number up to 150 which is not prime would have a factor of 13 or less (because 13 × 13 = 169). But how does his 'sieve' work?

> **PRACTICAL TASK** PRACTICAL TASK **PRACTICAL TASK** PRACTICAL TASK
>
> Before reading on to see how Eratosthenes tackled the problem, see if you can establish all the prime numbers between 1 and 150. Time yourself to see how long it takes, then repeat it using Eratosthenes' 'sieve'. Was the sieve any quicker?

As all the prime numbers up to150 need to be established, we need to work with a 150 grid. Starting at 2 (1 is not prime – see above), put a ring around it as it must be prime (i.e. have only 2 factors). Now shade in all the multiples of 2 in the table. Then put a ring around the next unshaded number, in this case 3, which must also be prime. Now shade in all the multiples of 3 in the table. The next unshaded number is 5, which is also prime. Put a ring around it and shade in all the multiples of 5. Do the same with the next unshaded number and so on. However, the wonderful thing about the Sieve of Eratosthenes is that it is not necessary to keep going for every unshaded number. If the multiples of all numbers up to 13 are considered, then the remaining unshaded numbers must also be prime, owing to the previously stated fact that any number less

1	②	③	4	⑤	6	⑦	8	9	10
⑪	12	⑬	14	15	16	17	18	19	20
21	22	23	24	25	26	27	28	29	30
31	32	33	34	35	36	37	38	39	40
41	42	43	44	45	46	47	48	49	50
51	52	53	54	55	56	57	58	59	60
61	62	63	64	65	66	67	68	69	70
71	72	73	74	75	76	77	78	79	80
81	82	83	84	85	86	87	88	89	90
91	92	93	94	95	96	97	98	99	100
101	102	103	104	105	106	107	108	109	110
111	112	113	114	115	116	117	118	119	120
121	122	123	124	125	126	127	128	129	130
131	132	133	134	135	136	137	138	139	140
141	142	143	144	145	146	147	148	149	150

Figure 7.1 The Sieve of Eratosthenes

than 150 which is not prime will have a factor of 13 or less. Hence the prime numbers are 'sieved' out.

The Greek mathematician Euclid (c. 330–275 BC) wrote about prime numbers in his *Elements.* It was in these volumes that he proved that there is an infinite number of prime numbers. Some very large primes have been calculated using computers. At the time of writing the largest known prime number is $2^{57885161}-1$, which has about 17.4 million digits!

Prime numbers lead to the study of prime factors. Numbers that are not prime numbers are called composite numbers. Composite numbers can be made by multiplying together other numbers, e.g. 16 can be made by multiplying 4 × 4, 2 × 8, 2 × 2 × 4, and so on. However, it is possible to multiply together just prime numbers to obtain a composite number. For 16:

$$2 \times 2 \times 2 \times 2$$

This is called prime factorisation.

The prime factors of 12 are:

$$2 \times 2 \times 3$$

PRACTICAL TASK PRACTICAL TASK **PRACTICAL TASK** PRACTICAL TASK

Find the prime factors of the following numbers:

24   35   18   42   100

Place value and ordering

Place value is used within number systems to allow a digit to carry a different value based on its position, i.e. the *place* has a *value*. Building on the areas already discussed in Chapter 6, children need to understand what each digit represents in a two-digit number, a three-digit number, a four-digit number and so forth. Partitioning is a very useful strategy to help children develop this understanding. In Key Stage 2, children are expected to multiply whole numbers and decimals by 1,000, giving the potential for a very large number of digits, and thus extending their understanding of our decimal place value system further.

Fundamental to children's understanding of place value is the use of 0 as a place holder. This means that in the number 206, the zero is 'holding' the tens column and showing that there are no tens there. Before our number system used a symbol for zero it would have been necessary to write '2 hundreds and six' as there was no other way of showing the column was empty. A clear understanding of place value is vital if children are to develop effective and efficient mental calculation strategies; yet it is an area in which children can very easily develop misconceptions.

For more on place value, see Chapter 2 in **Primary Mathematics: Knowledge and Understanding** *from Learning Matters (2014).*

Misconceptions

Many misconceptions which children develop in the area of Number are related to a poor understanding of place value. The child who reads 206 as twenty-six will have the same conceptual misunderstanding as the child who writes 10,027 when asked to write one hundred and twenty-seven. Both of these errors occur because the child focuses on the zeros as the fundamentally important digits in the numbers 10, 100 and so forth and not on the place value of the numbers. When asked, 'What is a hundred?' they might well respond, 'It has two zeros'. The child then applies this understanding to the reading and writing of number. Hence 206 is read as 20 and 6, so it is twenty-six.

It is quite clear here that the child has a very limited understanding of place value. In order to correctly read, write and identify numbers children need to understand that the position of each digit is of great significance and that zero can be used as a place holder to show that a column is empty. There are some quite clear implications for teaching to ensure children do not develop this misconception and also to remedy it if it already exists.

For more on misconceptions related to Number, see Hansen (2014) **Children's Errors in Mathematics** *from Learning Matters.*

Children need to be introduced to the importance of the position of a digit and equally must be able to state what each digit represents in a multi-digit number. This should be reinforced with the partitioning of numbers into, for example, hundreds, tens and ones. Place value cards are a useful resource when partitioning numbers. Using these, children can easily partition larger numbers, can identify the value of individual digits and equally can see how zero is used as a place holder.

For example, 325:

Through practical activity, the use of appropriate resources, discussion and an emphasis on correct mathematical vocabulary, children will move towards a much clearer and accurate understanding of these concepts.

EMBEDDING ICT EMBEDDING ICT **EMBEDDING ICT** EMBEDDING ICT

The Primary National Framework developed some useful interactive teaching programs (ITPs) to support the modelling of mathematics for learners. These programs can be used effectively on an IWB in class, alongside other practical manipulatives, to help children as they construct their understanding of mathematical concepts. One of these resources is the place value ITP. This ITP enables the manipulation of place value cards electronically, an invaluable resource for whole-class or large-group modelling. A further ITP related to place value is Moving digits, for use with children in Key Stage 2 as they explore multiplication and division of whole numbers and decimals by 10, 100, 1000. To find ITPs, search for 'NNS ITPs'.

For more on decimals, see Chapter 2 of **Primary Mathematics: Knowledge and Understanding** *(2014) from Learning Matters.*

A further misconception which children can develop related to place value is that of believing a number is larger because it has more decimal digits – for example, stating that 3.125 is larger than 3.14. The child will often state that this is true because, '125 is bigger than 14'. In this situation the child shows no understanding of the place value of digits after the decimal point.

As in the earlier misconception, children need to know the place value of digits, this time to the right of the decimal point. If they are introduced to the columns as the 1/10 (tenths) column, the 1/100 (hundredths) column, the 1/1,000 (thousandths) column and so on, they will not think of digits to the right of the decimal point in terms of those to the left, i.e. here they will not say '125' and '14', but 'point one two five' and 'point one four' instead. Actually looking at the fractional parts involved leads to a deeper understanding. For example, 3.125 can be seen as 3 and 1/10 (one tenth) and 2/100 (two hundredths) and 5/1,000 (five thousandths) which is the same as 3 and 125/1,000 (one hundred and twenty-five thousandths), while 3.14 can be seen as 3 and 1/10 (one tenth) and 4/100 (four hundredths) which is the same as 3 and 14/100 (fourteen hundredths). Expressed in terms of a common denominator this gives 3 and 125/1,000 and 3 and 140/1,000, hence 3.14 is bigger than 3.125.

For more on comparing fractions see Chapter 2 of **Primary Mathematics: Knowledge and Understanding** *(2014) from Learning Matters.*

Teaching to avoid these misconceptions, and remedying them if they do exist, is vital if children are to have a sense of the size of a number and where it fits into the number system. A sound understanding of place value is absolutely fundamental to developing this 'number sense'.

A SUMMARY OF **KEY POINTS**

➢ **In order to support the development of calculation strategies in the future, it is important that children recognise odd and even numbers.**

➢ **They must be able to count forwards and backwards in steps of different size.**

> ➤ Later, they need to learn to recognise multiples of numbers, including square numbers, and find factors of numbers.

> ➤ In Key Stage 2, children learn to understand our decimal place value system and count in fractional and decimal parts.

> ➤ They need to understand how to count through zero into negative numbers.

M-LEVEL EXTENSION > > > > M-LEVEL EXTENSION > > > >

Devise a bank of practical activities, resources and opportunities to give a real-life context to number activities. Include as many ICT programs as you can. Make sure that you know what is available in school and via the school's virtual learning environment (VLE), but also consider the internet.

Try some of the following websites:

www.bbc.co.uk/cbeebies

www.atm.org.uk

www.m-a.org.uk

www.microsoft.com

www.ncetm.org.uk

www.ase.org.uk

www.tes.co.uk

Why is it important to set children's development of the understanding of number in real-life scenarios?

REFERENCES REFERENCES **REFERENCES** REFERENCES REFERENCES

DfE (2011) *Teachers' Standards*. Available at: www.gov.uk/government/publications/teachers-standards (accessed 13/4/14).

DfE (2013) *Mathematics Programmes of Study: Key Stages 1 and 2. National Curriculum for England.* London: DfE. Available at: www.gov.uk/government/uploads/system/uploads/attachment_data/file/239129/PRIMARY_National_Curriculum_-_Mathematics.pdf (accessed 13/4/14).

Maclellan, E. (1997) 'The importance of counting', in Thompson, I. (ed.) *Teaching and Learning Early Number.* Buckingham: Open University Press.

FURTHER READING FURTHER READING **FURTHER READING**

Barber, D., Cooper, L. and Meeson, G. (2007) *Learning and Teaching with IWBs: Primary and Early Years.* Exeter: Learning Matters.

DfES (2000) *Mathematical Vocabulary.* London: DfES.

Gillespie, H., Boulton, H., Hramiak, A. J. and Williamson, R. (2007) *Learning and Teaching with Virtual Learning Environments.* Exeter: Learning Matters.

Hansen, A. (ed.) (2014) *Children's Errors in Mathematics: Understanding Common Misconceptions in Primary Schools.* London: Sage/Learning Matters.

Haylock, D. (2010) (4th edn) *Mathematics Explained for Primary Teachers.* London: Sage.

Maclellan, E. (2008) 'Counting and why it matters', in Thompson, I. (ed.) *Teaching and Learning Early Number.* Maidenhead: Open University Press/McGraw-Hill.

Mason, J., Burton, L. and Stacey, K. (2010) (Revised edn) *Thinking Mathematically.* Harlow: Pearson Education Limited.

Ofsted (2009) *Mathematics: Understanding the Score. Improving practice in mathematics teaching at primary level.* London: Ofsted.

Thompson, I. (2010) (2nd edn) *Issues in Teaching Numeracy in Primary Schools.* Maidenhead: Open University Press.

Williams, P. (2008) *Independent Review of Mathematics Teaching in Early Years Settings and Primary Schools.* Nottingham: DCSF.

8
Arithmetic

Introduction

Within arithmetic at Key Stage1, children develop confidence and mental fluency with whole numbers, counting and place value. This involves working with numerals, words and the four operations, including with practical resources. In lower Key Stage 2 children become increasingly fluent with whole numbers and the four operations, including number facts and the concept of place value. This should ensure that pupils develop efficient written and mental methods and perform calculations accurately with increasingly large whole numbers. At this stage, pupils develop their ability to solve a range of problems, including with simple fractions and decimal place value. In upper Key Stage 2 children develop their ability to solve a wider range of problems, including increasingly complex properties of numbers and arithmetic, and problems demanding efficient written and mental methods of calculation. With this foundation in arithmetic, children are introduced to the language of algebra as a means for solving a variety of problems.

Progression in aspects of arithmetic

This chapter will address four main issues: understanding arithmetic and operation relationships; mental recall and mental calculation; pencil and paper methods; and using a calculator and checking results. Throughout the chapter common misconceptions will also be raised and addressed.

Understanding arithmetic operations and relationships

'Sum like it not!'

Many teachers incorrectly use the word 'sum' when referring to all calculations. This term should only be used when working with addition calculations. When you are working on subtraction, multiplication or division questions, you should refer to them as 'number sentences', 'equations' or 'calculations' instead.

Addition and subtraction

The ability to count reliably is a prerequisite for any meaningful calculation to take place. Counting forwards and backwards in steps of different size is an important skill for young children to develop. In Key Stage 1 children need to know by heart all the pairs of numbers that sum to 10. Children who can count forwards and backwards to 10 will have little difficulty spotting a pattern and filling in the missing numbers in the following:

$$10 = 10 + 0$$
$$10 = 9 + 1$$
$$10 = 8 + 2$$
$$10 = 7 + 3$$
$$10 = \square + \square$$
$$10 = \square + \square$$
$$10 = \square + \square$$
$$10 = \square + \square$$
$$10 = \square + \square$$
$$10 = \square + \square$$
$$10 = \square + \square$$

For more on counting, see Chapter 7.

Children need to understand the operations of addition and subtraction and the relationship between the two operations. Being able to count forwards and backwards with ease will facilitate the understanding of this inverse relationship. Activities that emphasise the relation between addition and subtraction are important at an early stage. An example of such an activity is shown below:

For more on algebra, see Chapter 9.

Fill in the missing numbers

8 + 5 = 13	13 − 5 =	13 − 8 =
9 + 6 = 15	15 − 9 =	15 − 6 =
12 + 7 = 19	19 − 12 =	19 − 7 =
46 + 38 = 84	84 − 46 =	84 − 38 =

This familiarity with the inverse relationship between addition and subtraction is an important prerequisite for algebra. Children can be given simple problems to solve that require an understanding of this inverse relationship:

I am thinking of a number. I add 7 to this number and the answer is 15. What was the number I was thinking of?

I am thinking of a number. I take away 4 from this number and the answer is 9. What was the number I was thinking of?

Children should be encouraged to find the quick way to solve these problems by using the inverse operations.

In the same way that addition and subtraction are introduced to children as inverse operations so halving and doubling are introduced. Children in Key Stage 1 are expected to be able to solve simple problems mentally by doubling and halving. They should be able to solve the following:

I am thinking of a number. I double it and the answer is 8. What was the number?

I am thinking of a number. I halve it and the answer is 5. What was the number?

Multiplying and dividing

Just as addition and subtraction were introduced as inverse operations so multiplication and division need to be seen as inverse to each other.

It is, however, more complicated since children need to understand the various guises that multiplication and division take. In the first instance, multiplication needs to be introduced as repeated addition. For example:

$5 + 5 + 5$ can be written as 5×3, i.e. it is a mathematical shorthand

$15 \div 5$ can then be seen as asking how many times we can take 5 from 15.

A common misconception that children have is that division always makes numbers smaller. It is important that they encounter examples where this is not the case. Children need to be asked questions such as:

How many times can be $\frac{1}{2}$ taken from 15?

How many times can $\frac{1}{4}$ be taken from 10?

$15 \div \frac{1}{2}$ $\qquad$ $10 \div \frac{1}{4}$

Meeting examples like this will allow children to make correct generalisations. It will allow them to conclude correctly that:

$$15 \div \frac{1}{2} = 15 \times 2 \text{ and } 10 \div \frac{1}{4} = 10 \times 4$$

Next they need to see how multiplication can be used to describe an array. For example:

$$\begin{array}{cccc} \square & \square & \square & \square \\ \square & \square & \square & \square \end{array} \quad 4 \times 2 = 8$$

$$2 \times 4 = 8$$

It is useful to spend some time emphasising this aspect of multiplication since it is fundamental for an understanding of long multiplication. Children need to understand the distributive property of multiplication over addition if they are to understand long multiplication algorithms. The diagram below helps to show children why:

$$2 \times 13 \qquad = \qquad (2 \times 10) \qquad + (2 \times 3)$$

□□□□□□□□□□□□□ = □□□□□□□□□□ □□□

□□□□□□□□□□□□□   □□□□□□□□□□ □□□

For more on this see Chapter 2 of **Primary Mathematics: Knowledge and Understanding** *(2014) from Learning Matters.*

Children need to be able to generalise this rule and see that:

$2 \times (\nabla + \square) = (2 \times \nabla) + (2 \times \square)$ is true for any numbers we place in ∇ and $\square$

From arranging arrays children will also be able to see that the operation of multiplication is commutative, i.e. $a \times b = b \times a$.

In order to see division as the inverse of multiplication, children could be asked to group 26 into 2 rows and that this can be written as $26 \div 2 = 13$.

This grouping can also demonstrate that $26 \div 2 = (20 \div 2) + (6 \div 2)$, i.e. division is right distributive over addition.

It is important that children understand this property of division since it underpins the long division algorithm and, later on, work in algebra.

> **PRACTICAL TASK** PRACTICAL TASK **PRACTICAL TASK** PRACTICAL TASK
>
> Say which of the following are correct and which are incorrect. Try to do it by looking at the structure rather than calculating the answers.
>
> $17 \times 9 = (10 \times 9) + (7 \times 9)$ $\qquad$ $15 \times 8 = (8 \times 8) + (7 \times 8)$
>
> $8 \times 23 = (8 \times 20) + (8 \times 3)$ $\qquad$ $128 \times 8 = (120 \times 8) + (8 \times 8)$
>
> $104 \div 4 = (100 \div 4) + (4 \div 4)$ $\qquad$ $1{,}072 \div 8 = (1000 \div 8) + (72 \div 8)$

In fact they are all correct. The last two examples help to explain why the tests for divisibility by 4 and 8 work.

A common misconception that children have is that multiplication always makes numbers bigger. It is not surprising that they come to this conclusion since in all the above examples this is the case. Children need to be given examples where multiplication makes the number smaller. This is possible if multiplication is understood as a scaling. The following questions place multiplication in this context:

> This tower is 6 cubes high. Make a tower that is 3 times as high.
>
> This line is 4 centimetres long. Draw a line that is twice as long.

Children can then be introduced to fractional scalings, for example:

> A tower is 8 cubes high. Build a tower that is half as high.
>
> This line is 12 centimetres long. Draw one that is a quarter of the length.

Children can then be shown that these can be written as:

$$8 \times \frac{1}{2} = 4 \text{ and } 12 \times \frac{1}{4} = 3$$

In order to increase children's understanding and efficiency in multiplying and dividing they need to reflect on some interesting properties of our number system. Their attention needs to be drawn to the fact that multiplying and dividing by powers of 10 is particularly easy in our number system.

Multiplying by 10, for example, simply moves all the digits one place to the left.

H	*T*	*U*			*H*	*T*	*U*
	3	2	$\times 10 =$		3	2	0

It is important to emphasise that the numbers have moved rather than say a zero has been added. Children who simply add a zero may develop the misconception that $2.3 \times 10 = 2.30$.

Similarly, dividing by 10 simply moves all the digits one place to the right:

H	*T*	*U*			*H*	*T*	*U*
4	6	0	$\div 10 =$			4	6

Again it should be emphasised that the digits have moved rather than say a zero has been removed. Children who remove a zero may develop the misconception that $203 \div 10 = 23$ or that $1.07 \div 10 = 1.7$

Children should be encouraged to investigate what happens when numbers are multiplied and divided by 100.

In this way they will be able to convert pounds to pence and metres to centimetres efficiently.

We have emphasised the inverse relationship between addition and subtraction and between multiplication and division. It is also important that children can decide when it is appropriate to use each of these mathematical operations. They should have the opportunity of solving word problems involving numbers in 'real life'.

Start with simple one-operation problems, for example:

> How many more is 68 than 42?
>
> Find a pair of numbers with a difference of 15.
>
> What is the sum of 24 and 35?
>
> Which three numbers could have a total of 60?
>
> There are 6 eggs in a box. How many in 7 boxes?
>
> A bus seats 52 people. There are 60 people on the bus. How many are standing?
>
> What are the factors of 12?

Lead up to multi-step operations:

> There are 36 children in a class. Half of them have flavoured crisps. One third of them have plain crisps. How many children have crisps?
>
> For her picnic, Asmat spent £2.88 on apples, £3.38 on bananas and £3.76 on oranges. Will a £10 note cover the cost?

THE BIGGER PICTURE THE BIGGER PICTURE **THE BIGGER PICTURE**

When you are planning opportunities for children to solve real-life word problems, remember that they can come up naturally in other subjects, for example science, design technology, geography, history, PSHE and PE. Be on the lookout for these as they reinforce links in learning and allow children to practise their skills in using and applying mathematics.

Mental recall and mental calculation

Addition and subtraction

Knowing by heart simple addition and subtraction facts is a prerequisite for efficient mental arithmetic. In Key Stage 1 children should know all pairs of numbers that add to 10. They should be taught to use these facts to solve related problems, for example:

> $6 + 4 = 10$ What is $6 + 5$?
> $8 + 2 = 10$ What is $8 + 3$?
> $5 + 5 = 10$ What is $5 + 7$?

Similarly children should be taught to derive simple subtraction results from known facts:

$10 - 6 = 4$ What is $11 - 6$?
$10 - 7 = 3$ What is $12 - 7$?

They should be taught to use the commutative and associative properties of addition to solve problems in efficient ways. They should be taught to rearrange addition problems, for example:

$4 + 28$ $7 + 8 + 3 + 2$ $26 + 17 + 14 + 13$

can be calculated more efficiently if calculated as:

$28 + 4$ $7 + 3 + 8 + 2$ $26 + 14 + 17 + 13$

Similarly children should be taught to use the properties of subtraction. They should be able to find the following quickly:

$7 + 9 - 9$ $8 + 7 - 6$ $78 - 25 - 18$

by considering:

$7 + 0$ $8 + 1$ $60 - 25$

They should discover that subtraction is not commutative: $7 - 6$ does not give the same answer as $6 - 7$!

Knowing doubles is useful when adding and subtracting. For example, $8 + 9$ can be derived from knowing double 8. Children should be able to derive the following by Year 2:

$25 + 26$ $38 + 42$ $19 + 21$ $102 - 51$

from knowing:

$25 + 25 = 50$ $40 + 40 = 80$ $20 + 20 = 40$ $51 + 51 = 102$

Using number tracks and number lines

Number tracks can help young children to learn to add by counting on and to subtract by counting back. For example, you may enlist the help of a hand-puppet frog who jumps along the classroom number track, or use a programmable robot to go forward three steps ($+3$) on the carpet number track or back four steps ($- 4$).

REFLECTIVE TASK

Samira has been using a number track to solve some questions. She provides the following answers:

$3 + 4 = 6$ $2 + 3 = 4$ $8 - 3 = 6$ $6 - 2 = 5$

What has Samira done incorrectly? How might you help her to remedy this?

Samira has counted on and back and included the number she started at. This could be remedied by asking her to play a board game with some friends. It is unlikely that she will count the same number again in this context, especially if she is trying to reach the end first! You could then talk to Samira about transferring her skills on the board game to the number track.

Older children will find number lines a useful aid for mental arithmetic. They may also use a ruler as an aid. Most classrooms display 1–100 number lines on the walls or board as an aid.

Children can be encouraged to imagine a number line when solving addition and subtraction problems. Finding 17 + 8, for example, is more easily found by considering 17 + 3 + 5 on a number line.

Similarly 34 – 8 could be imagined to be 34 – 4 – 4.

Alternatively it could be viewed as 34 – 10 + 2.

Children should be encouraged to think flexibly. It is good practice to ask them to explain their way of tackling the question so that they can share their approaches and learn from one another.

Some problems are more easily answered by partitioning both numbers. For example, 35 + 24 can be partitioned into (30 + 20) + (5 + 4).

PRACTICAL TASK PRACTICAL TASK **PRACTICAL TASK** PRACTICAL TASK

Jot down notes to show how you could expect children to answer these calculations:

$$1) \ 45 + 46 \qquad 2) \ 40 - 19 \qquad 3) \ 101 - 99$$

Try to think of a number of possible ways.

1. A child might know that double 45 is 90 and one more is 91. Alternatively, they might add 40 + 40 (which is 80) and then add 5 + 6 (which is 11), making 91.

2. A child might know that 19 is close to 20, so 40 – 20 is 20. They will then need to add one to compensate for the extra one they took away, making an answer of 21.

    Alternatively they may take 10 away from 40, leaving 30 and then take the 9 away, leaving 21. Finally, a child may use the inverse calculation, 19 + ? = 40.

3. A child should notice that these two numbers are close together and use a counting on method – (99), 100, 101 – to find the difference of 2.

To find out about calculating with decimal numbers see Chapter 2 of **Primary Mathematics, Knowledge and Understanding** *(2012) from Learning Matters.*

Multiplication and division

Knowing by heart all multiplication facts is a necessity for children and they are expected to know up to 12 × 12 by the end of Year 4. On their own, however, the knowledge of these facts is not sufficient. Children need to be able to use these facts to work out related problems. They need to understand, for example, that if 9 × 7 = 63 then this implies that 63 ÷ 9 = 7 and 63 ÷ 7 = 9.

Children should be encouraged to relate division facts to the corresponding multiplication facts:

For more on grid multiplication see the section later in this chapter.

$56 \div 7 = 8$ Tell me a multiplication fact using the numbers 56, 8 and 7.

$9 \times 6 = 54$ Tell me a division fact using the numbers 6, 9 and 54.

They should be able to use the inverse relation between multiplication and division to try the following type of problem:

The problems on the right relate to the statements on the left.

Draw a line between each statement and its corresponding question:

$77 \div 11 = 7$	$54 \div 9 = 6$
$9 \times 8 = 72$	$7 \times 9 = 63$
$36 \div 4 = 9$	$11 \times 7 = 77$
$6 \times 9 = 54$	$72 \div 8 = 9$
$63 \div 7 = 9$	$4 \times 9 = 36$

They should be able to use simple multiplication facts to derive more complicated results. For example, $6 \times 3 = 18$ can be used to derive $6 \times 30 = 180$. This is a useful technique when children are using grid multiplication. Children should be encouraged to try the following type of task: if you know that $6 \times 3 = 18$, what else can you work out?

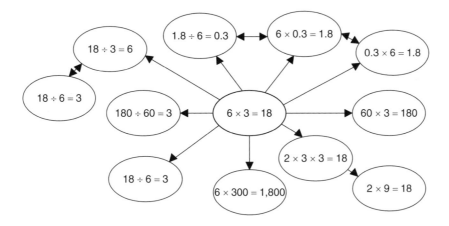

When children are completing this task, encourage them to draw the links they can see between the different number sentences they make.

Being able to multiply by 10 and 100 allows children to carry out related multiplications. A quick way to multiply by 5, for example, is to multiply by 10 and halve the result. For example, 18 × 5 is a half of 18 × 10 which is 90. The same approach can be used for 25 × 88:

$$25 \times 88 = \tfrac{1}{2} \text{ of } 50 \times 88 = \tfrac{1}{2} \text{ of } \tfrac{1}{2} \text{ of } 100 \times 88 = 2{,}200$$

This method can be generalised and is called halving and doubling. To calculate 14 × 3 we can halve the 14 and double the 3 and find 7 × 6 instead. Children should be taught to do the following by using this technique:

16 × 5	48 × 25	18 × 3
4.5 × 4	7 ½ × 8	32 × 50

Children should be taught to extend their multiplication facts. For example, use the fact that 12 × 12 = 144 to find 12 × 13 by adding 12 to 144.

Children can then attempt the following type of questions:

26 × 4	18 × 9	16 × 8
49 × 4	99 × 5	89 × 3

and similarly attempt associated division problems:

104 ÷ 4	510 ÷ 5	828 ÷ 4

When children understand that multiplication is distributive over addition and subtraction they can be taught how to do the following:

Find the cost of 5 T-shirts each costing £9.99.

Find the cost of 8 articles costing 63p, 8 articles costing 18p and 8 articles costing 19p.

Find 17½% of £80.

as:

$$5 \times £10 - 5 \times 1p = £49.95$$

$$8 \times (63p + 18p + 19p) = 8 \times £1 = £8$$

$$10\% \text{ of } £80 + 5\% \text{ of } £80 + 2\tfrac{1}{2}\% \text{ of } £80 = £8 + £4 + £2 = £14$$

By the time they leave primary school children are expected to be able to calculate simple percentages mentally. They should be taught how to find 10% and then make a suitable adjustment.

For example, to find 80% of £90, first find 10% of £90 and multiply the result by 8. Similarly 5% of £90 is half of 10% of £90.

Children should be able to use this technique on the following questions:

For more on this see Chapter 2 **Primary Mathematics: Knowledge and Understanding** (2014) from Learning Matters.

20% of £60	70% of £80	90% of £60
30% of £40	5% of £120	15% of £40

Pencil and paper methods

Addition and subtraction

For children in Key Stage 1 the emphasis is on mental calculation. Initially pencil and paper is used for recording their mental calculations in number sentences.

They should be taught how to use symbols such as □ or Δ to stand for unknown numbers.

For more on mental methods of arithmetic, see Chapter 3 of **Teaching Arithmetic in Primary Schools** (2014) from Learning Matters.

REFLECTIVE TASK

It is important for children to develop a flexible approach to number from a young age. By introducing symbols such as □ or Δ to represent a missing number, early algebraic foundations are set. However, introducing these does not come without difficulties. How might you encourage children to work out the answers to these number sentences?

$$1)\ 7 - 3 = \square \qquad 2)\ \square + 3 = 10 \qquad 3)\ \square - \Delta = 10$$

1. You might want to use a number track to demonstrate the counting back strategy. You might ask the child to hold up seven fingers, count down three, then count how many are remaining. (You might also do this with counters, teddies or pop-up people, or any other resource.)

2. This is a more difficult type of question for children to answer and research shows that it is often the first stumbling point in written calculations for children. It is essential that you teach the child to 'just think of it as 10 − 3' because although you are highlighting the inverse operation as a method to complete the calculation, you have not actually considered what the question is asking. In this case it is asking, 'I am starting at a number and counting on three to get to ten. What number have I started at?' or 'I am thinking of a number. When I add three more I get to ten. What number am I thinking of?' Alternatively, you may also want to demonstrate by having a plastic cup with seven counters already in it. Count in three more counters and have the children count that there are ten. Ask them to think about how many were in there to start with. Finally, because this is a number bond to ten, children may be able to use their fingers to partition ten into a seven and a three.

3. This is an open-ended question because there are an infinite number of possible solutions. At Key Stage 1 you will probably be expecting the majority of children to come up with the number bonds to ten and find the patterns in that list. You could use Cuisenaire Rods or coloured counters to show the patterns also:

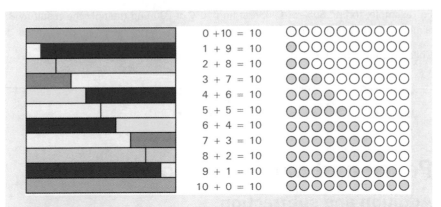

0 +10 = 10
1 + 9 = 10
2 + 8 = 10
3 + 7 = 10
4 + 6 = 10
5 + 5 = 10
6 + 4 = 10
7 + 3 = 10
8 + 2 = 10
9 + 1 = 10
10 + 0 = 10

(At Key Stage 2 you want most children to consider answers involving fractions and decimals such as $4\frac{1}{2} + 5\frac{1}{2} = 10$ or $2.35 + 7.65 = 10$ or negative numbers such as $-9 + 19 = 10$.)

When children are able to carry out multiplication and division calculations mentally they can use pencil and paper to record their results, for example:

$$9 \times \square = 18 \qquad \square \times 7 = 21 \qquad \square \times \triangle = 12$$

$$\triangle \times \triangle = 25 \qquad \square \div 6 = 7 \qquad 32 \div 4 = \square$$

Using a number line to help with addition and subtraction is particularly recommended within the non-statutory guidance of the National Curriculum.

RESEARCH SUMMARY RESEARCH SUMMARY RESEARCH SUMMARY

Findings from the Trends in International Mathematics Science Survey (TIMSS, 2003) indicate that the way children visualise addition and subtraction has a marked effect on their ability to solve problems. Dutch children as young as 6 are particularly proficient at solving addition and subtraction problems involving numbers as large as 100. To solve 100 − 28, for example, Dutch children would use an empty number line (ENL), as shown below:

counting back first to 90 then 80 and then down a further 8 to 72.

Alternatively children who realise that 28 is 2 less than 30 might count back 30 to 70 and then go forward 2:

Children are also encouraged to count up from 28 to 100 as shown below:

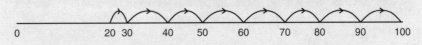

In the Netherlands these three approaches to the same problem are taught at the same time. Children are encouraged to appreciate the relationship between the three methods and be able to change between formats.

The last method is particularly useful when we want to give someone change in a shop.

Presented with the following problem:

> You are a shopkeeper. A chocolate bar costs 28 pence. Someone gives you a pound coin. Work out how much change you should give him.

a pupil should be encouraged to use an ENL approach counting up from 28 to 100.

PRACTICAL TASK PRACTICAL TASK **PRACTICAL TASK** PRACTICAL TASK

Here are some ENLs that some fictitious children have used for subtraction problems. Next to each one write the problem the child is solving and explain how they have tackled each one.

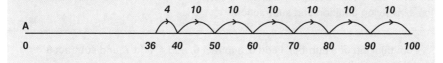

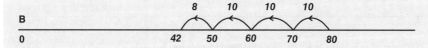

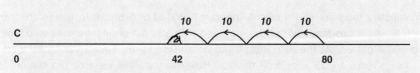

A The problem was to subtract 36 from 100. The child has counted on from 36 to 100. The answer of 64 is found by adding the numbers on each arc.

B The problem was to subtract 38 from 80. The child counted back 3 tens and then 8 units to find the answer 42.

C The problem was to subtract 38 from 80. This child counted back 4 tens and then went forward 2 units.

The ENL is also used for addition. To calculate 34 + 26 a child could use the ENL to add 10 and 10 and 6 to 34 as shown:

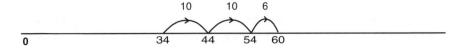

The ENL is a particularly useful aid since it mirrors the way we work mentally. Faced with solving the problem 47 + 29 mentally most people would solve it in one of two ways:

- first add 20 to 47 giving 67 then add 9 to give 76; *or*
- first add 30 to 47 giving 77 then subtract 1 to give 76

Each of these mental methods can be demonstrated using the ENL.

The two approaches are shown below:

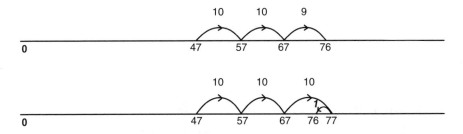

Children can be encouraged to use this approach to solve more complicated problems involving addition and subtraction:

> I am thinking of a number. I add 5, subtract 6, add 4, add 7, and subtract 8.
>
> The answer is 13. What was the number I thought of?

This kind of problem is particularly suited to solving by using the ENL.

Imaginative teachers might wish to present this kind of problem to young children as follows: 'A bus stops at the bus stop and 5 people get on. At the next stop 6 get off and 4 get on. At the next stop 7 get on and 8 get off. The driver looks round and sees there are 13 people on the bus. How many people were on the bus at the start?'

Children could also be encouraged to write their own stories to accompany ENL calculations. Calculating 7 – 6 + 4 is far less interesting than making a story to match 7 – 6 + 4 = 5! Writing a story also helps a child to make sense of what the calculation is asking them to do. It is also a useful assessment method for a teacher to check children's understanding.

In Year 2 children are expected to know that addition can be done in any order. An advantage of using the ENL is that it makes it more obvious that addition is commutative and associative. Recording the results of the following calculations on the ENL reinforces some of the basic rules of arithmetic:

$$17 - 4 - 6 \qquad 17 - 6 - 4$$

$$12 + 8 + 6 \qquad 12 + 6 + 8$$

$$12 - 5 + 4 \qquad 12 + 4 - 5$$

For more on the development of written methods of arithmetic, see Chapter 4 of **Teaching Arithmetic in Primary Schools** *(2014) from Learning Matters.*

Formal written methods

By the end of lower Key Stage 2, children are expected to be able to add and subtract numbers with up to 4 digits using the formal written methods of columnar addition and subtraction where appropriate. Below is the exemplification from the National Curriculum.

789 + 642 becomes	874 − 523 becomes	932 − 457 becomes	932 − 457 becomes
``   7 8 9
+ 6 4 2
─────────
1 4 3 1
1 1
``	``` 8 7 4
− 5 2 3
─────────
3 5 1
``	``` 8 12 1
9̶ 3̶ 2
− 4 5 7
─────────
4 7 5
``	``` 1 1
9 3 2
− 4̶ 5̶ 7
5 6
─────────
4 7 5
``
Answer: 1431	Answer: 351	Answer: 475	Answer: 475

(DfE, 2013, p. 46)

Multiplication

Children are often introduced to long multiplication via grid (or tabular) multiplication.

In this multiplication method each part of the first number is multiplied by each part of the second and the products are added. The distributive law is emphasised by this approach. So 35 × 24 is written as:

	30	5	
	600	100	20
	120	20	4

600 + 100 + 120 + 20 = 840

For more on formal written methods of addition and subtraction, see Chapter 5 of **Teaching Arithmetic in Primary Schools** *(2014) from Learning Matters.*

As well as illustrating clearly how the multiplication method works, this method provides a foundation for the later idea of multiplying out a pair of brackets: (30 + 5)(20 + 4) = (30 × 20) + (5 × 20) + (30 × 4) + (5 × 4).

Older children will be expected to multiply a three-digit number by a two-digit number and this method can easily be extended as shown:

For more on methods of multiplication, see Chapter 2 of **Primary Mathematics: Knowledge and Understanding** *(2014) from Learning Matters.*

345×36

	300	40	5	
	9,000	1,200	150	30
	1,800	240	30	6

In this example six numbers need to be added together to find the answer:

$$9,000 + 1,200 + 150 + 1,800 + 240 + 30 = 12,420$$

As children become familiar with this method they can dispense with the lines.

For more on Gelosia multiplication, see Chapter 2 of **Primary Mathematics: Knowledge and Understanding** *(2014) from Learning Matters.*

A popular way for older children to record multiplication of larger numbers is to use a variation of grid multiplication called Gelosia (or lattice) multiplication. Examiners have commented for several years that children who adopt this approach have a higher success rate.

To find 345×36, the working is set out as follows:

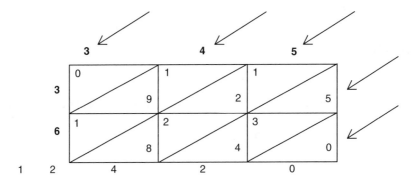

Starting at the right-hand side and adding the numbers inside the grid in the directions of the arrows gives the answer 12,420. This is a modification of grid arithmetic: the six products are found but they are added together more efficiently.

REFLECTIVE TASK

Can you work out how the Gelosia method above works? Explain your answer using correct place value terminology.

Formal written methods

By the end of lower Key Stage 2, children are expected to be able to multiply two-digit and three-digit numbers by a one-digit number using formal written layout. Below is the exemplification from the National Curriculum.

24 × 6 becomes

```
      2  4
   x     6
  ─────────
   1  4  4
      2
```

Answer: 144

342 × 7 becomes

```
      3  4  2
   x        7
  ────────────
   2  3  9  4
      2  1
```

Answer: 2394

2741 × 6 becomes

```
      2  7  4  1
   x           6
  ───────────────
   1  6  4  4  6
      4  2
```

Answer: 16446

(DfE, 2013, p. 46)

By the end of upper Key Stage 2, children are expected to be able to multiply multi-digit numbers up to 4 digits by a two-digit whole number using the formal written method of long multiplication. Below is the exemplification from the National Curriculum.

24 × 16 becomes

```
      2
      2  4
   x  1  6
  ─────────
   2  4  0
   1  4  4
   3  8  4
```

Answer: 384

124 × 26 becomes

```
   1  2
   1  2  4
   x     2  6
  ────────────
   2  4  8  0
      7  4  4
   3  2  2  4
   1  1
```

Answer: 3224

124 × 26 becomes

```
   1  2
   1  2  4
   x     2  6
  ────────────
      7  4  4
   2  4  8  0
   3  2  2  4
   1  1
```

Answer: 3224

(DfE, 2013, p. 46)

Division

Children's first introduction to division is repeated subtraction.

This approach can also be used for division by more 2 or 3 digit numbers. Consider the following problem:

> Coaches can transport 53 children.
>
> How many coaches will be needed to transport 1,300 children?

1,300	10 buses
530	
770	10 buses
530	
240	2 buses
106	
134	2 buses
106	
28	1 bus

Total number of buses needed is 25

For more on formal written methods of addition and subtraction, see Chapter 5 of **Teaching Arithmetic in Primary Schools** *(2014) from Learning Matters.*

For more on repeated subtraction, see Chapter 2 of **Primary Mathematics: Knowledge and Understanding** *(2014) from Learning Matters.*

A child doing the problem this way needs to be able to calculate 53 × 10 and 53 × 2 mentally. Research has shown that children who adopt this method have a far higher success rate. By keeping the word 'buses' in the working, they are far less likely to forget about the 28 pupils who need a bus to transport them! Another advantage of setting the work out in this way is that as children's mental arithmetic improves they can adopt quicker and more efficient methods. Once the child can calculate 53 × 20 and 53 × 4 mentally the problem can be laid out as follows:

1,300 1,060	20 buses
240 212	4 buses
28	1 bus

As children get older and have less need for the context being included in the working they can dispense with 'buses' and simply focus on the arithmetic.

Formal written methods

By the end of Year 5, children are expected to be able to divide numbers up to 4 digits by a one-digit number using the formal written method of short division and interpret remainders appropriately for the context, and by the end of Year 6 this is extended to dividing numbers up to 4 digits by a two-digit number. Below is the exemplification from the National Curriculum.

98 ÷ 7 becomes

$$\begin{array}{c} 1\ \ 4 \\ \hline {}^{\ \ 2} \\ 7\ |\ 9\ \ 8 \end{array}$$

Answer: 14

432 ÷ 5 becomes

$$\begin{array}{c} 8\ \ 6\ \ r2 \\ \hline {}^{\ \ 3} \\ 5\ |\ 4\ \ 3\ \ 2 \end{array}$$

Answer: 86 remainder 2

496 ÷ 11 becomes

$$\begin{array}{c} 4\ \ 5\ \ r1 \\ \hline {}^{\ \ 5} \\ 1\ \ 1\ |\ 4\ \ 9\ \ 6 \end{array}$$

Answer: $45\frac{1}{11}$

(DfE, 2013, p. 46)

By the end of Year 6, children are expected to divide numbers up to 4 digits by a two-digit whole number using the formal written method of long division, and interpret remainders as whole number remainders, fractions, or by rounding, as appropriate for the context.

432 ÷ 15 becomes

```
          2  8  r12
   1  5 | 4  3  2
         3  0  0
         1  3  2
         1  2  0
            1  2
```

Answer: 28 remainder 12

432 ÷ 15 becomes

```
          2  8
   1  5 | 4  3  2
         3  0  0      15x20
         1  3  2
         1  2  0      15x8
            1  2
```

$$\frac{\cancel{12}}{\cancel{15}} = \frac{4}{5}$$

Answer: $28\frac{4}{5}$

432 ÷ 15 becomes

```
          2  8 · 8
   1  5 | 4  3  2 · 0
         3  0
         1  3  2
         1  2  0
            1  2  0
            1  2  0
                  0
```

Answer: 28·8

(DfE, 2013, p. 46)

For more on formal written methods of addition and subtraction, see Chapter 5 of **Teaching Arithmetic in Primary Schools** *(2014) from Learning Matters.*

Fractions

Fractions were given a prominent place in the 2014 primary mathematics National Curriculum in England. At the beginning of Key Stage 1 children are taught half and quarter as 'fractions of' discrete and continuous quantities by solving problems using shapes, objects and quantities. For example, they recognise and find half a length, quantity, set of objects or shape. Children connect halves and quarters to the equal sharing and grouping of sets of objects and to measures, as well as recognising and combining halves and quarters as parts of a whole. Towards the end of Key Stage 1 children will use fractions as 'fractions of' discrete and continuous quantities by solving problems using shapes, objects and quantities. They will connect unit fractions to equal sharing and grouping, to numbers when they can be calculated, and to measures, finding fractions of lengths, quantities, sets of objects or shapes. They will meet $\frac{3}{4}$ as the first example of a non-unit fraction. Children will be able to count in fractions up to 10, starting from any number and using the $\frac{1}{2}$ and $\frac{2}{4}$ equivalence on the number line (for example, $1\frac{1}{4}$, $1\frac{2}{4}$ (or $1\frac{1}{2}$), $1\frac{3}{4}$, 2). This reinforces the concept of fractions as numbers and that they can add up to more than one.

In lower Key Stage 2, children connect hundredths and tenths to each other and to place value, decimal measures and to division by 10. They begin to understand unit and non-unit fractions as numbers on the number line, and deduce relations between them, such as size and equivalence. They also use the number line to connect fractions, numbers and measures. Children understand the relation between unit fractions as operators (fractions of), and division by integers. Children will also understand the relation between non-unit fractions and multiplication and division of quantities, with particular emphasis on tenths and hundredths. They continue to recognise fractions in the context of parts of a whole, numbers, measurements, a shape, and unit fractions as a division of a quantity. They make connections between fractions of a length, of a shape and as a representation of one whole or set of quantities. Pupils use factors and multiples to recognise equivalent fractions and simplify where appropriate (for example, $\frac{6}{9} = \frac{2}{3}$ or $\frac{1}{4} = \frac{2}{8}$). Children practise adding and subtracting fractions with the same denominator, to become fluent through a variety of increasingly complex problems beyond one whole. They are taught throughout that decimals and fractions are different ways of expressing numbers and proportions. They practise counting using simple fractions and decimals, both forwards and backwards.

By the end of upper Key Stage 2, children practise, use and understand addition and subtraction of fractions with different denominators by identifying equivalent fractions with the same denominator. They start with fractions where the denominator of one fraction is a multiple of the other (for example, $\frac{1}{2} + \frac{1}{8} = \frac{5}{8}$) and progress to varied and increasingly complex problems. Children also use a variety of images to support their understanding of multiplication with fractions. This follows earlier work about fractions as operators (fractions of), as numbers, and as equal parts of objects, for example as parts of a rectangle. Children use their understanding of the relationship between unit fractions and division to work backwards by multiplying a quantity that represents a unit fraction to find the whole quantity (for example, if $\frac{1}{4}$ of a length is 36cm, then the whole length is $36 \times 4 = 144$cm). They practise calculations with simple fractions and decimal fraction equivalents to aid fluency, including listing equivalent fractions to identify fractions with common denominators. Children can explore and make conjectures about converting a simple fraction to a decimal fraction (for example, $3 \div 8 = 0.375$). For simple fractions with recurring decimal equivalents, pupils learn about rounding the decimal to three decimal places, or other appropriate approximations depending on the context. Children multiply and divide numbers with up to two decimal places by one-digit and two-digit whole numbers. They multiply decimals by whole numbers, starting with the simplest cases, such as $0.4 \times 2 = 0.8$, and in practical contexts, such as measures and money.

For more on arithmetic with fractions, see Chapter 6 of **Teaching Arithmetic in Primary Schools** *(2014) from Learning Matters.*

Using a calculator and checking results

Children in the latter part of Key Stage 2 who are working at level 6 are expected to use a calculator effectively. Several skills are required to achieve this:

- to be able to check results by making sensible estimates;
- to know how a calculator prioritises operations;
- to be able to interpret the calculator output.

EMBEDDING ICT EMBEDDING ICT **EMBEDDING ICT** EMBEDDING ICT

When you introduce the use of calculators to children, you will probably want to use a big talking calculator via the IWB, or you may wish to use another modelling program or resource. Check with the class teacher, maths subject leader or ICT co-ordinator what is already available in school or via the VLE.

Estimating

Being able to estimate results is an important skill. If the calculator output is of the wrong magnitude it is helpful if a pupil can detect this immediately. Before resorting to the calculator the child needs to have some idea what the answer is going to be. If, for example, a number is being multiplied by a fraction less than 1 then the child should be aware the result will be smaller.

Before teaching children how to use a calculator they should be able to do the following type of questions:

Choose the approximate answers to the following:

208 + 305 + 769 + 638	*a* 180	*b* 1,800	*c* 18,000	*d* 18,0000
52 × 49	*a* 250	*b* 2,500	*c* 25,000	*d* 250,000
2873 ÷ 38	*a* 70	*b* 700	*c* 7,000	*d* 70,000
345 × 0.5	*a* 17	*b* 170	*c* 1,700	*d* 17,000
2,001 − 1,998	*a* 3,000	*b* 300	*c* 30	*d* 3

In fact they should not even be resorting to a calculator for the last question!

Prioritising operations

It is important for children and teachers to know how a calculator prioritises operations. Most calculators used in primary schools simply work from left to right. For example, 4 + 8 × 2 − 5 would be calculated as 19. Scientific calculators used in secondary schools, however, would give 15 for this expression. These calculators give precedence to multiplication and division. It is useful, therefore, for all the children to be using the same type of calculator. In order, however, to carry out calculations on a simple calculator children will often need to use brackets to prioritise operations. The following type of question is an example where children will need this skill:

Adult tickets cost £3.40. Child tickets cost £2.10.

Find the total cost of 37 adult tickets and 68 child tickets.

Children should be taught to enter this in the calculator as (37 × 3.40) + (68 × 2.10)

Time needs to be spent on converting word problems into the appropriate format for a calculator. Using a calculator, practise changing the following type of word problems into calculator format as Year 5 or 6 children would be expected to.

1. Winston has £8.60 in his piggy bank at the start of the year. Each month he saves the same amount. At the end of the year he has £86.60. How much did he save each month?

2. Emma saves £3.20 each week for 18 weeks. Peter saves £2.70 a week for 26 weeks. Who has saved more and by how much?

3. A plant grows 7 metres in 3 years. If it grows at the same rate each year how much did it grow in the first year? How much will it have grown in 6 years?

4. A bus can carry 53 passengers. How many buses are needed to carry 8,438 people?

Interpreting the calculator output

1. A child should enter the calculation as $(86.6 - 8.6) \div 12$ or $(86.60 - 8.60) \div 12$. The calculator output is 6.5. It is important that children realise that the answer is £6 and 50 pence and not £6 and 5 pence.
2. A child might enter the calculation on a calculator as $(18 \times 3.20) - (26 \times 2.70)$. The calculator output is −12.6. The child needs to be able to interpret this negative result as meaning that Peter saves more, by £12 and 60 pence.
3. A child might enter $(7 \div 3) \times 6$ to solve the second part of the question. The calculator output on a simple calculator is 13.9999999. Children need to be taught why the calculator gives this result and that the result needs to be rounded to 14.
4. $8,438 \div 53$ entered on the calculator gives 159.20754. Children need to be taught to consider the context of the question. In this example it is inappropriate to round the answer to the nearest whole number since 11 people would not be transported!

Examiners have commented for several years that one of the greatest difficulties that children have when using calculators is in deciphering the output. Most calculators display ERROR if an illegal operation is punched into the calculator. Children and teachers need to be able to interpret this message. It can mean the calculation is beyond the capability of the memory or that an illegal operation has been carried out. The following inputs would cause a simple calculator to display ERROR:

$$900,000 \times 900,000$$
$$\sqrt{} \; +/-16$$

The first is beyond the memory capability of a simple calculator and the second is asking the calculator to find the square root of a negative number.

Misconceptions

Several misconceptions have been identified throughout this chapter. Many of these involve children's confusion over place value, which is why it is essential that they have a firm foundation in place value and are able to calculate effectively mentally before moving on to written calculations.

Standard algorithms

Ayesha is asked to add the following numbers:

25, 175, 50, 200, 5

She tackles the problem as follows:

$$
\begin{array}{r}
25 \\
175 \\
+50 \\
200 \\
\underline{5} \\
1625
\end{array}
$$

What does this tell you about her understanding of addition?

Firstly it is clear that Ayesha does not yet have a sufficient understanding of place value to tackle column addition and should be using a different method. This example really encourages mental calculation. If she wanted to use a written method, an expanded written form would be far more appropriate.

Many of the misconceptions children develop in the area of calculation arise as a result of lack of understanding of the standard algorithms. In the past it was assumed that all children could learn algorithms by heart and apply them. Research has shown that unless pupils understand the algorithms they use, errors will creep into their work. Their lack of understanding means they find it difficult to detect errors in their working. For this reason far more emphasis is now placed on non-standard algorithms and jottings. Only when children are confident should they be moved onto standard algorithms. Many educators would argue that standard algorithms, although more efficient, are of little benefit since children should be resorting to calculators for more difficult calculations. For further information on misconceptions in calculation read Fiona Lawton's chapter in Hansen (2011).

A SUMMARY OF **KEY POINTS**

In order to support the development of calculation strategies it is important that children:

➢ know basic number bonds;

➢ know multiplication tables up to 10 × 10;

➢ are able to use these facts to derive new facts;

➢ practise mental arithmetic regularly;

➢ are able to use a range of resources including the empty number line (ENL) to support their mental calculations;

➢ understand the inverse relation between addition and subtraction and between multiplication and division;

➢ be allowed to continue using non-standard algorithms where necessary;

➢ can use a calculator efficiently.

M-LEVEL EXTENSION > > > > M-LEVEL EXTENSION > > > >

At the end of this chapter, in the section dealing with common misconceptions, reference was made to the fact that some educators would argue that children should be using a calculator for more difficult calculations, rather than using standard algorithms, even though these are more efficient than non-standard methods of calculation. Use the internet to research this view and the opposing viewpoint. Talk to your mentor/class teacher and the subject leader for mathematics in your school. What do they think? Take time to reflect on this issue. Where do you stand?

REFERENCES REFERENCES **REFERENCES** REFERENCES REFERENCES

DfE (2011) *Teachers' Standards.* Available at: www.gov.uk/government/publications/teachers-standards (accessed 13/4/14).

DfE (2013) *Mathematics Programmes of Study: Key Stages 1 and 2. National Curriculum for England.* London: DfE. Available at: www.gov.uk/government/uploads/system/uploads/attachment_data/file/239129/PRIMARY_National_Curriculum_-_Mathematics.pdf (accessed 13/4/14).

Hansen, A. (ed.) (2011) *Children's Errors in Mathematics: Understanding Common Misconceptions in Primary Schools.* London: Sage/Learning Matters.

TIMSS (2003) *Trends in International Mathematics and Science Survey* (third survey). Available at: http://nces.ed.gov (accessed 11/5/11).

FURTHER READING FURTHER READING FURTHER READING

Clausen-May, T. (2005) *Teaching Maths to Pupils with Different Learning* Styles. London: Paul Chapman Publishing. Utilising models and images, this practical guide supports you in teaching mathematics to all children in your classroom.

English, R. (2014) *Teaching Arithmetic in Primary Schools.* London: Sage/Learning Matters.

Frobisher, L., Monaghan, J., Orton, A., Orton, J., Roper, T. and Threlfall, J. (1999) *Learning to Teach Number: A Handbook for Students and Teachers in the Primary School.* Cheltenham: Nelson Thornes.

Haylock, D. (2005) (3rd edn) *Mathematics Explained for Primary Teachers.* London: Paul Chapman.

Thompson, I. (ed.) (2008) (2nd edn) *Teaching and Learning Early Number.* Buckingham: Open University Press. A collection of papers from key mathematics educators, drawn together to discuss a range of important issues in teaching and learning number.

Wright, R. J., Martland, J., Stafford, A. K. and Stanger, G. (2006) *Teaching Number in the Classroom with 4–8 year olds.* London: Paul Chapman Publishing. This research-based book is based on nine principles and has task design as a central focus.

9
Algebra

Introduction

The experience many people will recount of their own algebra learning with things 'jumping over the equals and changing the sign' or 'change the side, change the sign', did little to develop an understanding of algebra and even less to encourage an interest in and enjoyment of the subject! Algebra is firmly rooted in patterns, and the creation, extension and expression of patterns is fundamental to algebra. This needs to be our starting point with children if we are to support them as they develop a clear understanding of algebra and come to marvel at its elegance.

REFLECTIVE TASK

From your own learning of the subject, think of all the words, phrases and activities you associate with algebra. As you work through this chapter, think about how your own learning of algebra is similar to or different from the progression presented.

RESEARCH SUMMARY RESEARCH SUMMARY **RESEARCH SUMMARY**

Algebra is one area of mathematics that children have traditionally encountered later in their mathematics learning and one where they have worked in the abstract. Annie Owen (2005) argues that in fact children should, and do, encounter algebraic concepts much earlier. Granted the algebra they encounter may not closely resemble the activities many people recall when considering their own learning; however, she contends that as children move beyond the primary years and beyond school, they will be required to effectively use experimentation, recognition, application and communication. These are all fundamental skills developed when exploring algebra in the form of repeating patterns, structural patterns and sequences in the primary years. Studying these algebraic concepts equips children for more complex algebra in the upper primary years as they are introduced to functions, equations and symbolic representation.

To underpin their understanding of algebra, children need to be confident with:

- properties of numbers and number sequences;
- reasoning about numbers or shapes and making general statements about them;
- using letters and symbols to represent unknown numbers or variables.

Progression in aspects of algebra

Although algebra is only formally introduced in the National Curriculum in Year 6, many of the tasks that children carry out from EYFS and beyond are pre-algebraic in nature. In this chapter, we will be considering three main aspects that contribute to the development of children's understanding of algebra: the vocabulary that they need to use, number sequences and spatial patterns, and how children learn to generalise.

Vocabulary

In order to communicate confidently and competently within this area of mathematics, children need to be able to use appropriate mathematical vocabulary. Children need to be able to understand and use the following vocabulary to support their learning of algebraic concepts:

problem	solution	inverse
method	explain	predict
reason	pattern	relationship
compare	repeating pattern	show me
puzzle	symbol	equation
diagrams	pictures	odd, even
solve	order	
count in ones, twos, fives, tens...		
test	reasoning	strategy
sign	operation	rule
sequence	property	formula
criterion/criteria	generalise	general statement
construct	term	represent

THE BIGGER PICTURE   THE BIGGER PICTURE   THE BIGGER PICTURE

When you are planning English activities that are designed to encourage children to spell more independently, don't forget to include work based on other areas of learning and aspects of the wider curriculum as well as those met within English sessions. Specialised vocabulary needed for topics in subjects such as mathematics, science, history, geography and RE are sometimes learnt as 'one-offs' or irregular words, but they can often be chosen to highlight and reinforce particular spelling patterns that you are currently working on and added to that week's spelling test list. Even if the subject vocabulary seems to 'stand alone', why not include a batch of mathematical words instead of your usual word list and ask parents to help their children to learn both the spellings and meanings of the words? This could be an excellent way of approaching those terms that have special meanings in mathematical English or those that have a different meaning in mathematics to their meanings in ordinary English. See Chapter 7 of *Primary Mathematics: Knowledge and Understanding* (Learning Matters, 2014) for more on this.

Number sequences and spatial patterns

Algebra only appears as a specific content area in the National Curriculum in Year 6. However, there is a clear progression in pre-algebra throughout the primary curriculum by learning about number sequences, starting with counting in steps of different sizes from and back to zero, then one, then any number and recognising multiples of numbers. By the end of lower Key Stage 2 children are expected to count back through zero into negative numbers, count in steps of fractional size, recognise and extend sequences of square numbers and make general statements about odd and even numbers. This is extended by the end of upper Key Stage 2 where children will be able to use simple formulae, generate and describe linear number sequences, express missing number problems algebraically, find pairs of numbers that satisfy an equation with two unknowns and enumerate possibilities of combinations of two variables.

For more on counting and on the properties of numbers and number sequences, see Chapter 7.

Alongside the learning of number sequences, children also start to investigate patterns within shape and space. They start by recreating patterns, then extending

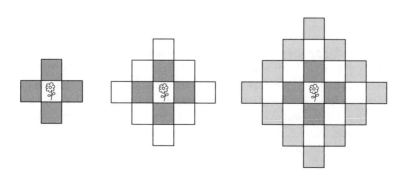

them; they then talk about the patterns and go on to describe them. This gradually leads to a recognition that number patterns can be generated from spatial patterns, and that these patterns can be expressed generally, at first in words and then using symbols.

An example of this move from spatial pattern to number sequence to generalised rule is shown below, with possible expectations for children at different stages.

The diagram above shows the number of slabs around a flowerbed in the garden. Each picture has a different number of slabs depending on how many 'rows' there are. This pattern could be given to children in either Key Stage 1 or 2 but their responses would be very different depending on their previous experiences and understanding.

PRACTICAL TASK PRACTICAL TASK **PRACTICAL TASK** PRACTICAL TASK

In order to support your own subject knowledge development, before reading on have a go at generalising the number of slabs in each new 'row'.

In Key Stage 1 children might practically reproduce the pattern using a concrete resource like Multilink. They may extend the pattern to produce the next in the sequence:

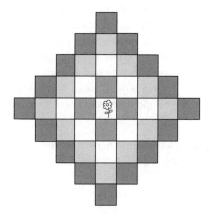

*To support your own subject knowledge development in this area, see Chapter 3 in **Primary Mathematics: Knowledge and Understanding** (2014) from Learning Matters.*

By Year 2 you could expect a child to be able to tell you that the number pattern for the number of slabs in each 'row' is 4, 8, 12, 16 and that the next 'row' would have 20 slabs. By Year 4 you could expect to find children generalising the sequence in words, for example: 'The numbers in the sequence are multiples of 4'. By Year 6 the children should have progressed from generalising in words towards generalising more in symbols. Thus you should find children who are able to find the nth term of this sequence, i.e. the number of slabs in the nth 'row' is equal to 4n.

Generalising

In the preceding example the children were expected to generalise the pattern, first in words and later using symbols. But how do children learn to generalise? It is certainly true that many people undertaking courses of initial teacher training were never taught to generalise patterns themselves. Those who were, tend to have encountered the topic as part of a GCSE syllabus purely in an abstract context. This means that many students are having to teach an aspect of mathematics they have not fully learnt or understood themselves. This can prove quite challenging, but meeting the challenge reaps great rewards.

In order to ensure children develop fully within mathematics, it is important that they encounter a clearly planned progression within algebraic concepts from a young age. In the area of generalising this means they need to start with general statements and find examples to match the statement. Examples include:

(Year 1) All triangles have three sides:

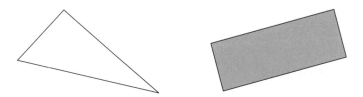

The white shape is a triangle but the grey shape is not a triangle.

(Year 3) Any odd number is one more than an even number:

$$23 = 22 + 1 \qquad 15 = 14 + 1$$

The general statements that children encounter get more and more challenging throughout the key stages. By Year 6 you should expect children to be able to find examples to match statements such as:

If you add three consecutive numbers, the sum is three times the middle number:

$$4 + 5 + 6 = 15 = 3 \times 5$$

For more on triangle numbers see Chapter 7.

Or:

Any square number is the sum of two consecutive triangular numbers:

$$4 = 1 + 3 \qquad 25 = 10 + 15 \qquad 64 = 28 + 36$$

As children become increasingly confident in finding examples to match general statements they need to be given the opportunity to start to express general relationships in words (in about Year 4). This might be within a real-life context, e.g. finding the number of days in any number of weeks, or within a purely mathematical context, e.g. explaining a number sequence. Into Year 5 children should start to record the general relationships they express in writing. For example, if given the sequence:

$$1, \ 4, \ 9, \ 16, \ 25, \ \ldots$$

you might expect a child to express the relationship as follows:

> *This is the sequence of square numbers. A square number is when a number is multiplied by itself, for example $2 \times 2 = 4$. To find the 10th square number you would need to multiply 10×10 and to find the 27th square number you would need to multiply 27×27.*

*To support your own subject knowledge development in this area, see Chapter 3 in **Primary Mathematics: Knowledge and Understanding** (2014) from Learning Matters.*

By Year 6 you can expect children to be able to express their relationships in symbols. For example, in order to find the formula for the nth term of the sequence:

$$3, 6, 9, 12, 15, \ldots$$

they will first need to recognise that the numbers are multiples of three and that the sequence starts at 1×3. Once they have seen this they need to express the nth term as $3 \times n$ or $3n$.

From this it can be seen that it is vital for children to encounter a gradual and progressive development in being introduced to algebraic concepts. If they start in the Foundation Stage and build on previous learning, then algebra should not be an abstract mathematical mystery to them.

Misconceptions

One possible misconception that children might develop when encountering symbolic representation within algebra occurs when children interpret the algebraic symbols as shorthand for words, for example:

$$2\mathbf{a} + 3\mathbf{b} \text{ is not shorthand for 2 apples plus 3 bananas.}$$

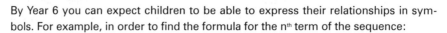

PRACTICAL TASK PRACTICAL TASK **PRACTICAL TASK** PRACTICAL TASK

Before reading on, think about why this might be counterproductive when children are learning algebra.

In fact if the equation was 2a + 3b = 5, then one possible solution would be a = 1 and b = 1, i.e. a = b, but an apple can never equal a banana!

The easiest way to ensure children do not develop this misconception is not to teach it. Although you may have experienced this yourself when you were being taught algebra, it is just as easy to plan to teach this aspect of the subject in a more meaningful way. By introducing children to the use of letters to represent variables before they start to generalise symbolically, they become familiar with the concept. Using letters which are completely different to the words in the relationship also helps to prevent this misconception, e.g. if generalising the number of days in any number of weeks, using *a* and *b* would be better than using *d* and w, which the children might interpret as abbreviations for days and weeks.

THE BIGGER PICTURE   THE BIGGER PICTURE   THE BIGGER PICTURE

When you are planning to teach children about generalising expressions, make sure that you are confident with this area yourself so that you are able to deal with any misconceptions that children may have. Check out some of the useful revision sites such as BBC Bitesize to practise your own skills in this area. See Chapters 3 and 7 of *Primary Mathematics: Knowledge and Understanding* (Learning Matters, 2014) for more on this.

Teaching using strategies that ensure children understand algebraic concepts in a meaningful way supports a fuller knowledge and awareness of the fundamental role algebra plays in mathematical communication. It is not a peripheral area that is encountered briefly then left alone again with relief – it is the essence of all mathematical recording and interaction. It should be brief, elegant and meaningful!

A SUMMARY OF **KEY POINTS**

In order to support the development of algebraic understanding, it is important that children:

> count forwards and backwards in steps of different sizes;
> recognise, recreate and describe number and spatial patterns;
> extend number and spatial patterns;
> learn to use appropriate mathematical vocabulary to support their learning of algebraic concepts:
> find examples to match general statements;
> express general relationships orally;
> express general relationships in writing;
> express general relationships symbolically.

M-LEVEL EXTENSION > > > > M-LEVEL EXTENSION > > > >

Look back at the Research Summary of the work of Owen (2005). Think about her argument that children encounter algebraic concepts much earlier than in upper Key Stage 2. Reread Chapter 6 of this book and Chapter 3 of the companion book in the series, *Primary Mathematics: Knowledge and Understanding* (Learning Matters, 2014). Can you create a progressive scheme of work, starting in the EYFS, that shows how children's knowledge and understanding of algebraic concepts will develop through Year 6?

REFERENCES REFERENCES **REFERENCES** REFERENCES REFERENCES

DfE (2011) *Teachers' Standards*. Available at: www.gov.uk/government/publications/teachers-standards (accessed 13/4/14).

Owen, A. (2005) 'In search of the unknown: a review of primary algebra', in Anghileri, J. (ed.) *Children's Mathematical Thinking in the Primary Years: Perspectives on Children's Learning*. London: Continuum International Publishing Group.

FURTHER READING   FURTHER READING   FURTHER READING

Anghileri, J. (2006) *Teaching Number Sense*. London: Continuum.

DfES (2000) *Mathematical Vocabulary*. London: DfES.

Durkin, K. and Shire, B. (eds) (1991) *Language in Mathematical Education, Research and Practice*. Buckingham: Open University Press.

Hansen, A. (ed.) (2014) (3rd edn) *Children's Errors in Mathematics: Understanding Common Misconceptions in Primary Schools*. London: Sage/Learning Matters.

Haylock, D. (2010) (4th edn) *Mathematics Explained for Primary Teachers*. London: Sage.

Haylock, D. and Cockburn, A. (2002) *Understanding Mathematics in the Lower Primary Years*. London: Paul Chapman Publishing.

Mason, J., Burton, L. and Stacey, K. (2010) (Revised edn) *Thinking Mathematically*. Harlow: Pearson Education Limited.

Ofsted (2009) *Mathematics: Understanding the Score. Improving practice in mathematics teaching at primary level*. London: Ofsted.

Thompson, I. (2010) (2nd edn) *Issues in Teaching Numeracy in Primary Schools*. Maidenhead: Open University Press.

Williams, P. (2008) *Independent Review of Mathematics Teaching in Early Years Settings and Primary Schools*. Nottingham: DCSF.

10
Measures

Introduction

Children need to realise that, although we can theoretically talk about measures with great accuracy, in reality all practical measurement is an approximation. As children progress through their primary years, there is an expectation that these approximations will become more and more accurate. This occurs as they become increasingly able to use measuring equipment and read scales with greater accuracy. A good understanding of measures is vital for all children as so many everyday tasks involve either an accurate measure of something or an estimate. Shopping, cooking, decorating, driving and arriving somewhere on time, all involve different measurement concepts. It is amazing to think just how many times in the day you encounter measurement without necessarily being consciously aware of it.

PRACTICAL TASK PRACTICAL TASK PRACTICAL TASK PRACTICAL TASK

Note down all the times you encounter a measurement concept during a 24-hour period. Classify your list into different types of measures and identify whether the measure was an estimate or accurate. Remember to include time, pints (either milk or beer!), oven temperatures, distances on road signs and so on. You will probably be amazed just how many there are.

Progression in aspects of measures

In this chapter, we will be considering three main aspects that contribute to the development of children's understanding of measures: the vocabulary that they need to use, non-standard and standard units, and progressions in the main areas of common measures.

Vocabulary

Measurement is one area of mathematics where a great deal of vocabulary is developed from the very early stages. The types of activities that can be done to support the development of this language in the early stages have been covered in Chapter 6. This chapter will continue with the development of measurement concepts as they advance from that point.

For more on misconceptions see later in this chapter.

At all times, constant reinforcement of appropriate and accurate vocabulary within measures is very important. Misconceptions can easily develop, with children confusing concepts and using them as if they were interchangeable. In order to help prevent this, careful consideration needs to be given to the selection and use of mathematical vocabulary.

As children move through Key Stage 2, they quite enjoy playing with the words used to describe units of measures. It is an interesting task to ask them to compare the language of measurement with other words in social usage in order to support an understanding of the size of the units. For example, you could ask them what is a centipede? a century? a centimetre? Or what is a millipede? a millennium? a millilitre?

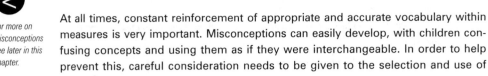

THE BIGGER PICTURE   THE BIGGER PICTURE   **THE BIGGER PICTURE**

When you are planning to teach children about the vocabulary of measures, consider setting it in a wider real-life context of topic work.

Our system of measures has been developed over thousands of years. The use of different units and the history of measures make for interesting study at upper Key Stage 2 and allow opportunities for good cross-curricular links. Children can study units of measurement used in the different ancient civilisations and also look at the historical development of units of measure in our own society. The earliest recorded units of length were based on body parts, for example:

- the cubit – the forearm from the elbow to the tip of the middle finger;
- the span – the tip of the thumb to the tip of the little finger on an extended hand;
- the reach – on outstretched arms, the tip of one middle finger to the tip of the other;
- the hand – the width of a hand (fingers closed) from the edge of the palm to the edge of the thumb (still used to measure the height of horses);
- the foot – the Romans divided this measure into 12 inches, but it was originally based on the length of a foot.

Children will enjoy practical measuring activities using these non-standard units.

Prior to adopting the metric system of measures, the UK used the imperial system for measuring. This system was first described officially in the Magna Carta (1215) and is still in quite common usage today. Since the beginning of the year 2000, however, metric units have had to take precedence over imperial units in retailing. Unlike the imperial system, in the metric system there are clear connections between the units. For example:

Imperial units: *Metric units:*

12 inches	= 1	foot	1 m = 100 cm = 1,000 mm
3 feet	= 1	yard	
1,760 yards	= 1	mile	
4 gills	= 1	pint	1 litre = 100 cl = 1,000 ml
2 pints	= 1	quart	
8 pints	= 1	gallon	

Non-standard and standard units

Children start measuring by making direct comparisons of lengths, weights, etc. They then move on to use uniform non-standard units to measure. Uniform non-standard units are things like Multilink cubes, yoghurt pots, drinking straws and so on. These are all objects that are of uniform size/mass, but they are not a standard unit of measurement. At this stage children are also introduced to standard units of measure, initially metres, litres, kilograms and centimetres. They can be encouraged to use these measures for direct comparison – for example, find something shorter than a metre, something that holds more than a litre or something lighter than a kilogram.

By Year 3 children are generally expected to use the following standard units of length, weight/mass and capacity to estimate, measure and record measurements:

Length:	*Weight/mass:*	*Capacity:*
centimetre	gram	millilitre
metre	kilogram	litre
kilometre		

In Year 4 children start to consider area. Again, here uniform non-standard units form a very sound introduction to measuring area. Multilink cubes, coins, sheets of

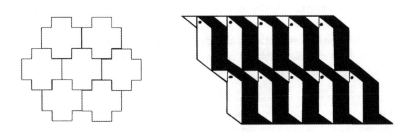

paper, either A4 or newspaper, etc. are very useful units depending on the size of the area to be measured. Another way of using uniform non-standard units when introducing area is to consider tessellations. A tessellation is where a shape fits together with a number of exact copies with no gaps or overlaps; see examples on p.179.

As with all uniform non-standard units, tessellations can be used to encourage children to recognise the need for standard units of measure. By asking simply, 'How many crosses does it take to cover the paper?' and then, 'How many penguins?' children can be guided to the need for standard units if we are to communicate measurement effectively.

By the end of Key Stage 2 the range of standard units children are expected to understand and use has increased to include:

Length:	*Weight/mass:*	*Capacity:*	*Area:*
millimetre	gram	millilitre	square millimetre
centimetre	kilogram	centilitre	square centimetre
metre	tonne	litre	square metre
kilometre			

In Year 5 children should understand and use approximate equivalences between metric units and common imperial units such as inches, pounds and pints, so this should include:

Length:	*Weight (/mass):*	*Capacity:*
mile	pound	pint
yard	ounce	gallon
foot		
inch		

Having considered vocabulary and standard and non-standard units, we will now briefly outline the expected progression in different areas of measurement.

Progression in measuring length

- Use comparative language (e.g. longer than, shorter than) to directly compare two lengths, then more than two lengths.
- Measure using uniform non-standard units.
- Estimate, measure and compare using standard units: metre, then centimetre, then millimetre, including their abbreviations.
- Use a ruler to draw and measure lines to the nearest centimetre, then half centimetre, then millimetre.
- Explain the relationship between kilometres and metres, and metres and centimetres, then centimetres and millimetres, and convert between them.
- Calculate the perimeters of rectangles and other simple shapes, then regular polygons, then simple compound shapes (shapes that can be split into rectangles).
- Know the imperial unit of length.

The circumference is the distance around the edge of a circle and, as such, is closely linked to perimeter. Once children can calculate the perimeter of rectilinear shapes they can move on to explore the circumference of circles. Eratosthenes (c. 276–194 BC) rather incredibly managed to calculate a value for the circumference of the Earth. Having heard of a well at Syene (now modern-day Aswan) where sunlight only struck the bottom at midday on the summer solstice, he was able to use this fact together with measurements taken at the same time in Alexandria to perform his calculation, which gave a circumference of about 40,000 km. Present-day calculations give a distance of 40,024 km. So, over 2,000 years ago he managed to calculate the Earth's circumference incredibly closely!

Progression in measuring area

- Calculate areas of rectangles and other simple shapes using counting methods and standard units, cm^2.
- Understand that area is measured in square centimetres (cm^2).
- Understand and use 'length x breadth' for the area of a rectangle.
- Calculate the area of simple compound shapes (shapes that can be split into rectangles).
- Calculate and compare the area of rectangles (including squares), and including using standard units, square centimetres (cm^2) and square metres (m^2) and estimate the area of irregular shapes.
- Recognise when it is possible to use formulae for area of shapes.
- Recognise when it is possible to use formulae for area and volume of shapes.
- Calculate the area of parallelograms and triangles.

Area and perimeter (see *Length* above) are frequently taught alongside each other as children focus on different measurement properties of shapes. It is interesting to consider whether a shape with a fixed area will always have the same perimeter and vice versa. Let us look at a shape with an area of 4 cm^2 – using squared paper will make the task easier.

This shape has an area of 4 cm^2.
Its perimeter is equal to 8 cm.

This shape has an area of 4 cm^2.
Its perimeter is equal to 10 cm.

PRACTICAL TASK PRACTICAL TASK **PRACTICAL TASK** PRACTICAL TASK

Try doing the same activity, but this time keep the perimeter fixed. Do all shapes with a perimeter of 10 cm have the same area?

Progression in measuring weight/mass

- Use comparative language (e.g. heavier than, lighter than) directly to compare two weights, then more than two weights.
- Measure using uniform non-standard units.

- Estimate, measure and compare using standard units: kilogram, then gram, including their abbreviations.
- Suggest suitable measuring equipment and read scales to the nearest labelled division, then unlabelled division.
- Explain the relationship between kilograms and grams, and convert between them.
- Know the imperial units of a pound (lb) and an ounce (oz).
- Know the metric and imperial equivalence of lb and kg, and oz and g.
- Convert between different units of metric measure (for example, kilometre and metre; centimetre and metre; centimetre and millimetre; gram and kilogram; litre and millilitre).

Mass can be defined as the amount of matter in an object and weight is the downward force of the object, calculated as the mass multiplied by the force of gravity. Hence the units of mass are kilograms and grams and the unit of weight is the newton.

THE BIGGER PICTURE THE BIGGER PICTURE THE BIGGER PICTURE

When you are planning work on measuring weight/mass, consider setting it in a cross-curricular context. The newton is named after Sir Isaac Newton (1642–1727). The story frequently relayed involves Newton observing an apple falling in his orchard. He realised that the force pulling the apple towards the Earth was the same force that held the Moon in orbit and thus was the first to explain gravitational force. Children will enjoy some drama work on this – acting out the story will give them opportunities to explain what gravity is, and this can then be linked to study of the Earth and beyond in science at Key Stage 2, including when learning about the gravity on the Moon and the other planets in the Solar System.

Progression in measuring capacity

- Use comparative language to directly compare two capacities (e.g. by filling and emptying containers), then more than two capacities.
- Measure using uniform non-standard units, e.g. yoghurt pots.
- Estimate, measure and compare using standard units: litre, then millilitres, including their abbreviations.
- Suggest suitable measuring equipment and read scales to the nearest labelled division, then unlabelled division.
- Explain the relationship between litres and millilitres, and convert between them.
- Know the imperial units of a pint, then a gallon.
- Know the metric and imperial equivalence of litres and pints and gallons.

At Key Stages 1 and 2 capacity is studied but not volume. Volume is the amount of three-dimensional space an object takes up. Capacity applies to containers and is equal to the amount of liquid a container can hold when full. For example if you are buying a 2-litre bottle of lemonade this means the amount of liquid in the bottle is equal to 2 litres. But is the capacity of the bottle actually 2 litres?

PRACTICAL TASK PRACTICAL TASK **PRACTICAL TASK** PRACTICAL TASK

Investigate some containers that you have as a result of shopping. Look at the liquid volume of the purchase you have made, e.g. 2 litres of lemonade, and compare this to the actual capacity of the container. How much 'empty space' are you purchasing? (Don't worry, as long as you get the 2 litres of lemonade that is advertised, the empty space is free!)

Progression in measuring time

- Sequence familiar events.
- Know the days of the week in order, the seasons of the year, then months of the year.
- On an analogue clock, read o'clock time, then half hour, then quarter hour.
- Know the relationship between units of time: second, minute, hour, day, week, then month and year.
- Read time on a 12-hour digital display.
- Read the time to 5 minutes on an analogue and 12-hour digital clock, then to the nearest minute.
- Use a.m. and p.m.
- Read simple timetables.
- Read the time on a 24-hour digital clock and use 24-hour notation.
- Use a calendar to calculate time intervals.
- Appreciate different times around the world.

There is a great deal of language associated with time that needs to be developed with children from the Foundation Stage upwards. It is interesting to consider how people have developed these concepts as society has become more and more sophisticated. The most primitive peoples measured time solely in terms of day or night and the passing of the seasons. As calendars were developed the year was divided into months based on lunar cycles. We can now measure time with an incredible degree of accuracy – indeed the most recent addition is the atomic clock which will only gain or lose one second every 1.7 million years. So there is no excuse for being late with one of those!

Misconceptions

Mass and weight

A common misconception held by children is to confuse mass and weight. These words are frequently used socially as if they were interchangeable. This means that, outside the classroom, children may encounter the language applied to the wrong concept, which could cause confusion.

Clearly mathematically there is a difference between mass and weight. Mass is the amount of matter contained within an object and it is measured in grams and kilograms, whereas weight is a measure of the downward force of the object measured in newtons. The weight is dependent on the force of gravity; hence if you were to stand on the Moon your weight would decrease as the Moon has a lower gravitational force than the Earth; however, your mass would remain unchanged. In the National Curriculum, 'mass/weight' is used in Key Stage 1 but 'mass' is the preferred term in Key Stage 2.

It is clear that some people will be very concerned about using 'weight' in Key Stage 1 as it is technically simply wrong. However, the reality is that children come to school with a knowledge of 'weighing' things. The approach suggested builds on this knowledge and starts to introduce the vocabulary of the different units. As the children progress into Key Stage 2 and Key Stage 3 the concepts of mass and weight will be explored in greater depth. Probably this means that as a society we will continue to use the two as if they were synonymous, but being over-pedantic at all times can be very counter-productive to learning. Simply make sure you know the difference between mass and weight and can explain it to children if and when you need to.

Time

Time is another area of measurement where a number of misconceptions can develop. These are due to the amount and use of language associated with time and the quite complex way we measure time and divide our day.

One of the first things to consider is the language of time. Children are frequently told, 'wait a minute' or 'you can play for one more minute', both of which, in reality, are used to represent any amount of time. Other confusion can arise from time-related words such as daytime and night time. Children may well establish that they sleep at night time and play during daytime – except in the summer they appear to sleep during daytime and in the winter they play at night time! We should therefore not be surprised when children have little understanding of the length of time. Time passing is a very ephemeral concept. It cannot be touched or directly seen; it can only be 'seen' through measuring instruments or, longer term, through changes, e.g. from day to night.

Reading time is a further area for confusion. An analogue watch or clock has at least two hands, sometimes three. Children are expected to interpret time by reading the display. It is quite interesting to compare our expectations for reading the time with that of the utility companies for reading their meters. When reading an analogue clock face children from Year 1 are expected to interpret two hands on one dial (Year 1 – o'clock and half hour, Year 2 – tell and write the time to five minutes, including quarter past/to the hour and draw the hands on a clock face to show these times). If you are not at home when the utility company comes to read one of your meters you are left with a card. On the card you have to write the number if it is a digital display, if not, you simply draw the position of each hand on each dial. There is often no expectation that you, as an adult, should 'read' the number represented by the hands on the dials, an expectation we have of five year olds!

When introducing telling the time on an analogue clock face, it is important that the chosen resources accurately represent time passing on a clock face. For example, simply moving the big hand from 12 to 6 to change from 'o'clock' to 'half past' without moving the hour hand will not support children's understanding or ability to tell the time. A 'cog clock', one that links the two hands appropriately so that when one is moved, the other moves proportionately around the clock face, is a very useful resource.

Further confusion can result from the fact that time is not measured using a metric scale; hence if children try to add or subtract time using standard algorithms they are almost guaranteed an incorrect answer. Complementary addition bridging through the hour would be a far more effective method.

For more on complementary addition, see Chapter 2 of **Primary Mathematics: Knowledge and Understanding** *(2014) from Learning Matters.*

The complex nature of learning to tell the time and appreciate the passing of time has clear implications for planning and assessment. As a teacher you will need to be very clear in identifying the learning, in planning for that learning to take place and in recording your assessments in order to inform future development in this area. In your planning you will need to have clearly 'rehearsed' the lesson in order to anticipate any misconceptions and misunderstandings and have considered how you might address these.

For more on misconceptions related to time, see Chapter 7 of **Children's Errors in Mathematics: Understanding Common Misconceptions in Primary Schools** *(2014) from Learning Matters.*

EMBEDDING ICT EMBEDDING ICT EMBEDDING ICT EMBEDDING ICT

The National Numeracy Strategy developed some useful interactive teaching programs (ITPs) to support the modelling of mathematics for learners. These programs can be used effectively on an IWB in class, alongside other practical manipulatives, to help children as they construct their understanding of mathematical concepts. You are able to manipulate all the resources electronically, invaluable for whole-class or larger group modelling. A number of these ITPs can usefully be used to support the teaching of a number of concepts related to measures. These include:

Measuring cylinder

Measuring scales

Ruler

Tell the time

Thermometer

To find these on the internet, search for 'ITPs NNS' followed by the name of the ITP.

A SUMMARY OF **KEY POINTS**

In order to support the development of understanding measurement concepts, it is important that children:

> ➢ recognise that all measure is approximate;
> ➢ use the appropriate language of measures confidently and accurately;

> ➢ can estimate and compare as well as measure, including using non-standard measures;
> ➢ can explain the need for standard units;
> ➢ understand and can use imperial measures still in everyday use;
> ➢ understand the relationship between different units of measure.

M-LEVEL EXTENSION > > > > M-LEVEL EXTENSION > > > >

Reflect on the issue of whether children should be taught the correct meanings of the terms 'weight' and 'mass' from the start of their work on measures. Research the differing viewpoints and discuss these with experienced colleagues, including your mentor/class teacher, and the subject leader for mathematics in your school. If the correct terminology is used from the EYFS onwards, would this cause tensions with the social use of the terms, including the usage within the child's family?

REFERENCES REFERENCES **REFERENCES** REFERENCES REFERENCES

DfE (2011) *Teachers' Standards*. Available at: www.gov.uk/government/publications/teachers-standards (accessed 13/4/14).

DfEE/QCA (1999) *Mathematics: the National Curriculum for England.* London: HMSO.

FURTHER READING   FURTHER READING   FURTHER READING

Barber, D., Cooper, L. and Meeson, G. (2007) *Learning and Teaching with IWBs: Primary and Early Years.* Exeter: Learning Matters.

Gillespie, H., Boulton, H., Hramiak, A. J. and Williamson, R. (2007) *Learning and Teaching with Virtual Learning Environments.* Exeter: Learning Matters.

Hansen, A. (ed.) (2014) (3rd edn) *Children's Errors in Mathematics: Understanding Common Misconceptions in Primary Schools.* London: Sage/Learning Matters.

Haylock, D. (2010) (4th edn) *Mathematics Explained for Primary Teachers.* London: Sage.

Thompson, I. (2010) (2nd edn) *Issues in Teaching Numeracy in Primary Schools.* Maidenhead: Open University Press.

11
Geometry

Introduction

A good spatial understanding is important for children as they compare, classify, investigate and solve problems within mathematics. Spatial activities can be the springboard for work in other mathematical areas including number, algebra and handling data.

RESEARCH SUMMARY RESEARCH SUMMARY RESEARCH SUMMARY

Some research in a few spatial areas is cited here. Mathematics education journals are a useful source of further papers.

Angles

Clements and Burns (2000) used Logo (software in common use in schools in various versions) to research the development of an understanding of angles. They found children learned about turns by integrating two schemes, turn as body movement and turn as number. The children could easily use these two schemes separately, but there was a gradual intertwining and integration of them. This led to the gradual construction of mental images and manipulations of these images to 'stand in for' what was a physical strategy. This is an 'image scheme', that is an 'internalised dynamic mental image acquired through bodily experience'.

Geometric development

The van Hiele model of geometric development (cited in Monaghan, 2000) details a possible progression in developing a geometric understanding. It is probable that most children in the primary years will be working at levels 0 and 1 with some children moving into level 2.

Level 0 (Basic level): Visualisation

> Geometric figures are recognised by their shape as a whole, i.e. physical appearance, not by their parts or properties.

Level 1: Analysis

> Through observation and experimentation children begin to discern the characteristics of figures. These properties are then used to conceptualise classes of shapes. Figures are recognised as having parts and are recognised by their parts. Relationships between properties cannot yet be explained and definitions are not understood.

Level 2: Informal deduction

> Children can establish the interrelationships of properties both within figures (e.g. in a quadrilateral, opposite sides being parallel necessitates opposite angles being equal) and among figures (a square is a rectangle because it has all the properties of a rectangle). Definitions are meaningful. Informal arguments can be followed or given. Formal proofs can be followed, but they cannot construct a proof starting from a different premise.

Level 3: Deduction

Level 4: Rigour

(For definitions of Levels 3 and 4 refer to the original paper – see References at the end of the chapter. Most primary-aged children do not pass Level 2.)

The spatial areas included within this chapter are:

- properties of 2-D and 3-D shapes, including symmetry;
- position, including co-ordinates;
- direction and angles.

It is possible to trace a progression within these areas.

Progression in geometry

The issues associated with early development have already been discussed in Chapter 6. This section will consider spatial development as it continues from that point. Throughout their primary schooling children move from using everyday language to describe shapes (at the lower end of Key Stage 1) to using precise mathematical vocabulary. They also have an ever-increasing range of shapes that they can recognise, describe and discuss. By the end of Key Stage 1 they will have encountered:

3-D shapes:	2-D shapes:	
cube	circle	hexagon
cuboid	triangle	octagon
pyramid	square	polygon
sphere	rectangle	quadrilateral
cone	pentagon	kite
cylinder	equilateral triangle	parallelogram
hemisphere	isosceles triangle	trapezium
prism	scalene triangle	semicircle
tetrahedron	rhombus	
polyhedron	oblong	
octahedron	heptagon	
dodecahedron		

For more on polygons and 3-D shapes see Chapter 5 of **Primary Mathematics Knowledge and Understanding** *(2014) from Learning Matters.*

But what do the children do with these shapes? There is a clear progression from using them to make models and pictures, ordering them by size, making repeating patterns and so on, to visualising properties such as parallel or perpendicular faces or edges, classifying using criteria such as size of angles, identifying nets, recognising transformations, using co-ordinates in four quadrants to describe position, using a protractor to draw acute and obtuse angles to the nearest degree and so on. This progression covers concepts from each of the areas of properties, position and angles.

Properties of 2-D and 3-D shapes

When comparing and describing 2-D and 3-D shapes, you should consider certain properties. These include the number of sides, edges, faces, the length of sides and edges, the area of faces, the size of angles, and so on. These properties are often referred to as *Euclidean* properties. They are named after the Greek mathematician Euclid (c. 330–275 BC) who described these properties in his *Elements*.

What other properties might children use to compare shapes?

PRACTICAL TASK PRACTICAL TASK **PRACTICAL TASK** PRACTICAL TASK

Classifying polygons

Given the following shapes, how might they be classified into different sets?

square	arrowhead
rhombus	irregular pentagon
regular hexagon	irregular heptagon
equilateral triangle	isosceles triangle

Symmetry

Children may well first encounter the subject of reflective symmetry when making folded 'butterfly' or 'blob' paintings.

They can extend their understanding through further creative activities such as cutting out paper chains of people. Peg boards and pictures only showing one half can be used to encourage the children to complete the pattern or picture so that there is a line of symmetry. To consider symmetry about more than one axis, paper can be folded into quarters and a 'snowflake' cut to introduce two axes of symmetry. Different shaped paper, with different numbers of folds, can introduce a different number of axes.

For more on reflective and rotational symmetry see Chapter 5 of **Primary Mathematics: Knowledge and Understanding** *(2014) from Learning Matters.*

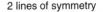

2 lines of symmetry

4 lines of symmetry

By upper Key Stage 2, children can be asked to find all the lines of reflective symmetry of any polygon, both regular and irregular.

If a child is to achieve level 5 by the end of Key Stage 2, he/she must be able to identify all the symmetries of 2-D shapes. Implicit in this statement is the need to identify rotational symmetry of 2-D shapes. In Year 6 children need to be able to visualise where a shape will be after a rotation through 90° or 180°, hence offering an appropriate opportunity to introduce consideration of rotational symmetry.

PRACTICAL TASK PRACTICAL TASK **PRACTICAL TASK** PRACTICAL TASK

Children often enjoy mathematics that is associated with them personally. As their understanding of symmetry increases, you could ask them to find all the symmetries of the letters in their name. Have a go yourself with your own name.

Position and co-ordinates

Children need to describe position from the EYFS onwards. Previously they were encouraged to use everyday language, but in the 2014 National Curriculum they start in Year 1 to use mathematical language, for example, 'higher than', 'on the edge of'. In Year 3 games such as Battleships can be used to introduce children to locating squares on grids, prior to introducing co-ordinates in the first quadrant in Year 4.

In addition to using co-ordinates to describe position, children also need to use a range of other mathematical language to describe location in space. This includes being able to identify and use the terms horizontal, vertical, diagonal (lines joining opposite corners), perpendicular and parallel.

Knowledge and understanding of the language of position and the use of co-ordinates will support children as they describe location and solve problems.

For more on Cartesian co-ordinates, see Chapter 5 of **Primary Mathematics: Knowledge and Understanding** *(2014) from Learning Matters.*

EMBEDDING ICT EMBEDDING ICT **EMBEDDING ICT** EMBEDDING ICT

Some really useful interactive programs (ITPs) were developed to support the National Numeracy Strategy and, although the requirement to have regard for the strategies has been removed, these materials are still available. The ITPs were designed to support the modelling of various aspects of mathematics, including shape and space:

Polygon enables you to draw and measure a range of polygons and use dynamic tools to manipulate them. **Symmetry** enables you to create and reflect simple images in a mirror line and predict where you think the image will appear – children can check on their predictions in a whole-class situation when this is used on the IWB.

Co-ordinates enable you to manipulate co-ordinates on a grid and to work in only the first quadrant, in the first two quadrants or in all four quadrants.

To find these ITPs online, search 'ITPs NNS' followed by the name of the specific ITP you are looking for.

Direction and angles

Building on the idea that angle is a measurement of something dynamic, children are introduced to 'turning' in Year 1. In addition children can recognise whole, half and quarter turns. By Year 2 they can specify a direction, either left or right, or clockwise or anti-clockwise. In addition they will know a right angle is a quarter turn. Degrees are introduced as a measure of turn in Year 5. Children start to draw and measure angles throughout Years 5 and 6 and use their understanding of these concepts to solve problems. Development of an understanding of these concepts can be enhanced very effectively by using ICT to support the children's learning. Both floor robots and 'logo' type software are very useful resources.

For more on angles, see Chapter 5 of **Primary Mathematics: Knowledge and Understanding** *(2014) from Learning Matters.*

Why are there 360° in a full turn?

The Greek astronomer Hipparchus of Nicaea (c. 170–120 BC) is thought to have first divided a circle into 360. He is thought to have obtained the number 360 from the early astronomers. They believed the Earth was stationary and all the stars rotated about it on a circular band divided into twelve parts. Each part was about 30 days, approximately one lunar cycle, hence 30 × 12, which gives 360. He did a great deal of work studying the Earth and calculated the length of a year to within $6\frac{1}{2}$ minutes of the figure we accept today!

At all stages throughout primary mathematics it is important to emphasise the dynamic nature of 'angle' as a measurement of turn. This should help prevent possible misconceptions developing as children progress through Key Stage 2 and into Key Stage 3.

THE BIGGER PICTURE   THE BIGGER PICTURE   **THE BIGGER PICTURE**

When you are planning work on shape and space, do not limit your thinking to work on paper or with practical resources, including ICT, within the classroom. What about the rest of the school building and its grounds? Are there shapes that you can explore and work on? For example, are there tile or brick tessellations? What about the shapes of windows? Are there any irregularly shaped rooms or corridors? What about the playground areas? Get hold of a floor plan of the school from the prospectus, the office or the site manager if you can, and invest in a tour of the site to look for possible places for children to visit and photograph. Check whether you need to undertake a risk assessment for this activity before you let the children loose!

Misconceptions

For more information on misconceptions, see Chapter 4 in Hansen (2014) **Children's Errors in Mathematics** *from Learning Matters.*

Many misconceptions that children develop in shape and space can be avoided with careful planning and consideration of how information is presented. If polygons are always shown as regular shapes 'sitting' on one side, then children's conceptual understanding of these shapes may be limited. For example, if a child is always presented with a triangle as in figure (a) below, then, when they encounter a triangle orientated as in (b), they frequently describe it as an 'upside-down' triangle.

(a)   (b)

For more on triangles, see Chapter 5 of **Primary Mathematics: Knowledge and Understanding** *(2014) from Learning Matters.*

In order to prevent this happening it is important to present a range of different triangles, both regular and irregular, in a variety of orientations:

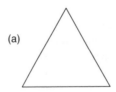

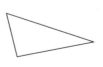

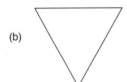

This will allow children to focus on the characteristics that are important when describing triangles, i.e. the number of sides and angles, and not focus on irrelevant details such as orientation. This is also the case when children are learning to distinguish different types of triangle when they need to focus on length of sides and sizes of angles.

This misconception is also revealed when children refuse to accept that any six-sided polygon is a hexagon, for example:

This is frequently due to the fact that they have always been presented with regular shapes when working with polygons. Again, they focus on specific characteristics that are not necessarily the key ones. It is vital that children encounter a range of polygons, both regular and irregular, in a variety of orientations, in order that this misconception does not develop.

For more on regular and irregular polygons, see Chapter 5 of **Primary Mathematics: Knowledge and Understanding** *(2014) from Learning Matters.*

A further misconception children can develop is related to social usage of language that is also used mathematically. An example of this is the child who is asked how many sides shape (a) below has, and replies '2'. When asked how many shape (b) has they also reply '2'. In desperation the teacher shows shape (c) and asks how many sides, the child replies '3'.

(a)   (b)   (c)

When asked to explain the child says that shape (a) has two sides and a 'bottom', shape (b) has two sides and a 'top' and shape (c) has three sides!

For more on language in mathematics, see Chapter 7 of **Primary Mathematics: Knowledge and Understanding** *(2014) from Learning Matters.*

This really demonstrates the importance of planning for the mathematical vocabulary that will be developed when teaching different aspects of shape and space in order to prevent children forming these misconceptions.

In all aspects of shape and space children can develop misconceptions. If they fail to understand that angle is dynamic, they may well be unable to order angles of different sizes correctly because they are focusing on irrelevant pieces of information. For example, looking at angles *a* and *b* below, a child may well state that *a* is larger than *b* because the 'arms' are longer in *a* than in b.

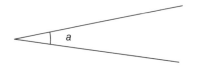

In order to avoid this misconception developing, children need to be introduced to angle as a measurement of turn. They need to have plenty of opportunity for practical exploration before encountering angles represented in this way. If they have engaged in these practical activities first, they will be able to apply their knowledge of angle as a measurement of something dynamic, i.e. turn, to this task successfully and not focus on irrelevant details such as the length of the 'arms'.

A SUMMARY OF **KEY POINTS**

In order to support the development of spatial understanding it is important that children are able to:

➢ **identify and name a range of polygons and polyhedra;**
➢ **describe, compare and classify shapes using Euclidean properties;**
➢ **identify the symmetries of 2-D shapes;**
➢ **use mathematical language and co-ordinates to describe position;**
➢ **recognise angle as a measurement of turn.**

M-LEVEL EXTENSION > > > > M-LEVEL EXTENSION > > > >

Find out more about the van Hiele model of geometric development as cited in Monaghan (2000). In particular, familiarise yourself with Levels 3 and 4. From your experience in schools so far, do you find this a useful model to describe how primary children learn about shape and space? Do you think that there are likely to be children in upper Key Stage 2, or perhaps younger children who are able, gifted or talented in mathematics, who will reach the higher levels of understanding? What activities could you devise to help children to progress through the levels?

REFERENCES REFERENCES **REFERENCES** REFERENCES REFERENCES

Clements, D. H. and Burns, B. A. (2000) 'Students' development of strategies for turn and angle measure'. *Educational Studies in Mathematics*, 41, 31–45.

DfE (2011) *Teachers' Standards.* Available at: www.gov.uk/government/publications/teachers-standards (accessed 13/4/14).

DfE (2013) *Mathematics Programmes of Study: Key Stages 1 and 2. National Curriculum for England.* London: DfE. Available at: www.gov.uk/government/uploads/system/uploads/attachment_data/file/239129/PRIMARY_National_Curriculum_-_Mathematics.pdf

Monaghan, F. (2000) 'What difference does it make? Children's views of the difference between some quadrilaterals'. *Education Studies in Mathematics,* 42, 179–96.

FURTHER READING   FURTHER READING   FURTHER READING

Hansen, A. (ed.) (2014) (3rd edn) *Children's Errors in Mathematics: Understanding Common Misconceptions in Primary Schools.* London: Sage/Learning Matters.

Haylock, D. (2010) (4th edn) *Mathematics Explained for Primary Teachers.* London: Sage.

Haylock, D. and Cockburn, A. (2002) *Understanding Mathematics in the Lower Primary Years.* London: Paul Chapman Publishing.

Mason, J., Burton, L. and Stacey, K. (2010) (Revised edn) *Thinking Mathematically.* Harlow: Pearson Education Limited.

Ofsted (2009) *Mathematics: Understanding the Score. Improving practice in mathematics teaching at primary level.* London: Ofsted.

Thompson, I. (2010) (2nd edn) *Issues in Teaching Numeracy in Primary Schools.* Maidenhead: Open University Press.

12
Statistics

Introduction

In the Foundation Stage, learning arises from children's everyday experiences. As a result, developing mathematical ideas to solve problems, talking about, recognising and recreating simple patterns and sorting familiar objects and then presenting the results using pictures, drawings or numerals are all aspects of statistics that can be drawn out of their play.

Within the National Curriculum for Key Stage 1 children are expected to interpret and construct simple pictograms, tally charts, block diagrams and simple tables; ask and answer simple questions by counting the number of objects in each category and sorting the categories by quantity; and ask and answer questions about totalling and comparing categorical data. Statistics is extended in lower Key Stage 2. In this children are expected to interpret and present discrete and continuous data using appropriate graphical methods, including bar charts and time graphs, as well as solve comparison, sum and difference problems using information presented in bar charts, pictograms, tables and other graphs. By the end of upper Key Stage 2, children will be able to solve problems using information presented in a line graph and pie charts; complete, read and interpret information in tables, including timetables; and calculate and interpret the mean as an average.

This chapter will focus on the progression through the primary age range in statistics and some of the difficulties that children and teachers might find. For further information about these aspects of mathematics at a higher level of attainment or for your own subject knowledge, refer to the companion book in this series, *Primary Mathematics: Knowledge and Understanding* (Learning Matters, 2014).

Progression in aspects of statistics

In this section, we will be considering the main aspects that contribute to the development of children's understanding of statistics:

- collecting, sorting and organising data;
- representing, extracting and interpreting data;
- quantitative data and summary statistics.

Collecting, sorting and organising data

In order to model the collection of data, tasks are often undertaken by the teacher or jointly as a class in Key Stage 1. As an example consider young children sorting magnetic from non-magnetic material. The teacher has supplied the child with the magnetic and non-magnetic materials. The child is asked to sort the data into two groups and organise the data using appropriate diagrams. In this case it is appropriate to use a Carroll diagram, Venn diagram or tree diagram to organise the data. These diagrams are the most appropriate when the data have to be sorted and organised.

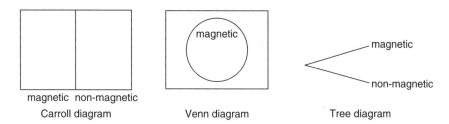

| Carroll diagram | Venn diagram | Tree diagram |

In each case the children physically place the actual magnetic material in one part of the diagram and the non-magnetic material in the other part of the diagram. This kind of activity where the children are sorting using one criterion is the most appropriate for young children in Key Stage 1. Normally, children sort into two sets themselves first and record in their own way before the teacher introduces this formal method of recording.

Progress can be made to sorting using two criteria. Suppose, for example, we wish to find out which materials are magnetic and which are made of metal. We can use the same kind of diagram but, because there are now two criteria, each diagram will have four parts instead of two.

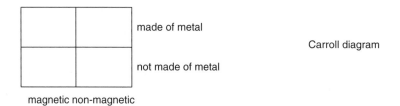

Carroll diagram

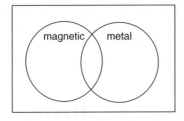

Venn diagram

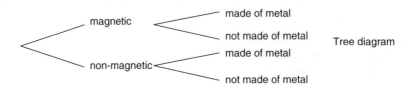

Tree diagram

Again the materials would be placed on the diagrams. These diagrams are useful for answering questions like 'Are all the metals magnetic?' In Key Stage 1 children classify using only one or two criteria. By Key Stage 3 children use similar diagrams to classify using more criteria and to solve problems involving probability.

For more detail on pictographs, see Chapter 6 of Primary Mathematics: Knowledge and Understanding (2014) from Learning Matters.

Representing, extracting and interpreting data

One clear implication of collecting data is how children go on to represent the data. For example, if the class wants to find out the most popular way of coming to school, a simple show of hands from the children is an efficient way of collecting the data. (The teacher will need to limit the number of choices.)

Bus ☺ ☺ ☺

Car ☺ ☺ ☺ ☺ ☺ ☺ ☺ ☺

Walk ☺ ☺ ☺ ☺ ☺ ☺ ☺ ☺ ☺ ☺ ☺ ☺

Bike ☺ ☺

This is called a pictogram or pictograph. They can be drawn horizontally or vertically with each icon representing one child. Questions such as 'How many more children walk than cycle?' can be extracted from this diagram. In turn the diagram is a simple way to interpret the answer.

Once the children realise that drawing icons is very time-consuming, then it is time to progress to **block graphs** where the icons are simply replaced by

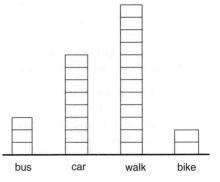

blocks. These diagrams do not require a side scale since the blocks can be easily counted.

For the purposes of answering the question 'Which is the most popular form of transport?' this is a perfectly adequate diagram.

When the frequencies become larger, however, it is inconvenient to have to count each block. The advantage of using **bar charts** can then be pointed out. A side scale is introduced and the frequencies can be read from the side of the graph.

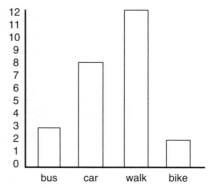

The progression is from pictogram to block graph to bar chart. In each of these cases the data being handled is categories, sometimes called qualitative. In other words the horizontal scale contains categories and not numbers. It is most appropriate at Key Stage 1 to pose questions that relate to categories data. Examples of appropriate questions are:

- 'What is our favourite cartoon character?'
- 'What is the most common eye colour?'
- 'What is the most popular way to travel to school?'

Another way to represent categories data is by using a **pie chart**. If we are interested in answering questions such as 'Do more children walk to school than cycle?' then a pie chart is a particularly useful diagram to use. This information can be quickly extracted. Pie charts are appropriate when we are asking questions about relative sizes.

Creating a pie chart by hand by calculating angles is complicated but with the advent of ICT they are now used extensively throughout the primary age range. Children should be encouraged to use data-handling packages such as *Number Box* to manipulate their data and produce appropriate diagrams. It is important, however, that children are familiar with correct terminology if they are to use the packages correctly.

Quantitative data

In Key Stage 2 children can begin to handle quantitative data. This is data that has a numerical value. Suppose, for example, the children want to find out the most common shoe size of the class. Shoe sizes are quantitative data, i.e. numerical. The children will first need to collect this data. This data can be collected quickly by a simple show of hands. A tally chart can then be drawn up:

Shoe size	Number of children
1	‖
2	‖‖
3	╫╫ ǀ
4	╫╫ ‖
5	╫╫ ‖ǀ
6	‖ǀ
7	ǀ

A frequency table can then be produced:

Shoe size	Number of children
1	2
2	4
3	6
4	7
5	8
6	3
7	1

The appropriate diagram to represent this data is a bar line graph:

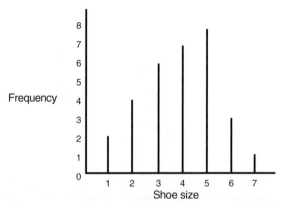

Shoe sizes are an example of *discrete* data. Shoe sizes only come in certain sizes. Other examples of discrete data are dress sizes, hat sizes, the number of children in a family, the number of goals scored in a soccer match. In general a bar line graph is the appropriate way to represent discrete data. This is logical since the vertical line needs to go to exactly above that particular numerical value.

Quantitative data can also be *continuous.* This is the kind of data that can take any value within a certain range. Examples of continuous data are time, distance, and speed. In Key Stage 2 children need to be able to interpret **line graphs**. The graph below is a line graph showing how the distance travelled by a car is related to the time it has been moving.

*For more detail on line graphs, see Chapter 6 of **Primary Mathematics: Knowledge and Understanding** (2014) from Learning Matters.*

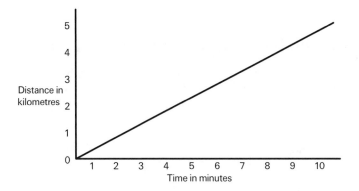

Children should be taught to interpret the graph and be able to answer questions such as:

- 'How far has the car travelled after 8 minutes?'
- 'How long does it take to travel 3 kilometres?'

Other line graphs that children can be introduced to are conversion graphs. For example, say that £10 can be exchanged for 16 euros. A conversion graph can be constructed and children asked to exchange pounds into euros and vice versa. Research shows that children find it easier to go from the horizontal scale to the vertical scale rather than the other way round. In the above example they find it easier to find how far the car has gone after 4 minutes rather than finding how long the car took to go 3 kilometres. It is worth spending time on reading conversion graphs both ways.

What should all graphs have?

Whether constructing graphs by hand or using a computer package it is necessary to highlight for children what information their graph must contain. Look at the generic bar graph template below. Note the information that must be on it in order to provide all the necessary information for people to interpret it.

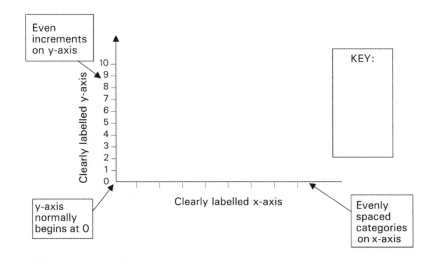

It is important to note that other types of graphs will still require the same precision in layout and presentation.

Constructing block graphs and bar graphs

A common hurdle for children is the move from constructing block graphs to bar graphs by hand. The difference is in the labelling of the y-axis. It might be helpful for you to consider this progression in relation to number lines and plotting co-ordinates:

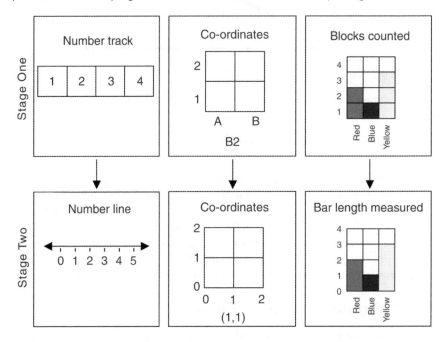

The move from using number tracks to number lines, from labelling squares in co-ordinate geometry to labelling points, and from creating block graphs to bar graphs all happen around similar times in school. Being aware of this shift occurring in several mathematics areas and making the links explicit to children may help to resolve their confusion.

EMBEDDING ICT EMBEDDING ICT **EMBEDDING ICT** EMBEDDING ICT

With easy access to wide and varied data on the internet, websites are a useful source of data for children to use in their cross-curricular work. For example, it is possible to search for and track over time the population sizes of villages, towns and cities to study population trends in history or geography.

As mentioned earlier in this chapter, the use of computerised data handling packages has meant that children are able to construct attractive, accurate graphs very simply and effectively. It is also possible to amend data and have an immediately updated graph. The use of the interactive whiteboard has also meant that skills involved in creating and interpreting graphs can be developed with the whole class efficiently. This is very welcome because a regular criticism of lessons prior to ICT inclusion was that children would spend whole lessons *creating* graphs but then did not *use* or *interpret* them, which is of course the main purpose of being able to handle data.

It is important to note, however, that computer packages will present *any* data in *any* way for you. This means that children can produce a line graph using discrete data which is nonsensical. For example, a line graph could be produced on a computer to represent shoe sizes in the class, but reading that 4.5 children wear size 11.75 shoes does not provide accurate data! Equally, when creating and interpreting pie charts, it is necessary for children to realise that they are comparing proportions.

Summary statistics

Older children progress to finding summary statistics. The easiest summary statistic to find is the mode. Indeed even in Key Stage 1 children are finding 'the most common eye colour' and 'the most popular way of travelling to school'. Children should be encouraged to call this the mode. In Key Stage 2 we introduce other averages such as the mean and median. Care should be taken, however, to find these statistics only when they are appropriate.

Consider the following example. As part of their History project a class of children was collecting data on the wages of miners. The table below (adjusted) shows the annual wages of the miners in their sample:

Miner	A	B	C	D	E	F	G	H	I	J	K
Wage(£)	2,000	2,000	2,000	2,000	2,000	2,500	3,000	3,000	3,000	4,000	5,500

The question the children wanted to answer was: 'Which summary statistic gives a true reflection of the average wage?'

For more detail on when mean, median and mode are best used, see Chapter 6 of **Primary Mathematics: Knowledge and Understanding** *(2014) from Learning Matters.*

PRACTICAL TASK PRACTICAL TASK **PRACTICAL TASK** PRACTICAL TASK

Before reading on, consider how you might answer this question: Which summary statistic do you feel gives a true reflection?

- The mode, the most common, is £2,000.
- The median, the wage of the middle miner F, is £2,500.
- The mean, the total wage bill divided by the number of miners, is £3,000.

From the management's viewpoint the total wage bill is very important. Consequently the mean is their most appropriate summary statistic because it is linked to the total wage bill. However, from the workers' standpoint what most people earn is of importance. The mode is their most appropriate summary statistic.

It would be misleading, however, for management to say the average wage was £3,000, just as it would be misleading for the workers to say the average wage was £2,000. It is important to state which average is being used.

Children should be taught to recognise when information is presented in misleading ways. It is a useful activity for children to find references to averages in newspapers and decide which average, the mode, median or mean, is being referred to.

An evaluation by HMI (Ofsted, 2002) challenged teachers' questioning in areas of the curriculum such as statistics. They provide an example from a Year 3 classroom where the teacher asked children to answer simple questions such as 'How many children like blue?' but did not ask more challenging questions such as 'How many more children like blue than orange?' The report also found that few schools make regular use of ICT during mathematics lessons. However, timetabled ICT time was commonly used to teach children how to use graphical presentations, data analysis and spreadsheet software.

In addition to this, the 2003 report from Ofsted highlighted the need for regular 'real-life' problems to develop skills such as interpreting data.

How can I be creative in statistics and developing cross-curricular links?

It is not uncommon for children in upper Key Stage 2 to be constructing graphs about their favourite pop stars or their favourite food. Quite frankly, this is no different to the skills required of them when in the Reception class they were answering questions about their favourite pets or food. In order to keep children interested and motivated it is necessary for them to see the purpose of their activity. The biggest challenge in setting questions for your children, or supporting them in choosing an appropriate question, is the level of challenge both mathematically and in other areas of the curriculum.

When you are planning statistics activities, if you wish to consider handling data discretely within mathematics lessons, one way to do this is to create a data-handling project with children where they answer a question of their choice in project groups. For example, they may collect data about adults' preferred car colour and present their findings to a car manufacturer. Another example might be to canvass children's preferred pet choices and present this information to a pet shop owner. Projects of this type can also benefit from having a guest speaker or organising visits for the children for them to see the purpose of their data collection, representation and interpretation. Another significant benefit is that the children recognise a purpose and gain a sense of the audience for their work.

If you are going to handle data in subjects other than mathematics lessons you may wish to consider teaching the skills of statistics within mathematics lessons and then use those skills in other lessons. Alternatively, you may use the double lesson time to integrate maths and another subject. Be aware of when the children are involved in mathematics and when they are engaged in other subjects, however, to ensure appropriate assessment opportunities.

REFLECTIVE TASK

REFLECTIVE TASK

For each of the questions below, consider how your children might gather data, present it and interpret it. Try to be as creative as you can. What cross-curricular links can you make with these ideas?

- How many tins does our class recycle?
- How do we get to school?
- Which is the best country performing in the world championships?
- What prices should we charge in the school canteen?
- What factors encourage people to move house?
- What effect does the weather have on wildlife?

Next time you sit down to look at your medium-term plans, think about where you can realistically make creative cross-curricular links in your teaching.

Misconceptions

The misconception many children have is that the graph is a picture rather than a scaled representation.

Teachers need to emphasise that each point on the line (for example in the graph showing the distance travelled by a car earlier in this chapter) represents a distance travelled in a particular time. In fact it is good practice for teachers to build the graph up from a set of points. Children can be encouraged to fill in missing values in the table (shown below) and then plot the points on a grid. The teacher can then discuss whether or not it is valid to join the points together to make a line. If the car is travelling at a constant speed then it is valid to join the points.

Time (in minutes)	Distance (in kilometres)
2	1
3	$1\frac{1}{2}$
4	2
5	
	3
7	
8	
9	
	5

Children will begin to appreciate that the straight line does not show a car going in a straight line but a linear relationship between distance travelled and time taken.

For further details about misconceptions in statistics read Chapter 10 in *Children's Errors in Mathematics: Understanding Common Misconceptions in Primary Schools* (2014) from Learning Matters.

A SUMMARY OF **KEY POINTS**

In order to support the development of a child's understanding of statistics, it is important that children:

➢ approach statistics as essentially a problem-solving exercise;

➢ progress from collecting, sorting and organising data to representing, extracting and interpreting data;

➢ understand the difference between discrete and continuous data and know in which ways these should be represented;

➢ are enabled to use measures of average in relevant contexts.

M-LEVEL EXTENSION > > > > M-LEVEL EXTENSION > > > >

Reread the Research Summary about HMI's views (Ofsted 2002, 2003) on teachers' questioning in areas of the curriculum, including handling data, and the need for regular 'real-life' problems to develop children's skills in interpreting data. Look at more recent views (Ofsted 2008, 2009). Does the same picture still pertain? Start to devise a series of real-life problems for each year group from the EYFS to Year 6 that can be used to develop children's knowledge, understanding and skills in the area of handling data. For each investigation, write a list of relevant questions that will probe children's understanding and challenge them to use appropriate vocabulary in their responses. Can the same questions be used as part of your assessment of this aspect?

REFERENCES REFERENCES **REFERENCES** REFERENCES REFERENCES

DfE (2011) *Teachers' Standards.* Available at: www.gov.uk/government/teachers-standards (accessed 13/4/14).

Hansen, A. (ed.) (2014) *Children's Errors in Mathematics: Understanding Common Misconceptions.* London: Sage/Learning Matters.

Ofsted (2002) *The National Numeracy Strategy: The Second Year. An Evaluation by HMI.* London: Ofsted.

Ofsted (2003) *Mathematics in Primary Schools: Ofsted Subject Reports Series 2001/2, HMI* 806. London: Ofsted.

FURTHER READING   FURTHER READING   FURTHER READING

Haylock, D. (2005) (3rd edn) *Mathematics Explained for Primary Teachers.* London: Paul Chapman.

Hopkins, C., Gifford, S. and Pepperell, S. (2009) (3rd edn) *Mathematics in the Primary School: A Sense of Progression*. London: Routledge.

Hopkins, C., Pope, S. and Pepperell, S. (2004) *Understanding Primary Mathematics.* London: David Fulton.

Ofsted (2009) *Mathematics: Understanding the Score.* London: Ofsted.

Suggate, J., Davis, A. and Goulding, M. (2006) (3rd edn) *Mathematics Knowledge for Primary Teachers*. London: David Fulton.

Thompson, I. (ed.) (2003) (2nd edn) *Enhancing Mathematics Teaching*. Maidenhead: Open University Press.

Glossary

abscissa: the first number in a pair of Cartesian co-ordinates. The abscissa always represents the distance along the x-axis.

angle: a measurement of turn.

approximation: an inexact result adequate and appropriate for a given purpose.

arc: a curved line that forms part of the circumference of a circle.

associative law: numbers can be regrouped to simplify a question while making no difference to the answer. It is true for addition and multiplication:
$$(a + b) + c = a + (b + c) \quad (a \times b) \times c = a \times (b \times c)$$

average: the general term used for using one number to represent a set of data.

bar graph: a graph that uses bars to represent data.

bar-line graph: a graph that uses lines to represent data.

block graph: a graph used to display discrete data where one block can represent one or many item(s) of data.

BODMAS: the order of precedence given to the operations when working out complex expressions. It stands for:

    B – brackets
    O – of
    D – division
    M – multiplication
    A – addition
    S – subtraction

or BIDMAS, where the 'I' represents indices.

box and whisker plot: a graphical representation that allows for comparison of two sets of data.

capacity: how much liquid volume a container can hold when full.

Cartesian co-ordinates: a pair of numbers that locate a point on a plane with reference to two axes (can also refer to three axes in order to locate a point in three dimensions).

chord: a straight line connecting any two points on a curve. When a chord passes through the centre of a circle it is called the diameter.

commutative law: the order in which the operation is performed makes no difference to the answer. It is true for addition and multiplication:
$$a + b = b + a \quad a \times b = b \times a$$

congruence: shapes are said to be congruent if they are the same shape and size.

conjecture: a hypothesis, something that has been surmised or deduced.

conservation: understanding that the quantity of matter remains unchanged regardless of its arrangement.

continuous data: data that is measured. Every item of data can be placed along a continuum, for example, lengths of leaves.

counter-example: disproving an assertion by finding an exception.

cumulative frequency: a table displaying the running total of a set of data.

cumulative frequency curve: a graph of the running total of a set of data.

data: a set of facts, numbers or information.

decimal: a fractional number expressed using places to the right of the decimal point.

deduction: a conclusion based on a set of true statements.

denominator: the bottom number in a fraction, representing the number of fractional parts the unit has been divided into.

discrete data: data that can be counted. Every item of data can be placed in a category, for example, colours of cars.

distributive law: one operation is 'distributed out' over another operation. It is true for multiplication over addition and multiplication over subtraction:
$$a \times (b + c) = (a \times b) + (a \times c) \qquad a \times (b - c) = (a \times b) - (a \times c)$$
It is also true that division is 'right distributive' over addition and subtraction (i.e. the division needs to be on the right side of the brackets):
$$(a + b) \div c = (a \div c) + (b \div c) \qquad (a - b) \div c = (a \div c) - (b \div c)$$

dividend: within the operation of division, the number that is divided by another number.

divisor: within the operation of division, the number that divides another number.

edge: the line where two faces join (i.e. the intersection of two plane faces of a solid).

enlargement: each measurement is multiplied by a scale factor in order to enlarge or reduce an image.

equation: a statement that two expressions are equal.

estimation: the rough answer (a judgement of an approximate value or amount).

exhaustion: a proof that is arrived at by considering all possibilities.

experimental probability: the number between 0 and 1 that is found by dividing the number of outcomes by the total number of trials.

expression: a general term used to describe mathematical terms.

face: the flat surface of a solid shape (i.e. parts of planes).

factor: a number that divides another number exactly, for example 8 is a factor of 32, but 5 is not.

fraction: a fraction is expressed as the quotient of two numbers, the dividend is the numerator, the divisor the denominator.

frequency diagram: a table displaying continuous data grouped into classes.

frequency histogram: a graph displaying continuous data grouped into classes.

function: a rule that changes or maps one number on to another.

gradient: the slope of a graph.

imperial measure: introduced in the Magna Carta in 1215, for example, pints, gallons, miles, etc.

independent events: events when the outcome of one event does not affect the outcome of another event, for example, flipping two coins.

index form: a concise way of writing repeated multiplication of a number by itself, for example, $10 \times 10 \times 10 \times 10 = 10^4$.

inequality: a statement that one quantity is greater or less than another.

interquartile range: the interval between the upper quartile and the lower quartile in a set of data.

irrational numbers: the set of numbers that cannot be expressed in fractional form.

line graph: a graph used to display continuous data, where curves or line segments join points of measured data.

linear equation: takes the form $ay + bx + c = 0$. A linear equation can always be represented as a straight line graph.

lower quartile: the value one quarter of the way along a set of ordered data.

mass: the amount of matter contained in an object.

mean: the sum of the values in a set of data divided by the total number of items in that set.

median: the middle value of a set of ordered data.

minuend: the quantity from which another quantity is to be subtracted.

mode: the value that occurs most often in a set of data.

mutually exclusive events: events which, having happened, exclude any other outcome from occurring in that same event, for example, throwing a 3 on a die excludes a 1 ,2, 4, 5 or 6 being thrown at the same time.

net: a flat shape that can be folded to form a solid.

numerator: the top number in a fraction representing the number of fractional parts.

ordering: putting a collection of items in order from smallest to biggest/biggest to smallest according to weight, length, thickness, etc.

ordinate: the second number in a pair of Cartesian co-ordinates. The ordinate always represents the distance along the y-axis.

parallel: lines travelling in the same direction but which will never meet.

percentage: fractions with a denominator of 100. They can also be represented as decimals, for example $\frac{1}{4} = \frac{25}{100} = 0.25 = 25\%$.

perpendicular: two lines are said to be perpendicular if they meet at right angles.

pi (π): an irrational number found when the circumference of a circle is divided by the diameter. It is approximately equal to 3.141592...

pictograph: a graph used to display discrete data where one picture/symbol can represent one or many item(s) of data.

pie chart: a circle graph cut into sectors.

place value: place value is used by number systems that allow the same digit to carry different values based on its position.

Platonic solids: the five regular polyhedra, comprising the regular tetrahedron, the cube, the regular octahedron, the regular dodecahedron and the regular icosahedron.

polygon: a plane shape with straight sides and many angles.

polyhedron (pl. polyhedra): a solid formed from many flat faces.

prism: a solid shape with a uniform cross section.

probability: used to measure the likelihood of certain events occurring in the future.

probability scale: a scale from 0 to 1 that is used to measure the likelihood of an event occurring, with 0 being impossible and 1 being certain.

proportion: compares part of a quantity with the whole, for example, a ratio of 1:3 results in proportions of 1 out of 4 and 3 out of 4.

pyramid: a solid that has a polygon base and all other faces triangular.

quotient: the result when one number is divided by another number.

range: the interval between the greatest and least values in a set of data.

ratio: a comparison between two quantities.

rational numbers: the set of all numbers that can be written as fractions.

real numbers: the set of rational numbers and irrational numbers combined.

reduction: combining different parts of an equation to make it simpler.

reflection: when a shape is reflected, a mirror image is created. The shape and size remain unchanged and the two images are congruent.

reflective symmetry: also sometimes called line symmetry. A shape is said to have reflective symmetry if it can be folded so that one half fits exactly on top of the other half.

restoration: simplifying an equation by performing the same operation on each side.

rotation: rotation involves a turn around a fixed point. The shape and size remain unchanged, the two images are congruent.

rotational symmetry: a shape is said to have rotational symmetry if it looks the same in different positions when rotated about its centre.

scattergraph: a graph representing two types of data plotted as co-ordinates.

sector: a wedge from a circle (like a slice of pie).

sigma: means 'the sum of'. The symbol for sigma is Σ.

similarity: shapes are said to be similar if all the angles are the same size and the shapes are the same but of different size, i.e. one is an enlargement of the other.

simultaneous linear equations: two linear equations which have a common solution.

standard form: sometimes called standard index form as it uses powers of 10, i.e. 10 expressed in index form. It is a shorthand way of writing very small and very large numbers that would require a huge number of digits if written in full.

statistics: statistics help us to bring order to data and to draw information from it.

subtrahend: the number or term to be subtracted.

Système Internationale (S.I.): determines the units of measurement used in the metric system, for example, millimetres, kilograms, litres, etc.

terms: algebraic quantities that are separated from each other in expressions by operations.

theoretical probability: the number between 0 and 1 that is found by dividing the number of actual outcomes by the total number of possible outcomes.

transitivity: a mathematical relationship used to compare two objects or events, e.g. if A is shorter than B, and B is shorter than C, then A must be shorter than C.

translation: this takes place when a shape is moved from one place to another just by sliding it (without rotating, reflecting or enlarging).

upper quartile: the value three-quarters of the way along a set of ordered data.

vertex: the point of intersection of edges.

volume: the amount of three-dimensional space an object occupies.

vulgar fraction: a fraction expressed by numerator and denominator, not decimally; used in ordinary calculations; (the original meaning of the word 'vulgar' was 'as used by ordinary people').

weight: the force exerted on a body due to gravity.

y-intercept: the point at which a graph crosses the y-axis.

12.4.06

Leadership in Nursing

To my mother – the most effective leader I know.
And she is well over 40.

For Churchill Livingstone

Senior Commissioning Editor: Alex Mathieson / Jacqueline Curthoys
Project Editor: Pat Miller
Project Manager: Jane Shanks